Uruguay

W. H. Koebel

Alpha Editions

This edition published in 2024

ISBN : 9789362096432

Design and Setting By
Alpha Editions
www.alphaedis.com
Email - info@alphaedis.com

As per information held with us this book is in Public Domain.
This book is a reproduction of an important historical work. Alpha Editions uses the best technology to reproduce historical work in the same manner it was first published to preserve its original nature. Any marks or number seen are left intentionally to preserve its true form.

Contents

INTRODUCTORY NOTE .... - 1 -
CHAPTER I .... - 2 -
CHAPTER II .... - 9 -
CHAPTER III .... - 18 -
CHAPTER IV .... - 25 -
CHAPTER V .... - 33 -
CHAPTER VI .... - 39 -
CHAPTER VII .... - 52 -
CHAPTER VIII .... - 58 -
CHAPTER IX .... - 65 -
CHAPTER X .... - 72 -
CHAPTER XI .... - 80 -
CHAPTER XII .... - 90 -
CHAPTER XIII .... - 98 -
CHAPTER XIV .... - 107 -
CHAPTER XV .... - 114 -
CHAPTER XVI .... - 124 -
CHAPTER XVII .... - 133 -
CHAPTER XVIII .... - 141 -
CHAPTER XIX .... - 149 -
CHAPTER XX .... - 158 -
CHAPTER XXI .... - 165 -
CHAPTER XXII .... - 171 -
CHAPTER XXIII .... - 179 -
CHAPTER XXIV .... - 186 -
CHAPTER XXV .... - 194 -

CHAPTER XXVI ....- 203 -
CHAPTER XXVII ....- 214 -
APPENDIX..- 224 -

INTRODUCTORY NOTE

The author has to tender his cordial thanks for the extreme courtesy and for the invaluable assistance rendered during his stay in the country by the Uruguayan officials, and by the British Minister Plenipotentiary, Mr. J. R. Kennedy.

He is desirous of expressing the obligations under which he has been placed by Mr. C. E. R. Rowland, British Consul at Montevideo, for general assistance and information on the seal fisheries; Señor José H. Figueira, for the description of the aboriginal tribes; Señor Ramos Montero, for the commercial technicalities of the pastoral industry; and Mr. V. Hinde, for the paper on the British railways in Uruguay.

Thanks are due to a number of British residents, both in Montevideo and the Campo, greater than it is possible to enumerate individually. The author would more especially acknowledge the courtesy of Messrs. Stapledon, W. J. Maclean, H. Hall-Hall, C. W. Baine, Temple, R. Booth, Piria, Adams, R. B. Harwar, L. L. Mercer, Warren, and J. Storm.

Mr. R. A. Bennett, who accompanied the author for the purpose of photography, displayed an unremitting zeal that must be gratefully recognised. He is responsible for much of the information on Mercedes, the Swiss colony, and the frontier town of Rivera.

CHAPTER I

SURVEY

Geographical situation of the Republic—Boundaries and area—Uruguay as an historical, commercial, and financial centre—The respective positions of Uruguay and Paraguay—Disadvantages of a buffer State—A land of sunshine and shadow—The history of Uruguay—The blending of industry and warfare—Vitality of the nation—Instances of self-sacrifice—A South American Switzerland—A freedom-loving folk—Deeds of arms and the undercurrents of commerce—Montevideo in the eyes of the casual traveller—Factors that make for the progress of the Banda Oriental—Influence of railway—Coming cessation of the North American beef shipments—Temperament of the Uruguayan—Distinction between Argentine and Uruguayan politics—The clans of the Banda Oriental—The birthright of party convictions—Education in Uruguay—National points of honour—Liberty accorded the foreigner—The courtesy of officials—An incident at the customs-house—Popularity of the English—A gratifying situation—Satisfactory international relations—The work of Mr. R. J. Kennedy, the British Minister Plenipotentiary—Uruguay's pacific foreign policy—Careful finance—Army and navy—General progress of the nation.

Uruguay may be described as a republic of comparatively small dimensions sandwiched in between the great territories of Argentina and Brazil, and bounded on the south by the Southern Atlantic Ocean and the estuary of the River Plate. Its actual area, 72,100 square miles, is less than that of the British Isles, and thus the Banda Oriental, to use the name by which the State is locally known, enjoys the distinction of being the smallest of the South American republics. But, although this distinction applies to actual area, it serves for remarkably little else in the country. Indeed, an astonishing amount is packed within the frontiers of Uruguay. In the first place it is a land where much history has been made. Secondly, to turn to its industrial assets—although I do not intend to deal with the commercial side of the Republic more fully than can be helped—it is a country where many cattle are bred. Lastly, it is a place in which no less than fifty million pounds sterling of English money are invested. Thus the small Republic, as an investment field, ranks third in importance amongst all the States of South America, a fact that is realised by remarkably few outside its own boundaries.

Uruguay and Paraguay are frequently confused by those quite unfamiliar with South American affairs, owing to the similarity of the nomenclature. In actual fact the two countries have very little in common, save in their political situation. Both separated themselves from the River Plate Provinces in the course of the War of Independence, since which time both have served as buffer States between Argentina and Brazil. The position of such is seldom enviable at the best of times. Upon Uruguay it has worked with an especial degree of hardship, since even before the days of her independence it was upon her suffering soil that the too frequent differences between Spaniard and Portuguese were fought out.

A RURAL INN.

COUNTRY COACH AT LA SIERRA STATION.

To face p. 28.

As to the international jealousies of a later era, they have not been without their influence upon the domestic affairs of the central State. Thus on not a few occasions the result of foreign diplomacy has been civil war within the boundaries of Uruguay, with consequences that were necessarily disastrous to the nation. The Banda Oriental is a land of sunshine, it is true, but one of shadow too, which is logical enough, since without the former the latter cannot obtain. Its metaphorical sunshine is represented by the undoubted merits of its inhabitants, its temporary shadows by the circumstances in which they have found themselves placed.

He would be no real friend of Uruguay who strove to show that the march of the country has not been rudely arrested on innumerable occasions. Indeed, were it not for the conditions that have prevailed for centuries, the actual forward steps that the Republic has effected would be far less remarkable than is in reality the case. The history of Uruguay reveals a continuous medley of peace and war. Its swords have been beaten into ploughshares and welded back again into lethal weapons ere the metal had cooled from the force of the former operation.

Each series of such transformations, moreover, has occurred at intervals sufficiently short to destroy utterly the hopes and prosperity of an ordinary people. Over and over again the Uruguayans have strewn the battlefields with their dead; yet during each interval they have continued to plant the soil with its proper and more profitable seed. An extraordinary vitality on the part of the people joined to the natural wealth of the land have been the factors by means of which the small Republic has brushed away the results of its wars as lightly as though such convulsions were summer showers.

The history of Uruguay reveals an admirable amount of pure heroism. Apart from the fighting merits that are inborn and natural to the race, the most unsympathetic reader of its past pages cannot deny to it the innumerable instances of self-sacrifice that were the fruit of loftier ideals. Of the many vivid battle scenes that were painted in too deadly an earnest against their neighbours and even amongst themselves, there are few that are not relieved by some illuminating act of heroism, for all the utter ferocity and courage by which these conflicts were wont to be marked. Uruguay, in fact, was something of a South American Switzerland; but a Switzerland bereft of the lofty peaks and mountain tops that assisted the men of the Cantons against the Austrians, endowed, moreover, with a more restless and undisciplined folk of its own. Yet in many respects the resemblance holds good, and for one reason most of all. The Orientales rested not until they had won their freedom. Not once but several times they were forced to wrest it from the stranger ere it finally became secure.

At later periods, too, it is not to be denied that the greater bulk of the neighbouring nations has stood out remorselessly between Uruguay and the sunlight. There have been times when the small Republic has been ground between the great mills of Argentina and Brazil. Thus her progress—steady and all but continuous in spite of the civil wars and revolutions that have torn her—has been achieved all but unnoticed and entirely unapplauded. Europeans, and many South Americans too, read of the Uruguayan battlefields and deeds of arms, yet they learn nothing of the undercurrent of industry that has flowed onwards all the while beneath the turbulence of the wild warrings. Nevertheless, this progress has been very real, and that it must become apparent to the world before long is certain. Even to the present day Uruguay amongst nations has remained "a violet by a mossy stone, half hidden from the eye." To the ordinary person who passes between Europe and South America, Montevideo represents little beyond a whistling station between the two important halts at Buenos Aires and Rio de Janeiro. In justice to the Banda Oriental's neighbour be it said that this ignorance does not apply to the actual resident in Argentina, and least of all to the dwellers in Buenos Aires. To them the commercial importance and general attractions of Uruguay and its capital are well enough known. This interest, however, is merely local, and fails to extend beyond the familiar radius of the pleasant little Republic's influence.

Commercially speaking, it is difficult to understand how the factors that have now arisen to drag the Banda Oriental from its undeserved oblivion can well fail in their task. The linking of the country by railway with Brazil, the influence that the imminent cessation of the North American beef exportation is bound to exert upon a stock-breeding country, to say nothing of the internal progress already referred to, must undoubtedly result sooner or later in bringing the gallant little nation into the light of publicity.

A fusion of warring parties, an end of civil strife, and a strict attention to the less risky and more profitable business of the day should follow in the natural sequence of events. Very hale, hearty, and jovial though he is, it must be admitted that the Oriental is in deadly earnest when engaged in civil battle— as is the case with all who pursue a hobby to the detriment of a more lucrative occupation. Yet the substitution of gunshots for the suffrage is not only expensive, but, from the polling point of view, unpleasantly devoid of finality.

The distinctions between the political arrangements of Uruguay and Argentina are curiously marked. For generations the latter country has been governed by a succession of groups that have respectively formed and dissolved without leaving any marked cleavage in the society of the nation. Strictly speaking, Argentina possesses neither faction spirit nor party.

Uruguay, on the other hand, is concerned first and foremost with these very matters of party.

The history of the Colorados and the Blancos—the reds and whites—would in itself suffice to fill a volume. Probably in no other part of the world have the pure considerations of clan triumphed to such an extent over the general political situation. Until the present day the line between the rival camps has been as absolute as that between life and death. The position of either is immutable. Neither argument, mode of government, nor the vicissitudes of state are among the considerations by which they are affected. A man is born one of two things—a Blanco or a Colorado. This birthright, moreover, is to be exchanged for no mere mess of pottage; it is valued above the price of life itself. Such, at all events, has been the creed of the past, and to a large extent it still holds good, although the stress of modern influence is just beginning to leave its mark upon the cast-iron prejudices that are the relicts of another age.

At the same time, it must not be inferred from this that the Uruguayan is ignorant or small-minded. Far from it. Education enjoys an exceptionally high standard throughout the country, and a most liberal breadth of view is typical of the nation. This is readily admitted, and even insisted upon, by foreigners whose dealings with the native-born dwellers in the Republic have placed them in a position to render an accurate judgment. In internal politics, however, there are prejudices, considerations of clan, and points of honour that are not to be gauged from a purely commercial standpoint.

The foreigner in Uruguay is accorded a most complete liberty, and there are few of these who have resided for any length of time within its frontiers who have not become very truly attached to the land and its people.

It has frequently been my lot to pass over from Argentina to Uruguay, arriving at one of the minor ports that dot the middle reaches of the great river. But it so happened that I had never landed, bag and baggage, at the capital until the time came for a regular and organised spying out of the land. An incident at the start lent a very pleasing aspect to the visit. The customs-house officer, in whose hands lay the fate of the interior of my baggage, gazed from where it lay piled upon the official trestle in the direction of its owner. "Inglez?" he demanded in the curt tone of one in authority. When I had signified assent he smiled cordially, sketched with rapid fingers the magic chalk marks upon the impedimenta, and then motioned me to pass through the portals with all the honours of customs, locks unviolated, and straps in repose.

I have not introduced this incident from any personal motives. It merely affords an instance of a very genuine courtesy rendered to the nation through the medium of one of its most humble units. Yet it is from such attentions to a stranger that the trend of the general attitude may be gleaned. The English are not a little addicted to a frank confession of their unpopularity amongst the South Americans in general. The attitude may be the result of a certain pose, since they claim full credit for the respect that is undoubtedly theirs by right. Nevertheless, whether imagined or real, the idea obtains.

In Uruguay at the present moment the Englishman is so obviously *not* unpopular that it is gratifying to be able to proclaim the fact. Whatever the fates may have in store the existing understanding between the Uruguayans and the British is very cordial and complete. In words as well as in deeds it is perhaps advisable to let well alone. Yet it is satisfactory to reflect that innumerable practical proofs show that this mutual esteem which has existed for centuries has never been more firmly grafted than at the present day. There can be no doubt, moreover, that the present satisfactory phase is very largely due to the efforts of Mr. R. J. Kennedy, the British Minister Plenipotentiary and Envoy Extraordinary, whose tact and conscientious ability have won for him respect and popularity on the part of Uruguayans and resident British alike—a consummation to which it is the lot of sufficiently few ministers to attain.

Although internal disturbances may continue to arise from time to time, the position of Uruguay is now undoubtedly consolidated to a far greater extent than has ever been the case in former years. The nation that sprang into being at the commencement of the nineteenth century had to contend with indefinite frontiers at the best of times, and with the frequent waves of turbulence that swept inwards over the land from the greater centres of disturbance without its borders. Now for many decades an undisturbed peace has characterised the foreign affairs of the nation, and such differences as have occurred from time to time with the neighbouring republics have been settled in an essentially pacific and reasonable spirit.

A striking instance of this has occurred quite recently in the case of the vexed question concerning the delimitation of neutral waters in the River Plate. The rights affecting a great inland and international highway are naturally most delicate and difficult to adjust, as the past history of the entire river system here has proved on numerous occasions. In this particular instance had either Uruguay or Argentina shown any other but a fair and conciliatory spirit, the consequences cannot fail to have been serious in the extreme. As it was, the dispute was brought to a satisfactory and amicable conclusion, much to the credit of the respective diplomatists concerned.

For many years now the policy of the Banda Oriental Government has been practical and deliberate. In matters of finance extreme caution has been exercised, and economy in expenditure has been rigid. The result is now evident in the very favourable financial position of the Republic, since it is now endowed with more solid monetary sinews than has ever been the case before. The nation, moreover, is free from any excessive expenditure on its army and navy. Both branches of the service are on a small scale, and in this moderation Uruguay is undoubtedly wise; since, although the race possesses its fighting instincts to the full, the population and resources of the Republic would not allow it to compete either in numbers, guns, or ships with the armies of the neighbouring countries, or with the great naval armaments that are being brought together.

In the past there is no doubt that matters in Uruguay have been regarded with a certain amount of pessimism—a gloomy view for which the alleged instability of the Government was chiefly responsible. Were all that has been said on this head strictly accurate, there is no doubt that the condition of the country would be parlous indeed. On numberless occasions, however, the reports that have prevailed have been remarkable merely for their exaggeration. Frequently, moreover, such highly coloured—or rather darkened—pictures have been depicted to serve interests in Europe rather than in Uruguay. Commercially speaking, it is surely a matter for congratulation that even such a disturbing element as civil strife should have left the financial solidity of the Republic unimpaired.

This point of view, however, is merely the financial one—important enough in its place, but not sufficiently overwhelming to eliminate all the other interests at stake. The spirit of progress has been abroad, not only in the ethics of the pastures, banks, and business houses, but in the more subtle fields of science, literature, and art as well. This, however, is not the place in which to introduce details or statistics concerning the improvements in the various ramifications of the nation's existence. For the present let the statement suffice that in no direction has a retrograde movement been perceptible: on the contrary, a continuous progress has been evident in almost every matter from the curing of beef to the making of scholars—two products that are equally essential to the welfare of the land.

CHAPTER II

HISTORY

The discovery of Uruguay—Reception by the Indians—Juan de Solis and his fate—Navigation of the River Plate—Serrano and Magellanes—Rivalry between Spaniards and Portuguese—The first settlement in the Banda Oriental—Aggressive tactics of the Indians—Forts destroyed by them—Colonisation under difficulties—The introduction of cattle—A prophetic move—Intervention of the missionaries—Jesuit settlements established—Uruguay's isolation comes to an end—Influence of the livestock—Cattle-raiders—The first Portuguese invasion—Victory of the Spaniards, assisted by native auxiliaries—Treaties and their attendant troubles—The indecision of Old Spain—Partial extermination of the Indians—The town of Colonia as a bone of contention—Introduction of the first negro slaves into the provinces of the River Plate—Unrest on the Spanish main—Moreau, the buccaneer—The fate of his expedition—Portuguese invaders expelled by the Spaniards—A fort is constructed on the present site of Montevideo.

The early history of Uruguay needs but cursory recapitulation, since its episodes form part and parcel of the general discovery of the River Plate. Juan Diaz de Solis, the famous explorer of the great river, was the first leader in the Spanish service to set foot on Uruguayan soil. The precise point of his disembarkation is unknown, but it is certain enough that the spot lay somewhere just to the north of the island of Martin Garcia. His reception at the hands of the hostile Charrúa Indians, who at the time inhabited the district, was fatally inhospitable. Solis and many more of the landing party of fifty who accompanied him were slain by these natives almost as soon as they had landed, and the disheartened expedition returned to Spain.

It is supposed that Rodriguez Serrano was the first to sail the waters of the Uruguay River proper. In 1520, when anchored in the mouth of the River Plate on his way to the South, Magellane is supposed to have sent this subordinate of his some distance up the Uruguay. There is much, however, that is vague in the history of these particular waterways at this time. A certain material reason obtained for the mystery. The rivalry between the Spaniards and Portuguese tended towards a concealment on the part of each of discoveries that affected comparatively unknown and debatable areas. Thus there is no doubt that various Portuguese expeditions sailed the Uruguay River at this period; but the details of these are uncertain.

In 1527 Spain, fearing the possibilities of Portuguese influence, turned her attention once more to the great river system of the South. It was in that year that Cabot founded the fort of San Sebastian on the Uruguayan coast. This, at the confluence of the San Salvador River with the Uruguay, was the first Spanish settlement in the country. Its existence was short-lived. Attacked by the Charrúa Indians in 1529, the fort was destroyed and many of its garrison slain.

After this little was heard of the Uruguayan coast until, in 1552, Irala, the famous Governor of the River Plate, ordered Captain Juan Romero to found a settlement on that shore. Juan Romero set out with an expedition of 120 men, and founded the settlement of San Juan at the mouth of the river of the same name. This attempt was likewise unsuccessful. The Charrúas had to be reckoned with, and two years later the place was abandoned on account of their incessant attacks.

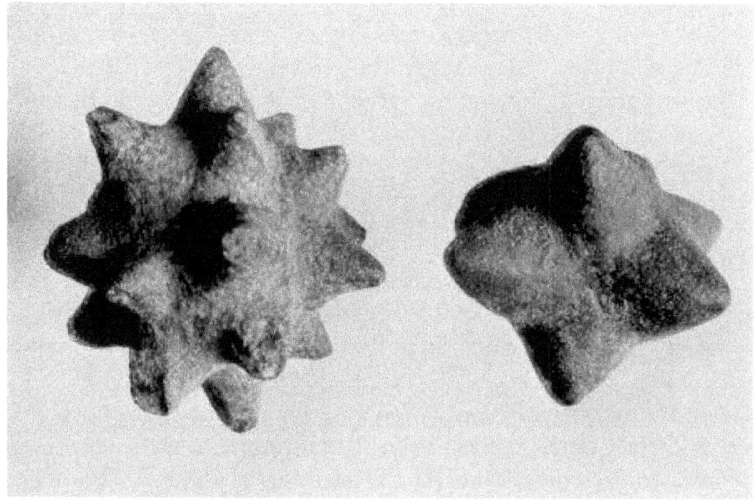

INDIAN MACE HEADS.

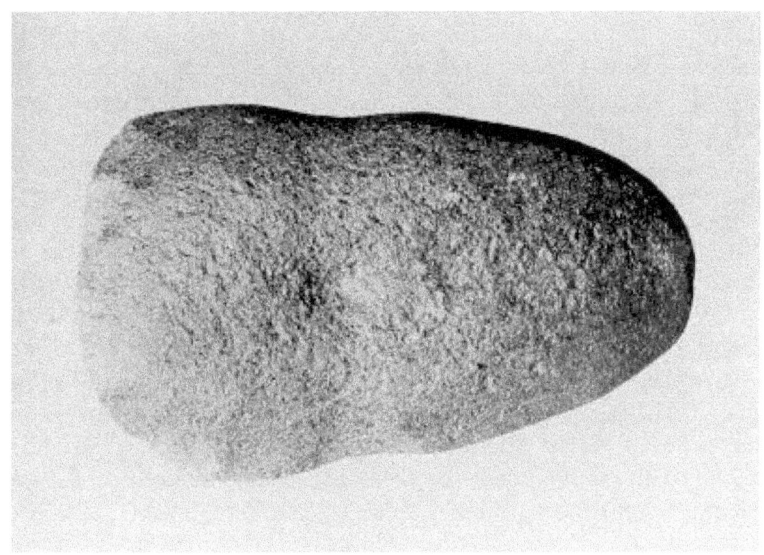

INDIAN STONE AXE.

To face p. 38.

In 1573 another noted *conquistador*, Zarate, on the completion of his voyage from Europe, arrived at the island of San Gabriel. He founded a settlement on the neighbouring Uruguayan mainland, and the Charrúas for once received him with comparative hospitality. Nevertheless it was not long ere hostilities broke out, by reason of the Spaniard's own arrogance, it is said. In the end the Europeans were completely defeated by the famous chief Zapicán, losing over one hundred soldiers and various officers. The Spaniards then retired to the island of San Gabriel, leaving the aboriginal tribe in possession of the new township, which they immediately destroyed.

A short while after this Juan de Garay, afterwards famed as the founder of the modern Buenos Aires, arrived near the scene of the disaster. With a diminutive force (it is said by some that his expedition comprised no more than twelve cavalry and twenty-two infantry) he attacked Zapicán's army of a thousand men. The result was the rout of the Indians, in the course of which Zapicán and many other leading caciques perished. This action was fought in the neighbourhood of ruined San Salvador, and Zarate founded a new settlement on the ruins of the old. Triumph, however, was short-lived, for the Indians remained as fiercely persevering as ever, and three years later their aggressive tactics caused the establishment to be abandoned once again.

In 1603 it is said that Hernando Arias de Saavedra, the first colonial-born Governor of the River Plate, led an expedition of five hundred men against the Charrúas. Hernandarias, by which name the Governor was popularly known, was a famous warrior of whose prowess and feats of arms much is told. For all that, according to report, the defeat of the Spanish force was so complete that only Hernandarias, thanks to his tremendous personal strength, escaped from the field alive. It is probable, however, that this version of the fight is, to say the least of it, exaggerated.

The next move of Hernandarias in the direction of the Banda Oriental was of a more pacific nature. With a rare touch of wisdom and foresight he shipped from Buenos Aires to Colonia across the river one hundred head of cattle, and a like number of horses and mares. These, sent adrift to roam at their own sweet will in the new country, multiplied at least as fast as had been anticipated. The animals in question undoubtedly stand as the nucleus of the pastoral riches of to-day. Thus Hernandarias sent out wealth to the land that was closed to his men in order that it should seed and multiply until the time came for the European to take it over with the country itself.

In this earlier era of River Plate history the march of civilisation had been arrested at the first step in Uruguay on each occasion on which it had been undertaken. It was not until the beginning of the seventeenth century that success attended the endeavours of the Spaniards. In 1618 the first missionaries entered Uruguay. The Franciscan fathers Bernardo de Guzman, Villavicencio, and Aldao landed in that year at the mouth of the Rio, and converted to Christianity many members of the more peaceably disposed tribes. In 1624 Bernardo de Guzman founded the first Uruguayan Jesuit settlement, Santo Domingo de Soriano, and a little later the missions of Espinillo, Viboras, and Aldao were established in the present provinces of Soriano and Colonia. Larger and more important missions were shortly afterwards founded in the north, and formed a more or less integral portion of the great Jesuit field in Paraguay. At one time there were no less than thirty-seven of these stations existing within the frontiers of the old Banda Oriental as they were then defined. In consequence of the later Brazilian encroachments, however, the sites of only seven of these—San Francisco de Borga, San Nicolas, San Juan Bautista, San Luis Gonzaga, San Miguel, San Lorenzo, and Santa Angel—lie within the boundaries of the present Republic.

While in the north of Uruguay the Indians, taught by the missionaries, were now beginning to occupy themselves with agriculture and grazing, in the south the herds introduced by Hernandarias were multiplying amazingly. These were responsible for the visits of many who came over from Argentina to slay the cattle and to collect their hides. They were licensed by the Cabildo of Buenos Aires, who received a third of the profits. In order to facilitate this traffic in hides, these *Faeneros*, as they were termed, gradually established themselves upon the banks of the Uruguay and its tributaries, and upon the ocean coast. Thus the names of Cufré, Pavón, Toledo, Pando, Solís, Maldonado, and many others have been bequeathed to the soil by the merchant adventurers who trafficked in those spots, since each named his settlement after himself.

No little competition was afforded these Faeneros by the *Changadores*, adventurers of a more reckless order who made their incursions into the country without licence and against the law. Corresponding precisely to the buccaneers of the farther north, they slew where opportunity offered, taking refuge in Brazil when pursued, until their growing numbers enabled them from time to time to offer armed resistance to the officers of the Crown sent to chastise them. Attracted by this commerce, pirates, whether of Portuguese or other nationality, would occasionally make descents, and would raid and harry the cattle in their turn. The Indians, for their part, were not slow in availing themselves of this new and convenient source of livelihood, and, according to a Uruguayan writer became "carnivorous from necessity and equestrian from force of imitation." In 1680 a more serious danger threatened the Banda Oriental. At the beginning of that year a Portuguese fleet came to anchor off the island of San Gabriel. Eight hundred soldiers and a number of colonist families were disembarked at Colonia del Sacramento on the mainland, where they founded a township. On learning of this invasion the Governor of Buenos Aires, José de Garro, immediately demanded the evacuation of the place. As a reply to this request, Lobo, the Portuguese commander, triumphantly produced a map on which Colonia was represented as in Brazilian territory. A strenuous geographical discussion ensued, at the conclusion of which Garro, having failed to convince the intruders of the inaccuracy of the chart by more subtle arguments, resolved to expel the enemy by force.

With this end in view he obtained the loan of three thousand Indians from the Jesuits, who were by this time becoming accustomed to the lending of men and arms for such patriotic purposes. With this force, stiffened by the presence of three hundred Spaniards, he captured the hostile settlement, taking prisoners the Portuguese Governor and garrison.

It is related that the Spanish general had prepared a striking *ruse de guerre* that was to serve in this assault. Four thousand loose horses were to be driven to the front of the charging forces, and upon these animals the first devastation of the artillery fire of the defenders was to expend itself. The Indians, however, whose destined place was in the vanguard, raised some powerful objections to this scheme of attack. Considering with reason that a backward rush of the wounded and terrified beasts—like that of the elephants of a previous age—would promise greater disaster to themselves than to the enemy, they protested against the living bulwark with its many possibilities. Thus the town was captured without the aid of the horses, and the first of the many combats that reddened the shore of Colonia ended in favour of Spain.

This triumph was short-lived. In 1681 Carlos II. of Spain in a weak moment signed a treaty by which Colonia was given back to Portugal, to be held by her until a definite decision could be arrived at concerning the vexed question of ownership. In the meanwhile it was arranged that the geographical arguments should be settled by the pontifical authorities, whose expert knowledge upon the point was doubtful. The Portuguese, moreover, in order to obtain an added salve to their dignity, stipulated that Garro should be deprived of his post. This was complied with; but the result did not in the least coincide with the Portuguese expectations. Garro himself must have smiled broadly when he learned that he was deprived of his command at Buenos Aires in order to take over the superior governorship of Chile!

In 1702 a campaign was waged against the Indians. The tactics of the majority of the tribes had remained consistently aggressive, and their predatory interest in the commerce of hides and dried meat had developed to a pitch inconvenient to the settlers. The war, although its scope did not include the entire aboriginal population, was one of extermination so far as it went, and at its conclusion the sections of the Charrúas, Bohanes, and Yaros in the neighbourhood of the River Yi had practically ceased to exist.

In the meanwhile Colonia, in the hands of the Portuguese, had become the centre of contraband operations by means of which merchandise was smuggled into the sternly closed port of Buenos Aires. As a point of vantage it served so admirably for this purpose, and so greatly to the profit of both the Portuguese and of the more unscrupulous residents of Buenos Aires, that in 1705 Philip V. of Spain ordered its recapture in earnest.

For this purpose two thousand Spaniards and four thousand Jesuit Indians assembled. After a six months' strenuous siege of the place the Portuguese garrison fled in a fleet that had been sent to their rescue, and Colonia passed back into the hands of the Spaniards. But the vicissitudes of the spot were not yet at an end. Oblivious of the past, Philip V. by the Treaty of Utrecht in 1713 ceded the town to the Portuguese. Garcia Ros, the Governor of Buenos Aires, was of sterner mould. Taking advantage of a loosely worded clause in the treaty, he limited the Portuguese ownership of the soil to the radius of a cannon-shot from the plaza of the town. By this means the inconvenience of the occupation was to a certain extent neutralised.

A GAUCHO RACE: THE START.

A GAUCHO RACE: THE FINISH.

To face p. 44.

About this time negro slaves were first introduced from Africa into the provinces of the River Plate. This measure had been originally urged by the famous Father Bartolomé de las Casas with a view of augmenting the local force of labour, and thus of alleviating the condition of the aboriginal races that in many parts were becoming exterminated on account of the excess of toil imposed upon them. This state of affairs, as a matter of fact, did not obtain in the Banda Oriental, where Indian and Spaniard stood entirely apart. Nevertheless an influx of negroes occurred in the province, and—though nothing can be said in favour of the morality of the proceeding—there is no doubt that, once arrived, their presence tended to benefit the industries of the land.

The period now was one of considerable unrest throughout the Spanish main. For some while the adventurers of other nations, seeking a share in the great riches of the South American provinces, had been knocking loudly at the gates that remained closely barred to them. Privateering and raids upon the coast had become more and more frequent, while the Spanish galleons, in continuous dread of attack, only put to sea for the purpose of long voyages in imposing numbers and beneath weighty escort. The River Plate, owing to the practical absence of the mineral traffic from its frontier, suffered far fewer depredations than fell to the lot of the gold and silver bearing countries to the north.

Yet the homelier riches of the pastoral districts were becoming known and appreciated to a certain extent. In consequence of this the waters of the River Plate from time to time had many unwelcome visitors. Privateers of all nationalities, although their enforced ignorance of the navigation forbade them to penetrate for any distance up the waters of the great streams themselves in the face of local opposition, harassed the coast-line, and occasionally landed in more or less formidable parties. One of the most notable of these was a French adventurer of the name of Moreau, whose buccaneering ideas were considerably in advance of those of the majority who were wont to harry these particular districts. Moreau's plan of campaign, in fact, savoured rather of regular warfare than of the more usual methods of the rapid raidings and retreats. Thus in 1720 he disembarked with a body of men and four cannon at Maldonado, where he fortified himself, and began to amass a great store of hides. Surprised by the Spaniards, he was forced to take to his ships in haste, with the loss of his guns and of his stock-in-trade. A few months later the Frenchman returned, accompanied this time by a force of over a hundred well-armed men, and prepared to settle himself for an extended stay in the country. Curiously enough, it appears to have been the unfortunate Moreau's fate to reverse the fighting rôles of the buccaneer and local resident, since, instead of surprising others, it was he who was caught unawares on either occasion. The termination of his second visit was more fatal than that of his first. Attacked when in an unprepared condition by the Spaniards, the defeat of the buccaneer force was complete. Moreau himself was slain, together with the greater part of his company, while the remainder were taken prisoners.

Freed from this source of danger, the inhabitants of the Banda Oriental were not long left without anxiety on another head. The Portuguese had never ceased to covet the rich land that might be made to serve as such a valuable and temperate pendant to their torrid northern areas. The River Plate stood to them in the light of a Rhine, and at the end of 1723 they awoke once more into aggressive activity. An expedition then left Rio de Janeiro consisting of four ships with three hundred soldiers. The force sailed to the point where the town of Montevideo now stands, at that time a lonely spot whose commercial and strategic importance was then for the first time discovered. Here the expedition landed, and in a short while its leaders had negotiated with the natives whom they found in the district, had supplied them with arms, and had founded a settlement. On learning of this aggression the Buenos Aires authorities determined to resist the attempt in earnest. Gavala, the Spanish Governor, collected a powerful fleet, and sailed in haste to the spot. The Portuguese, ascertaining the strength of the attacking force, abandoned their new settlement, and made off to the north without awaiting its arrival. Gavala then took possession of Montevideo in turn, and took measures in order to prevent a repetition of the incident. To this end he constructed a powerful battery on the spot, and supplied the fort with a garrison of a hundred Spanish troops, and with a thousand native auxiliaries.

CHAPTER III

HISTORY—*continued*

Founding of the city of Montevideo—Its first inhabitants—Inducement offered to colonists—The early days of the town—Successful rising of the Indians in the neighbourhood—Victory of the natives—Montevideo saved by Jesuit intervention—The Portuguese invade the northern provinces—The first Governor of Montevideo—Treaties and territorial cessions—Dissatisfaction of Jesuit Indians—Their defeat by combined Spanish and Portuguese forces—Vicissitudes of Colonia—The danger of hostile residents—A concentration camp of the old days—Expulsion of the Jesuits—Some incidents of the wars with the Portuguese—The foundation of urban centres—The English occupy themselves with the whaling industry on the coast—Discouragement of the enterprise by the King of Spain—A corps of Blandengues is created—The British invasion—Political effects of the occupation—The war of independence—Montevideo as the seat of the Spanish viceroyalty—Commencement of the agitation for freedom in Uruguay.

On the 24th of December, 1726, was founded the city proper of Montevideo. Its inception was sufficiently modest. Indeed, the spot commenced its urban existence on a human diet of seven families translated from Buenos Aires for the purpose. A little later twenty families were brought from the Canary Islands to add to the humble population. It is not a little curious to read how, even in those early days, the spirit of colonial enterprise was already manifest in the way that is now considered most up-to-date. Intending immigrants to Montevideo were each offered free transport from Buenos Aires, plots in the city and holdings in the Campo, two hundred head of cattle, one hundred sheep, and free cartage of building material. They were offered, beyond, tools, agricultural implements, and a remission of taxes for a certain period. The whole savours strongly of a modern immigration department. In any case, the inducements offered were considerable.

Two years after its foundation Montevideo received an important reinforcement of citizens, when thirty families from the Canary Islands and from Galicia were introduced into the place. Thus the small town was already beginning to make its mark upon the surrounding country, and at the end of 1728 it could count over two hundred inhabitants, four hundred troops, and a thousand Indians employed principally in the works of fortification. A couple of years later it was deemed worthy of a corporation.

Nevertheless, in this very year the growing settlement all but came to a bloody and untimely end. A rising of the Charrúa Indians in the immediate neighbourhood of Montevideo resisted all the efforts made to subdue it. Over one hundred Spaniards were slain and the royal forces put to rout. The natives, drunk with success, were on the eve of entering Montevideo and of slaughtering the inhabitants, when a Jesuit missionary, Padre Herán, intervened, and prevailed on the Indians to desist from their purpose.

Scarcely had this danger passed when another, and remoter, came into being to take its place. The restless Portuguese having given peace to the Banda Oriental for ten years, doubtless considered the period unduly prolonged, and thus invaded the Rio Grande on the northern frontier. Lavala's successor, Don Miguel de Salcedo, a ruler as impotent as the first had been strong, contented himself with besieging Colonia as a counter-stroke, while the Portuguese forces were left free to complete the conquest of Rio Grande. This they continued to hold, despite the terms of an armistice arranged in 1737 between Spain and Portugal.

For ten years after this no historical event of importance occurred to disturb the progress of Uruguay. In 1747 a rising of the Indians was utterly crushed at Queguay, and two years later Montevideo, now acknowledged as a town of importance, was accorded a Governor of its own. Don José Joaquin de Viana was the first appointed to the post. His opinion of its urgency is evident from the fact that he only took office in 1751.

By the treaty of 1750 King Ferdinand VI. of Spain ceded to Portugal the northern stretches comprising the Jesuit Missions of Uruguay and the present province of Rio Grande in exchange for Colonia. As a stroke of commercial diplomacy the bargain was undoubtedly a failure, since by its means Spain not only lost for ever two flourishing provinces, but, in addition, the Jesuits and their Indians were obliged to forsake the field of their labours, and to migrate in search of fresh country.

This, however, was not the case with all alike. A large number of the Indians, deeply attached to the neighbourhoods wherein lay their homes, refused to follow the missionaries, and in the end resisted the unwelcome decree. Pitted against the combined forces of Buenos Aires, Uruguay, and Brazil, their cause had not a momentary chance of success. After suffering various defeats, they were finally routed and almost exterminated at Caaibate in 1756, when the native loss amounted to 154 prisoners and 1,200 dead, at the very moderate Spanish cost of 4 dead and 41 wounded. The character of the action is sufficiently evident from the butcher's bill. A certain number of the surviving Indians were taken to Maldonado, and, settling there, formed the nucleus of the present town.

In the meanwhile Colonia, whose inhabitants by this time must have been rendered giddy by the continuous substitution of bunting, had again passed into the possession of the Portuguese. The recurrence of war between these and the Spaniards gave Pedro de Ceballos, an able and energetic Governor of Buenos Aires, an opportunity to act. In 1762 he surprised Colonia, captured it, and was in the act of invading the ceded territory of Rio Grande when the Treaty of Paris came inopportunely into being to stay him in his path of conquest, and to give back Colonia, that bone of contention, to the Portuguese once more.

This occurred in 1763, and Ceballos was powerless to struggle further against a fate that caused victory to be followed by the loss of provinces. Nevertheless, he took various measures towards the preservation of the remaining territory. One of the most important of these was concerned with the numerous Portuguese families that were settled along the eastern frontier of the country. Having reason to believe that these were hatching further warlike schemes in conjunction with the authorities across the border, Ceballos caused them to be taken south, and to be collected together in a small settlement in the neighbourhood of Maldonado, where they could remain under the watchful eye of the Uruguayan officials.

In 1767 the expulsion of the Jesuits from South America by King Carlos III. of Spain proved of no little moment to the Banda Oriental, since many of the Indians, wandering shepherdless and at a loss, came southwards, and became part and parcel of Uruguay. It was by means of twelve of these Indian families that the city of Paysandú, amongst several others, was founded, while the fields of Montevideo and Maldonado derived many new cultivators from this source.

It was but a very few years later that the trouble with the Portuguese broke out once again. Indeed, it would seem that indulgence in border feud had now become an ineradicable habit on the part of both sides. By the year 1774 the inhabitants of Brazil had once again passed over the north-western frontier, and had spread themselves over the country in such numbers as to render their presence a menace to Uruguay. In order to remedy the situation, Vertiz, the Governor of Buenos Aires, crossed from Buenos Aires to Montevideo, from which city he sallied out northwards with an army of four thousand men. Meeting with the Portuguese forces in the neighbourhood of the Santa Tecla range, he routed them and pursued them as far as the River Yacuy, depriving them of the lands they had usurped.

On the return of Vertiz to Buenos Aires, Portuguese aggression burst forth once again. Advancing from the east this time, they were repulsed in an attack on the town of San Pedro; but in 1776, returning with an army of two thousand men, they captured the place and possessed themselves of the district. The inevitable counter-stroke on the part of the Spaniards was to follow. Indeed, the scale of the struggle waxed steadily with the growth of the respective countries. Brazil was already the seat of a viceroyalty, and immediately after this last invasion the provinces of the River Plate were raised to the same status. Ceballos, then on a visit to Spain, was created first Viceroy, and was dispatched from Cadiz with a powerful fleet and with over nine thousand troops to avenge the incursion.

RUINED COLONIA.

ARTIGAS' MONUMENT.

To face p. 52.

With such forces as these at his disposal the task of Ceballos was an easy one. The Island of Santa Catalina was captured without a blow, and that bone of contention, Colonia, surrendered perforce after a few days of siege. Above its walls for the fifth time the flag of Spain was hoisted afresh. On this occasion the ill-omened place was destined to pay for the memories of the past, and its walls suffered in place of the garrison. In order to remove temptation from the minds of the northern enemy, Ceballos razed the elaborate fortifications to the ground and destroyed the more pretentious houses, amongst these being some of the best architectural specimens of the River Plate.

Having effected this, Ceballos was passing northwards with the intention of bringing back the Rio Grande Province once more within the fold of Buenos Aires, when his march was stopped by the news of another of those treaties between the mother-countries that seemed to materialise with unfailing regularity at moments so ill-timed for the interests of the Spanish colonies. By the terms of this Spain was left with the mines of Colonia, while the Island of Santa Catalina and the greater part of Rio Grande were ceded definitely to Portugal.

After this ensued an exceptionally lengthy era of peace, which was marked by the immigration of many families from Galicia and from the Canary Islands, and by the foundation of numerous towns, amongst these latter Canelones, Piedras, Rosario, Mercedes, Pando, Santa Lucia, San José, and Minas. As to the capital itself, by the year 1788 Montevideo had become a fairly important place, and could count a population of 6,695 Spaniards, 1,386 negro slaves, 562 liberated negroes, and 715 half-castes and Indians. A few years later the population was much augmented by the introduction of important numbers of negro slaves, a traffic that continued intermittently until 1825, when its continuance was prohibited by law.

At the end of the century an industry was initiated that might have led to important commercial results but for the action of the Spanish home authorities. The waters off the coast of Maldonado had long been famed as a whaling-ground, and at this period permission was given to the Englishmen engaged in the traffic to found establishments both at this place and at Punta de la Ballena. The result was a rapid but fleeting prosperity at both these points, since after a while the attitude of the Court of Spain changed. Fearful of the influence of the English upon the Uruguayans, the authorities offered to the new colonists the option of becoming Roman Catholics and of swearing allegiance to the King of Spain, or of abandoning the settlement. The latter alternative was chosen by the whalers, and Maldonado and Punta de la Ballena, in consequence, sank back into the lethargy of industrial torpor.

The instance is only one of the many in which the mother-country satisfied its conscience at the expense of its colony.

A corps of *Blandengues*, or Lancers, was formed in 1797, whose duties, beyond their military performances, were varied to a degree. Thus, in addition to the occasional brushes with the Indians that fell to their lot, they were employed as excise officials against the smugglers, as escorts of high officials, as ordinary police, and as official messengers. The corps was composed of picked men, and in its ranks served José Gervasio Artigas and José Rondeau, both bearers of names that were destined to become famous in Uruguayan history.

This body of cavalry was destined to be employed on active service very soon after its formation. In 1801 the Portuguese became active once more, and the first year of the new century was marked by their occupation of land in the north-west of the Banda Oriental. After various actions, Rondeau, with a force of Blandengues and dragoons, defeated the invaders and won back the greater part of the lost territory.

In 1806 occurred the first of the British invasions which, although materially fruitless in the end so far as our own country was concerned, were destined to influence the minds of the colonials and the future of the River Plate Provinces to a greater extent than is generally realised. The circumstances of the invasion that won to the British Crown for a very short while not only Montevideo, Maldonado, Colonia, and numerous lesser Uruguayan towns, but Buenos Aires in addition, afford bitter reading. Thanks to the colossal incapacity—to give his conduct no harder name—of the British Commander-in-Chief, General Whitlocke, the last troops of the British army of occupation had sailed away northwards from Montevideo by the beginning of September, 1807.

Although the matter ended for the British with the departure of the troops from the River Plate, the aftermath of the event took very definite shape in the Spanish colonies themselves. Not only had the inhabitants of the provinces learned their own power, but—more especially in the case of Montevideo—the seeds of commercial liberty had been sown amongst the local merchants and traders by the English men of business who had descended upon the place beneath the protection of the army. That the final leave-taking between the English and the Uruguayans should have been accompanied by actual cordiality and regrets is surely an astonishing circumstance that affords great credit to both sides. There can be no doubt, however, that this mutual esteem was in the first place fostered by an appreciation on the part of the residents of British laws and methods of trading.

Whether the germs thus left behind would have fructified so rapidly but for the chaotic condition of the mother-country is doubtful. As it was, scarcely had the smoke of these actions cleared away when it became necessary for the patriots of the River Plate Province to look once again to their primings in view of still more vital occurrences.

I do not propose to tell here the full story of the rebellion of the River Plate Provinces and of the revolution that ended in the complete overthrow of Spanish power in South America, since I have already roughly sketched these events elsewhere. So far as the main events are concerned, the transition from the colonial stage to the condition of independence was slower in the Banda Oriental than was the process upon the eastern bank of the great river. In Julio of 1810, when the Junta of Buenos Aires had already established itself to cast off the yoke of Spain, Montevideo still remained faithful to the mother-country, and rejected the advances of the Argentines.

Thus at the beginning of 1811 Montevideo found itself, if only for a short while, the seat of the viceroyalty of the La Plata Provinces, and from that point of vantage Elio, the Viceroy, declared war upon Buenos Aires. Almost immediately, however, the spirit of independence became manifest in Uruguay itself, and it is at this juncture that occurs the name that has perhaps stamped itself most deeply of all upon the history of the Banda Oriental.

CHAPTER IV

HISTORY—*continued*

The advent of Artigas—First revolutionary movements in Uruguay—The appointment of leaders—First successes of the Uruguayans—The germs of future jealousies—Montevideo besieged by the patriot forces—An incident of the investment—Spain appeals to Portugal for assistance—Invasion of Uruguay by the latter—The Buenos Aires Government concludes a treaty with the Spanish Viceroy—Raising of the siege of Montevideo—Position of Uruguay—Discontent of the Orientales—The exodus of the nation—Incidents of emigration to the Argentine shore—Montevideo in Spanish hands—The country overrun by Portuguese—Buenos Aires effects a treaty with the latter—Resumption of the campaign against the Spaniards—Disputes between the Argentine and Uruguayan leaders—Montevideo again besieged—Some battle incidents—Artigas reappears on the scene—Drastic measures towards an ally—A national Congress convened—Oriental deputies rebuffed by Buenos Aires—Artigas withdraws from the siege of Montevideo—Price set upon his head—War declared between Uruguay and Buenos Aires—The Argentine littoral provinces adhere to Artigas—Fall of Montevideo.

The personality of Artigas, the central figure of the Uruguayan revolutionary era, is fully described in a later chapter. It is necessary here, therefore, merely to give the record of historical occurrences, without laying stress on the individuality of the Oriental leader, a matter that is not easy of accomplishment, since the figure of Artigas seems to have dominated the field of action in whatever direction it lay.

Shortly after the outbreak of the revolution Artigas, who at the time was in the Spanish service, joined the patriot ranks after a violent quarrel with his brigadier. The Oriental fled across the river to Buenos Aires. Here he received a warm welcome, and was supplied with armed men and financial aid in order to foment the movement in his native country. Beyond this he received the official rank of lieutenant-colonel in the Army of Independence.

In the meanwhile the first stirrings of the war that was to come had already shaken Uruguay. With its capital, Montevideo, now the seat of the viceroyalty, the small province had remained more or less quiescent, lying, as it were, directly beneath the eye of Imperial Spain itself. But the awakening, when it occurred, was followed by a strenuous outbreak of activity. The first important rising took place at Paysandú, on the banks of the Uruguay River. This was crushed by the aid of the Spanish war vessels that lay in the stream. But the inhabitants, not in the least discouraged by this first check, rose again in greater numbers than before. A body of one hundred gauchos, ill-armed as it was, captured the town of Mercedes, and then, with augmented forces, marched on Soriano, which surrendered to them.

This success was the signal for a general rising throughout the country. At the beginning of 1811 the Spanish garrison found themselves in the midst of a definitely hostile population. From one frontier to another bodies of men were gathering together, forging weapons from agricultural tools, and arming themselves as best they could in order that they might take their share in the struggle for liberation that was already in active being. In March the towns of Maldonado, San Carlos, and Minas rose, and the country just to the east of Montevideo itself threw off the Spanish authority and came into possession of the insurrectionist companies.

On the 11th of April, 1811, Artigas returned to Uruguay in command of 150 men of the regiment of Patricios, and disembarked in the neighbourhood of that hub of all strife, Colonia. Here he was welcomed by a great number of armed countryfolk, who acclaimed him as chief of the Orientales. The movement now fairly under way, he established his headquarters at Mercedes. In the meanwhile the germ of future combinations had already been created by the appointment on the part of the Buenos Aires patriots of Rondeau as commander of the Uruguayans. Belgrano, first named for the post, had, disgraced, been deprived of it since his defeat by the Paraguayans.

Artigas's first collision with the royal forces occurred at Paso del Rey, the Spanish army being completely defeated. Reinforced by a second victorious column, under Benavidez, the Uruguayans followed up the retreating regulars, and forced them to surrender.

Artigas, the *Jefe de los Orientales*, had now at his disposal a force of over a thousand men. Meeting at Las Piedras with a royalist army of 1,230 men, the valour of the new levies was soon put to the test. Although the Spaniards possessed the advantage of artillery, they were in the end, after a desperate and prolonged fight that endured for half a dozen hours, defeated and forced to surrender.

The doings of the patriotic force came as a blow to the Spanish authorities at Montevideo. Urged by the first tremblings of the viceregal throne beneath him, Elio cast about him for an inducement to turn Artigas from his victorious course. To this end he sent messengers offering the chieftain a heavy monetary bribe to desert the patriot cause, and to take service again in the royalist cause. Whether any offering of any kind would have tempted Artigas is doubtful. But in any case the tender was eloquent of Elio's want of acquaintance with the Gaucho temperament, to which the possession of mere cash constitutes a matter of utter indifference. As it was, Artigas treated the offer with angry contempt.

The hour of the patriot leader's triumph was not without its sting. The battle of Las Piedras had won him the rank of colonel in the revolutionary forces, it is true; but Belgrano, after Suipacha, had risen to that of a general. And, although both the Buenos Aires Government and the official *Gazette*, using the soft soap of courtesy titles, referred continuously to Artigas by the honorary term of "General," the bitterness remained to give rise to future strife.

Three days after his victory Artigas marched to Montevideo, and laid siege to the headquarters itself of the Spanish régime. As a preliminary to the operation an exchange of prisoners, wounded and whole, was effected. Artigas then formally demanded the surrender of the garrison; Elio responded by various sorties, all of which were repulsed. The beginning of the siege was marked by a dramatic episode. Suspecting the revolutionary sympathies of some Franciscan monks domiciled in Montevideo, Elio decided to expel these from the city. The Franciscans were led through the streets with the utmost silence at the dead of night. Arrived at the gates, the officer in charge of the escort pointed with his sword at some sparks of light that twinkled faintly in the distance. "Go you with the butchers!" he commanded, and the priests passed out silently into the darkness to join the forces of Artigas. Their influence was doubtless exhilarating to the patriot cause, but there is no evidence to show that it was employed in the cause of mercy. A few days later forty Uruguayan families suffered a similar fate.

In the meanwhile Benavidez had laid siege to Colonia, the garrison of which, after a month's resistance, escaped by river to Montevideo. It was upon this latter place that the fortune of the Spanish dominion now hung. The scale of warfare was increasing in proportion to the importance of the issue. Shortly after the arrival of the reinforcements supplied by the Royalist fugitives from Colonia, Rondeau, in command of the Argentine troops, arrived to take charge of the attacking force, that now amounted to four thousand men. Artigas, now one amongst many, dropped in rank from commander to leader of horse.

Rondeau had contrived to drag two heavy guns to the spot, and with these he opened fire upon Montevideo. Galled by a continuous bombardment, Elio took a more desperate step than was justified even by his situation. Carlota, the Queen of Portugal and the sister of Ferdinand VII. of Spain, had been established in Rio de Janeiro since the invasion of the peninsula by the Napoleonic armies. To her the Viceroy, seeing the last foothold of power slipping from beneath him, sent an urgent message for assistance.

Ere the response to this appeal became evident the condition of the beleagured town had changed. Discouraged by the serious defeat at Huaqui of the army of Peru, the revolutionary leaders of Buenos Aires were already contemplating a retirement from before Montevideo, when the blow engineered by Elio took effect. A swarm of Portuguese, under command of General Diego de Souza, entered the Banda Oriental from the north with the purpose of overrunning the country. The Buenos Aires Government, appalled by the new turn that affairs had taken, made the utmost haste to conclude an armistice with Elio. By the terms of the treaty the patriot forces were to retire from Montevideo, and Spanish authority was to be recognised throughout Uruguay in exchange for the return of Souza's forces to Brazil. Thus Elio's unscrupulous move had succeeded for the time being, and the first siege of Montevideo came to an end. A month after its conclusion Elio retired to Spain. The command he had left was now no longer worthy of the highest rank, and the departed Viceroy was succeeded by Vigodet in the minor capacity of Captain-General.

Artigas had from the first bitterly opposed this treaty, by the terms of which the Orientales were to be left at the mercy of the Royalists. That he had right upon his side from his own point of view is undeniable, although it is difficult to see by what other means the Buenos Aires Government, caught between the Spaniards and the Brazilians, could have extricated themselves from their dilemma. The treaty once concluded, however, Artigas initiated a move that in itself proved the greatness of the man.

A general assembly of the patriotic Oriental families was sounded. Obedient to the call, they mustered in numbers that amounted to over thirteen thousand men, women, and children. Then followed the exodus, ordained by the stress of events, of which Artigas was the human instrument. Escorted by three thousand soldiers, the march of the families began. Carts filled with women and children, herds of cattle, troops of horses, companies of pack-mules, to say nothing of the riders themselves—the tragic procession toiled its long length northwards through the summer dust clouds struck up by the hoofs and feet from the crude earth roads. Mingled with the slowly advancing ranks, and lending still greater variety to the whole, went four hundred faithful Charrúa Indians, armed with bolas and spears.

Over the rolling hills of Uruguay struggled the human thread of emigrants. Death waited on the column in the shape of heat and hardship. But, though many children and many aged folk fell by the way, the great majority won through in safety to Salto, on the banks of the Uruguay; crossed the great river in boats, and took up their abode on the Argentine shore, awaiting with anxiety the hour that might permit their return to their native land.

In the meantime matters were passing from bad to worse in Uruguay. Once within its frontiers, the temptations of the promised land overcame any scruple on the part of the Portuguese concerning a too rigid adherence to the terms of the treaty. Under the convenient pretext of pacifying an already deserted country, Souza's army overran the smiling Campo, capturing towns and plundering where they might. The Spanish royalists, for their part, remained passive, and the sole opposition with which the Portuguese armies had to count was that rendered by the forces of Artigas, sent by him across the river. But, although they won a victory or two, the slender patriot bands were unable to stem the tide of invasion to any appreciable degree.

It is a little curious to remark what an endless wealth of complications appear to have attended every political move at this period. In this particular instance the introduction of a new element was productive of unexpected results. Thus, when the Buenos Aires Government, realising the gravity of the situation, proposed to send reinforcements to the assistance of Artigas, the move was checked by Elio, the Spanish commander, who, forgetful of the ties of blood, threatened to join cause with the Portuguese in the event of any such intervention. As an appropriate climax to the chaotic situation, the Buenos Aires powers turned to Paraguay for assistance. The latter, inclined to assent, began negotiation with Artigas direct, and, since the Argentine Government resented this slight upon its authority, and the negotiations themselves failed to fructify, the only outcome of importance was an increase in the mutual jealousies that already existed between Artigas and the Argentines.

Shortly after this, however, the tables were turned upon the Spaniards. An able stroke of diplomacy on the part of the famous Argentine, Belgrano, supported by British influence, resulted in a treaty with the Portuguese. Thus the Royalists, hoist by a second edition of their own petard, lay without allies at the mercy of the patriot forces.

Preparations for a fresh siege of Montevideo were at once begun. Don Manuel Sarratea, appointed Commander-in-Chief of the Argentine Army, marched to the Entre Rios shore to join his columns with those of Artigas. The inevitable jealousies between the Argentine and Oriental leaders came to a head almost immediately. Apart from a deep personal antagonism that separated the pair, a yet more potent reason made the rupture inevitable. Sarratea, representing the triumvirate of Buenos Aires, was determined to deal with Uruguay as a province of the new Republic of Argentina. Artigas, on the other hand, although willing to acknowledge the authority at Buenos

Aires from a federal point of view, insisted upon the independence of the State.

It was in these circumstances that Sarratea descended upon Artigas's mixed camp of soldiers and Uruguayan emigrant families upon the banks of the Uruguay. The results of the meeting were soon evident. Artigas, complaining bitterly that Sarratea had seduced from his allegiance not only his troops but the civilian elements of the settlement, resigned his colonelcy, and separated his division from the Argentine forces. The troops now remaining to him numbered rather less than a thousand men, under the command of Otorgués, Rivera, and Manuel Artigas.

In the meanwhile Sarratea, anxious that the credit for the capture of Montevideo should fall to his lot, had dispatched a force under Rondeau to lay siege once again to the town of contention that represented the headquarters of the Royalists. Arriving at the spot, he found that his task had already been forestalled to a certain extent by an independent Oriental, José Eugenio Culta. The latter *caudillo*, spurred onwards by the numerous examples of reckless initiative offered by the period, had collected a band of three hundred Gauchos. With these kindred spirits he was busily occupied in harassing the garrison to no little purpose.

With the arrival of Rondeau, in October of 1812, the siege of the devoted city began on an imposing scale, the army employed for the purpose soon amounting to two thousand men. Destined to drag out its length for almost two years, the first few months of the siege were marked by two events of importance. Vigodet, having received reinforcements from Spain, made a vigorous sally on the last day of the year. At early dawn sixteen hundred men burst out from the gates of the city, surprising and routing the besieging forces as they went, until they won the summit of the Cerrito hill itself, the headquarters of the American forces. With the yellow and red of Spain flaunting from this the Royalists forgot all but their success, and expended their energies in a jubilation that cost them dear. For Rondeau, gathering together his fugitive troops with an amazing rapidity, fell like a thunderbolt upon the cheering crowd, whose joyful clamour turned to groans and death gasps as the stricken mass went reeling back into the city.

An event of still greater importance occurred during the first month of the following year. Sarratea himself then journeyed to the camp before Montevideo. But he had company behind that he could not have failed to regard with considerable unease. Notwithstanding his late check, Artigas still remained a power to be reckoned with. Indeed, his vitality had risen to the occasion; he had flung out his summons far and wide, and his power was now infinitely greater than before. Thus, when Sarratea set out for Montevideo, Artigas followed grimly in his wake, having now no mean instrument by means of which to assert his rights—an army of five thousand men.

Arriving on the heels of his enemy at the point of hostilities, Artigas was not slow to act. Taking full measure of his advantage, he sent peremptorily to Rondeau, demanding the immediate dismissal of Sarratea from his office of Commander-in-Chief. The order thus given to a subordinate to deal with his superior was quite in accordance with the spirit of the times.

As Rondeau, however, did not immediately comply, Artigas took a very simple measure by which to prove that he did not intend to ask in vain. His Gauchos dashed full gallop into Sarratea's camp, and drove off with them all the horses that they found within the establishment. Seeing that a Gaucho army, unhorsed, is as a collection of fish on dry land, the matter was definitely settled by the act. Sarratea retired with the best grace he could muster to Buenos Aires, Rondeau remained in command, and the Oriental and Argentine leaders sat down to continue the investment of Montevideo, one jealous eye of each upon his fellow-chief, the other fixed more casually upon the beleaguered town.

During the comparative lull in active hostilities that followed Artigas busied himself in the affairs of the State that he was determined to see fully created. To this end he convened a national Congress of Uruguayans, of which he was, as a matter of course, elected President, in addition to being created Military Governor of the country. One of the first acts of the new Congress was to advertise its existence by the mission of deputies to the Junta at Buenos Aires. But, the Junta refusing to recognise either an independent Uruguay or its agents, the deputies returned home to spread the tale of the rebuff, and to increase the bitterness that already lay so deep between the Buenos Aires authorities and Artigas.

In January, 1814, the long series of incessant disputes was brought abruptly to a head by Artigas. In the dead of night he struck his hide tents, mounted his men, and his entire force rode away over the hills, leaving Rondeau and his army to continue the siege of Montevideo as best they might. The Buenos Aires authorities, furious at the defection, placed a price upon Artigas's head; and the Gaucho leader, equally incensed at this personal ultimatum, retaliated by declaring open war upon the Junta. Storming against the Buenos Airens, this born leader of men took his body—valued by his enemies at six thousand pesos, alive or dead—along the coast of the great river. So successful were his denunciations and the missions of his ambassadors that not only the littoral provinces of Entre Rios, Corrientes, and Santa Fé came spontaneously to his standard, but the comparatively remote province of Córdoba, following the example of the rest, proffered its allegiance.

It was not long ere the news of the rupture reached the ears of Vigodet in Montevideo. Thinking to derive profit from the occasion, he made a final appeal to throw in his lot with the royal forces. The Gaucho leader in his refusal is stated to have said that "with the Porteños [Buenos Airens] there was always time for reconciliation; with the Spaniards, never!" That the time for the former consummation was not yet ripe was evidenced by the almost immediate outbreak of active hostilities between the rival South American parties.

In the meanwhile Montevideo was giving out the last gasp of its imperial existence. The Spanish fleet that had assisted in its defence had been destroyed by Admiral Brown, the famous Irishman in Argentine service. Hunger and the lack of general necessaries both of livelihood and of war completed the work of arms. On the 20th June, 1814, Montevideo, after suffering intense privations, capitulated, and with its fall passed for ever the last vestige of Spanish power from the provinces of the River Plate.

CHAPTER V

HISTORY—*continued*

Conclusion of Spanish rule—Situation of the victors—Rival claims—Alvear defeats a Uruguayan force—Montevideo remains in possession of Buenos Aires—Rural Uruguay supports Artigas—Alliance of the Argentine littoral provinces with the Orientales—Some intrigues and battles—Success of the Uruguayans—Departure from Montevideo of the Buenos Aires garrison—The Uruguayans enter into possession of their capital—Some crude methods of government—Trials of the inhabitants—Growth of Artigas's power—The Buenos Aires directors undertake a propitiatory measure—A grim human offering—Attitude of the Uruguayan Protector—Negotiations and their failure—The civil progress of Uruguay—Formation of departments—The Portuguese invade the country once again—Condition of the inhabitants—Fierce resistance to the invaders—A campaign against heavy odds—The Portuguese army enters Montevideo—War continued by the provinces—Invasion of Brazil by the Oriental forces—Crushing defeats suffered by the army of invasion—Final struggles—The flight of Artigas—Uruguay passes under Portuguese rule.

The defeated eagle was fluttering slowly homeward with broken wing. But its departure did not leave the battlefield empty. It was the turn now of the victorious hawks to rend each other. Alvear had arrived from Buenos Aires, and was now in charge of the newly won city. Scarcely had he begun his work of organisation, however, when Otorgues, Artigas's chief lieutenant, appeared at Las Piedras in the neighbourhood of the capital, and in the name of his leader demanded that the place should be handed over to the Uruguayans. Alvear's answer was unexpected and to the point. Marching his army through the darkness, he fell upon Otorgues's forces in the middle of the night, shattering them completely.

Thus the Buenos Aires authorities remained for the time being masters of the city. As for their sway, the Montevideans broke out into bitter complaints that the Spanish dominion had been liberal and lenient by comparison. However this may have been, it is certain that those families noted for their allegiance to Artigas were subjected to severe penalties and restrictions.

Nevertheless the situation of the advocates of centralisation had now become critical. By a curious irony of fate the position of the Junta was exactly identical with that formerly held by the Spaniards. Montevideo lay in its power; but the remainder of the Banda Oriental as well as the Argentine provinces of Entre Rios, Correntes, and Santa Fé were completely subject to Artigas. Alive to the growing power of the Protector, the Buenos Aires Government opened negotiations for a treaty, flinging out in the first place an olive-branch in the shape of a degree not only relieving the head of the Gaucho leader of the dollars set upon it, but in addition proclaiming him to the world as *buen servidor de la patria*—"a worthy servant of the country." A meeting at Montevideo resulted in the evacuation of Montevideo on the part of nearly the entire Buenos Aires garrison. These departed by river; but, instead of returning to Buenos Aires, the troops landed at Colonia, marched inland to Minas, fell upon Otorgues, whose camp lay in that district, and completely routed the force of the unsuspecting lieutenant.

This achieved, the victorious army set out in search of Rivera, another of Artigas's commanders, who had recently surprised and destroyed a Buenos Aires column. In this latter leader, however, Dorrego, the Junta general, met with more than his match, and, suffering many casualties, was forced to retire to Colonia. Sallying out from here with reinforcements a little later, he was utterly defeated, and fled in haste to Corrientes, accompanied by some score of men who formed the sole remnant of his entire army.

Just as the fall of Montevideo crowned the doom of the Spanish power, so this final disaster marked the end of the occupation of the town by the Buenos Aires Government. A little more than a month after the event the troops of the garrison sailed across to Buenos Aires. The following day Fernando Otorgues entered the place at the head of his troops. The advent of the new Military Governor was hailed with enthusiasm by the inhabitants. The unfurling of Artigas's blue and white standard with its red bar was answered by illuminations and fireworks by the citizens.

For the first time in its history the capital of Uruguay lay beneath the command of a Uruguayan. By one of the first acts of the new régime a national coat of arms was instituted, and a flaming proclamation promised nothing short of the millennium. All this would have been very well had it not been necessary for this new benignity to be put immediately to the test. It then became evident to the depressed Montevideans that with each change of rulers their load of evils had increased. With his talents essentially confined to the field of battle, there was probably no man in Uruguay who possessed less of the lamb in his disposition than Otorgues. The temperaments of his subordinates, reckless at the best of times, had been further excited by merciless warfare. Thus the inhabitants, at the mercy of the utterly licentious Gaucho soldiers, continued to groan for relief in vain.

Artigas himself had not approached the city. From points of vantage along the great river system he had ceaselessly harassed the forces of the Junta, until Alvear, its director, goaded to exasperation, collected into an army every soldier that he could spare, and, determined to put all to the hazard, sent the imposing expedition against the Gaucho leader. The adventure involved complete disaster to the director. Ere it had passed the frontiers of Buenos Aires Province, the army, encouraged by Artigas, revolted, and its chief, Colonel Alvarez Thomas, returned to Buenos Aires to depose Alvear, with whose office he invested himself.

The power of the famous Oriental chief had now reached its zenith. The new director, Alvarez Thomas, acutely conscious of the Protector's power, thought of nothing beyond conciliation. Among the measures employed was one that redounded very little to his credit. Not satisfied with the public burning of the various proclamations hostile to the *Caudillo*, he bethought himself of a stake that should win for ever the regard of Artigas. To this end he arrested the seven chief friends of Alvear, and sent them as a combined sacrifice and peace-offering to Artigas's encampment. As a specimen of grim and sycophantic courtesy the callousness of the offering of seven bodies can scarcely have been exceeded in the world's history. But Artigas, contrary to the Director's expectation, failed to make the intended use of the gifts. Indeed, he treated them with no little consideration, and sent them back whence they came, bidding them tell Thomas that the General Artigas was no executioner.

The next move was of the legitimately political order. The voluntary acknowledgment of the independence of Uruguay was offered in exchange for the abandonment of the protectorate over the provinces of Entre Rios, Santa Fé, Córdoba, and Corrientes. This was also refused by Artigas, who maintained that the provinces of the River Plate should, though self-governing, be indissolubly linked.

During all this time Artigas remained at his encampment at Hervidero on the banks of the Uruguay River. From thence by a system of organisation that, though crude, was marvellously effective, he manipulated the affairs of the extensive region under his command, jealously watching the moves of doubtful friends and open enemies, and keeping his armed bands of remorseless Gauchos ceaselessly on the alert.

This continual state of minor warfare, however, did not altogether exclude the attention to civil matters. In addition to some tentative measures of administration in Córdoba and the Argentine littoral provinces, Uruguay was partitioned off into six departments, to each of which was allotted its Cabildo and general mechanism of government. These attempts naturally represented nothing more than a drop of progress in the ocean of chaos; but there is no reason to doubt that Artigas undertook the new and peaceable campaign with no little measure of whole-heartedness. In any case the new era proved as fleeting as any of its predecessors. It was the turn of the Portuguese once again to set in motion the wheel of fate upon which the destinies of Uruguay were revolving with such giddy rapidity.

It was in 1816 that the Portuguese invaded Uruguay for the second time since the natives of the land had started on their campaign of self-government. Their armies marched south from Brazil with the ostensible object of putting an end to the anarchy that they alleged was rampant under the rule of Artigas. The condition of the country was undoubtedly lamentable. Harassed by hordes of marauding soldiery or acknowledged bandits, the safety of lives and homes without the more immediate range of Artigas's influence was even more precarious than had been the case during the recent period of wild turmoil.

It is true that in the districts bordering on the headquarters of the Gaucho chief at Hervidero matters were very different. Indeed, so severe was the discipline imposed by the Caudillo, and so terrible the penalties following on theft, that it is said that beneath his iron rule a purse of gold might have been left on the public highway with as little chance of its removal as though it lay within the vaults of a bank.

But notwithstanding the disorder that prevailed in so many quarters, the disinterestedness of the motives that caused the Portuguese intervention need not be taken too seriously. There can be no doubt that the real object of the invasion was territorial possession rather than the amelioration of a state of turbulence that concerned Brazil to a very minor degree. To this end an imposing army of twelve thousand men marched southwards, striking Uruguay at the central point of its northern frontier.

Artigas braced himself for a desperate struggle, the final result of which could scarcely be doubtful. In order to distract the attention of the advancing army he became in turn the invader, and sent a force northwards to invade the Misiones territory that, lost to the Banda Oriental, now formed part of Brazil. The manoeuvre, though adroit, was rendered futile by the preponderance of the foreign troops. In a short while the scene of the conflict was transferred to the home country. Here the entire collection of Artigas's mixed forces made a stand. Men of pure Spanish descent, Gauchos, Indians, negroes, and a sprinkling of emigrant foreigners beyond—all these fought with a desperation that was in the first place rewarded by several victories. No human effort, however, could stave off the final result. Andresito, a famous Indian leader, Rivera, Latorre, and Artigas himself were in turn defeated, and in February of 1817 Lecor, at the head of the Portuguese army, entered Montevideo in triumph.

The fall of the capital did not end the war. Throughout the provinces the resistance continued unabated. On the water, too, the Uruguayans asserted themselves with no little success, and it is amazing to read that one or two of their privateers with the utmost hardihood sailed across the ocean to the coasts of Portugal itself, making several captures within sight of the Iberian cliffs. Indeed, that the authority of Artigas was still recognised to a certain degree is proved by a treaty between his Government and Great Britain that was concluded several months after the loss of Montevideo.

It was not long, however, ere the inevitable complications arose to render the situation yet more hopeless. The perennial disputes with Buenos Aires became embittered to such a degree that Artigas, in sublime disregard of the Portuguese forces already in the country, declared war against the Directorate. The primary outcome of this was the defection of several of his leaders, who, as a matter of fact, foreseeing the reckless declaration, had espoused the Buenos Aires cause just previous to its publication.

The sole hope of Artigas now lay in the provinces of Entre Rios and Corrientes. Even here had occurred a wavering that had necessitated a crushing by force ere a return to allegiance had been brought about. With these and the remaining Oriental forces he continued the struggle. But the tide of his fortune had turned. The beginning of the year 1818 witnessed the capture of two of his foremost lieutenants, Otorgues and Lavalleja, who were sent by the Portuguese to an island in the Bay of Rio de Janeiro. As a last effort, Artigas, daring the aggressive even at this stage, hurled his intrepid Gauchos and Misiones Indians once more over the frontier into Brazilian territory itself. A brilliant victory was followed by the inevitable retreat in the face of immensely superior forces. At Tacuarembo, in the north of the Banda Oriental, fell the blow that virtually ended the campaign. Here Artigas's army, under the command of Latorre, was surprised and completely routed with a loss that left the force non-existent for practical purposes. Shortly after this Rivera surrendered to the Portuguese, and with his submission went the last hope of success.

Artigas crossed the River Uruguay, and took up a position in Entre Rios. The hour of his doom had struck; but even then, with his forces shattered and crushed, he refused to bow to the inevitable. With extraordinary doggedness he scoured Entre Rios, Corrientes, and Misiones in an endeavour to sweep up the remaining few that the battles had spared, and yet once again to lead them against the Portuguese. But on this occasion there was no response. Sullen and despairing, the majority of the remnant turned from him, and in the end his officer Ramirez, Governor of Entre Rios, threw off his allegiance, and came with an expedition to expel him from the country.

Devoting themselves to this narrowed campaign, the two Gaucho leaders assailed each other with fury. Victory in the first instance lay with Artigas, despite his diminished following. Ramirez, however, received reinforcements from the Buenos Aires authorities, who had thrown the weight of their influence against their old enemy. It was against the allied forces that Artigas fought his last battle. When it was evident even to his indomitable spirit that all hope was at an end he marched northwards with a couple of hundred troops who remained faithful in the hour of adversity to the once all-powerful Protector.

At Candelaria he crossed the Paraná, and sought the hospitality of Gaspar Rodriguez Francia, the dreaded Dictator of Paraguay. The latter first of all imprisoned the fugitive—probably more from force of habit than from any other reason, since Francia was accustomed to fill his dungeons as lightly as a fishwife her basket with herrings.

After a very short period of incarceration, however, the autocrat came to a definite determination regarding his attitude towards the fugitive who had sought his protection. Releasing him, he treated him with a certain degree of liberality as well as with respect. Artigas was allotted a humble dwelling in the township of Curuguaty, far to the north of Asuncion, and in addition he was granted a moderate pension upon which to live. Here the old warrior, enjoying the deep regard of his neighbours, ended his days in peace, while the tortured Uruguay was incorporated with Brazil and passed under Portuguese rule.

CHAPTER VI

ARTIGAS

The human product of a turbulent era—Historical verdicts disagree—Opinions of Uruguayan and foreign historians—High-flown tribute—The cleansing of Artigas's fame—Prejudices of some local accounts—Uruguay at the time of Artigas's birth—Surroundings of his youth—Smuggling as a profession—Growth of his influence—His name becomes a household word—Artigas enters the Spanish service—The corps of Blandengues—Efficiency and promotion—Quarrel with the Spanish General—Artigas throws in his lot with the patriot forces—His success as a leader of men—Rank accorded him—Jealousy between Artigas and the Buenos Aires generals—Conflicting ambitions—The Portuguese invasion—Artigas leads the Oriental nation to the Argentine shore—The encampment at Ayui—Scarcity of arms and provisions—Battles with the Portuguese—The subalterns of Artigas—Otorgues and Andresito—Crude governmental procedure—Arbitrary decrees—The sentiments of Artigas—His love of honesty—Progress of the war—Complications of the campaign—Artigas as Protector—The encampment of Hervidero—Revolting tales—The exaggeration of history—Artigas refuses honour—His proclamations—Simple life of the commander—Some contemporary accounts—The national treasury—Final desperate struggles against the Portuguese—Rebellion of Ramirez—Fierce battles—Extraordinary recuperative power of the Protector—Final defeat of Artigas—Flight to Paraguay—The Protector in retirement.

The name of Artigas stands for that of the national hero of Uruguay. Within the frontiers of the River Plate countries and of Southern Brazil no such introduction would be necessary, since in those places have raged controversies as fierce as any of the battles in which the old warrior took part. To the average English reader, however, his name is necessarily unfamiliar, although it crops up now and again in the records of travellers who visited South America during the first quarter of the eighteenth century.

Artigas was essentially the product of a turbulent era. Born in 1764, he had remained comparatively obscure until forty-six years later, when the outbreak of the South American War of Independence sent him aloft with dramatic rapidity to a pinnacle of prominence from which he ruled nations and armies—with a result that is yet the subject of considerable dispute.

Perhaps never did the memory of a man meet with more honour in his own country, and with less favour without it. Argentine historians and European travellers of all nationalities have included him within the dark fold of the world's great criminals. From the mill of their analysis Artigas emerges as a bandit, murderer, traitor, a criminal who seized with audacity each of his thousand opportunities to outrage the laws of morality and decency. Apart from the testimony of the noted historians, two Swiss naturalists, Rengger and Longchamps, who penetrated to his country and whose report should be unbiassed, speak of him as one "whose life has been only a tissue of horrors, the great instrument of all the calamities which for ten years fell on the provinces of the confederation of Rio de la Plata." These convictions are echoed by a score of other authorities.

For the other side of the picture it is necessary to turn to the Uruguayan writers. Their views are at least as definite and unanimous as the others. According to one, Eduardo Muñoz Ximinez, "the austerity of Cato, the purity of Aristides, the temperament of the Gracchi, the nobility of Camillus, the generosity of Fabricius—these virtues, allied to heroism and determination, have been found united within the breast of none but Artigas." This represents but a solitary note, typical of the great chorus of praise that goes up from Uruguay.

Artigas, living, had little concern with compromise; dead, his spirit seems to have infected his historians with the same dislike of half-measures. In other respects this particular strand of history is as flexible as all the rest. For generations the feathers of Artigas's fame remained of undisputed black; now the active protests of the Uruguayans have initiated a cleansing process that promises to change the plumes to too blinding a white. Such impartial judgment as is possible induces the persuasion that the Argentine and foreign chroniclers, though writing in all good faith, have erred a little in relying too much upon the testimony of men who bore bitter personal enmity towards the Uruguayan leader. Artigas, in fact, reveals himself from out of the cloud of conflicting authorities as an essentially human being, swayed by the passions of the age and knowing many of its faults, wild as the age itself, but less sordid and more picturesque, and the author of some deeds, moreover, that, worked in the light of a more central and populous field, might well have sent his name to posterity with more assured honour.

Artigas was born at a time that, by courtesy, was termed one of peace. A treaty of the previous year had for a short while changed the open warfare between the Spaniards and Portuguese into an unofficial series of aggressions and frontier skirmishes. Scarcely, however, had the future Protector of

Uruguay attained to his twelfth year when the war broke out again, thus adding fresh fuel to the ceaseless minor hatreds and private feuds. Brought up, as one of his own apologists admits, in an atmosphere of rapine, revenge, and violence, the early surroundings of Artigas were sufficient to prepare him for the grim part he was destined to play. He could, moreover, lay claim to an especial sentimental stake in the country, since forty years before the date of his birth his grandfather had formed one of the heads of seven families who were sent from Buenos Aires in order to found the town of Montevideo.

Artigas, attained to manhood, became noted for physical prowess. As was inevitable in such a land, his unequalled tricks of horsemanship and feats of strength soon gave him an ascendency over the companions of his own age. Since Artigas himself vouchsafed little information on the subject, the details of this early career are at best vague. His enemies assert that he turned brigand, and captained a band of desperadoes. It is now practically certain that this was not the case, but that he devoted himself to smuggling there is no doubt. It must be remembered that in those days contraband was not necessarily a commerce of reproach. Although its active agents were essentially of a reckless type, there were others of considerable standing who were more or less directly interested in a traffic that they held a legitimate and profitable protest against the repressive fiscal measures of Spain.

It was in the sparsely populated hill country of the north that Artigas first learned to control men and to command expeditions. Once fairly settled to the work, unusually numerous convoys of laden horses and mules passed stealthily southwards from Brazil through the valleys, forests, and streams of the frontier districts, for the daring ventures of the Uruguayan leader met with phenomenal success. As a result his influence steadily increased among both the men of his own race and the semi-civilised Indians of the neighbourhood. The personality of the man with the hawk nose, blue eyes, and fair skin possessed the rare faculty of inspiring his followers with personal affection as well as with admiration. As the years went on his name began to ring in every mud cabin and reed hut, and the numbers of his adherents attained to formidable proportions.

In the meanwhile the general disorder of the country had increased to a pitch that demanded active measures for its repression. In 1797 the Spanish authorities raised a special corps of Blandengues, whose duties were fairly comprehensive. Picked men, they served as cavalry, police, as guards against Indian raids, and as a force to repress the smugglers. Imbued with a wholesome respect for his power, the Montevidean Government approached Artigas by way of the line of least resistance. The Uruguayan accepted an invitation to join the corps, and soon proved himself its most capable and efficient officer.

Thus we see Artigas in the blue-and-red uniform of the Blandengues, armed with a lance that sported a steel crescent below its point, chasing smugglers instead of being chased, arresting criminals, fighting with intruding Brazilians, and slaying rebellious Indians with the precautionary enthusiasm of the period. His vindication of justice was now as thorough as had formerly been his evasion of the fiscal laws. In 1802 a rapid series of promotion created him *Guarda General de la Campaña*, or guardian officer general of the rural districts. We next hear of him as taking part with his regiment against the British invaders of the country in 1807. Then, in 1810, began the South American War of Independence, and with its outbreak dawned the true career of the Uruguayan popular hero.

It was not, however, until nine months or so after the commencement of the campaign that Artigas threw in his lot with the patriot forces. The immediate cause was a quarrel with his superior officer, the Spanish General Muesa. Artigas, whose spirit was not tempered to verbal chastisement, gave back word for word, until the incensed general threatened to send him in chains to the neighbouring island of San Gabriel. That night the offended officer of Blandengues crossed the broad River Plate in a small boat, was received with acclamation by the Argentine leaders, and with their aid prepared an expedition that should free his country from the Spaniard. The motives that brought about this sudden adherence to the party of independence have been much in dispute. Hostile critics assert that the change of front was merely vindictive, and that it was the revengeful fruit of wounded pride that sent him to the patriot ranks. His supporters declare positively that the dispute was of importance only in so far as it gave him reason for the long desired severance of the link that bound him to the Spanish service.

Be this how it may, the figure of Artigas now looms with vastly increased bulk from the field of River Plate history. He is in command of armies now—which is the lot of many—winning battles with them, moreover, which is the luck of few. His official rank is that of Colonel, but the title of General is accorded him by all alike, whether his superiors or inferiors in grade. As for his own folk of Uruguay, they have grown to regard him as a being of almost superhuman power, and follow him with a devoted affection that speaks well for the temperament of the leader.

Indeed, it was at this period that the famous Uruguayan was first enabled to show his true mettle. His armies knew little of the pomp of war. The ragged companies looked up to a chief whose garb was little more warlike and pretentious than their own. The goodwill, however, that prevailed in the midst of the Uruguayan armies was not shared by the leaders of the united forces. Jealousy between Artigas and the Buenos Aires generals had already caused a breach that political dissensions rapidly widened. Nations were in the making, and the process was attended by an almost inevitable bitterness.

Buenos Aires urged a united republic, with its own town as the centre of government. Artigas strongly opposed this plan, proposing in its place a bond of self-governing provinces. Recriminations and threats were bandied to and fro between the rival patriots while the Spaniards, though closely besieged, yet retained Montevideo, and even while the Portuguese were moving from Brazil to the assistance of the monarchists.

At length the Portuguese peril loomed sufficiently large to outweigh every other consideration. With a view to stemming the foreign tide of invasion, the Buenos Airens patched up a treaty with the Spanish troops in Montevideo. The despairing measure was doubtless one of necessity, but it aroused deep passion in the mind of the Uruguayan leader, who protested that his country was forsaken, and given over once again to the mercies of the Spaniards. Collecting every available man, woman, and child, he led them to the north-west, and passed the great exodus over the River Uruguay to a haven of safety at Ayui, upon the Entre Rios shore. Meanwhile, Uruguay was overrun by the invading Portuguese and by the released Spaniards, who eddied out in all directions from Montevideo.

Artigas was now encamped for the first time with a translated nation and an independent army of his own. The condition of both was grimly tragic, pathetically humorous. For fourteen months almost the only shelter, that served for all alike, was afforded by the branches of the trees and the boards of the carts that had brought them. As for the army, it was composed of strangely heterogeneous elements. Honest countryfolk rubbed shoulders with professional criminals and cut-throats; Indians from the destroyed Jesuit missions went side by side with fierce-faced Gauchos; while townsmen, negroes, and a few adventurous foreigners made up the mixed gathering.

The men were in deadly earnest, since the example of Artigas seems to have inspired even the most depraved with a spark from his own fire. Had it been otherwise they would undoubtedly have succumbed to the disadvantages with which they had to contend. Arms were scarce. A certain favoured few were possessed of muskets and swords; but the weapon in chief use was the lance, the national arm of River Plate folk, the point of which, here at Ayui, was usually fashioned from the blade of shears or a knife, or from the iron of some other agricultural instrument. Many, however, had perforce to be content with a long knife, with the lasso and the sling—the *boleadores*—as subsidiary weapons. Yet even these proved by no means despicable in the hands of the men whose sole garment was the ragged remnant of a poncho tied about the waist, and who exercised with poles in preparation for the time when a musket should be in their hands.

It was with the aid of an army such as this that Artigas would cross the river to make his incursions among the hills of his native country, and would engage Portuguese and Spaniards alike in battles from which the desperate and motley companies of men would frequently emerge victorious. Artigas was now assisted by numerous minor chiefs, many of whom were of a character quite unfitted to stand the light of day. Otorques and Andresito were the most noted of these. The methods of the former were utterly brutal. Although the fact is contradicted, he is credited by many with the order to a subaltern officer to "cut the throats of two Spaniards a week in order to preserve the morale. Failing Spaniards, take two Buenos Airens for the purpose"!

Andresito was an Indian from the deserted Jesuit missions who commanded a considerable force of his own race. He appears to have interspersed his dark deeds with some evidence of better qualities and even of a grim humour. A coarse instance of this latter is supplied when he entered the town of Corrientes in the heyday of Artigas's power. On this occasion the Indian troops behaved with no little restraint towards the terrified inhabitants, and contented themselves with levying contributions towards the clothing of the almost naked army. This accomplished, Andresito determined to exhibit the social side of his temperament. He organised several religious dramas, and followed these by a ball in honour of the principal residents of the town. These, however, failed to attend, their reluctance to dancing with Indians overcoming their prudence. On learning the reason from some crassly honest person, the enraged Andresito caused these too particular folk to be mustered in the main plaza of the town. There he obliged the men to scour the roadway, while the ladies were made to dance with the Indian troops.

Although no merit or subtlety can be claimed for such methods, they at all events stand apart from the rest in their lack of bloodthirstiness. Compared with the sentiments revealed in a proclamation of Otorgues in taking possession of Montevideo, the procedure at Corrientes seems innocuous and tame. One of the clauses of this document decrees the execution within two hours of any citizen who should speak or write in favour of any other government, while the same fate was promised to one "who should directly or indirectly attack the liberty of the Province"! The humour in the employment of the word "liberty" is, of course, totally unconscious.

Such proclamations, naturally, served purely and simply as a licence for convenient murder. Employing lieutenants of the kind, it is little wonder that much of the guilt of their accumulated deeds should be undeservedly heaped upon Artigas's head. Not that the Commander-in-Chief himself was inclined to put a sentimental value upon human life; indeed, a delicacy on this point would be impossible in one who had passed through the scenes of his particular calling. In any case his hatred of robbery was deep-rooted and sincere. After the execution of three criminals of this type, he proclaims to his people at Ayui: "My natural aversion to all crime, especially to the horrible one of robbery, and my desire that the army should be composed of honourable citizens ... has moved me to satisfy justice by means of a punishment as sad as it is effectual." A little later he makes a similar appeal, adding, "if there be remaining amongst you one who does not harbour sentiments of honour, patriotism, and humanity, let him flee far from the army he dishonours"! Here we get the flowers of the south, earnestly thrown, but alighting in too earthy a bed! The poor army, with its impoverished, ragged loin-cloths, and with its lassos and slings, undoubtedly valued the occasional luxury of a full stomach at least as highly as the abstract virtues. Yet they probably heard the words with sincere admiration, feeling an added pride in their beloved leader who could employ such phrases. In any case—whether as a result of punishments or proclamations—the crime of robbery soon became rare almost to extinction within the sphere of Artigas's influence.

The war itself was each month growing more savage in character. Such virtues as the Uruguayan army possessed were recognised least of all by the Spaniards. Elio, the Viceroy, had erected a special gallows in Montevideo for the benefit of any prisoners that might be captured, while Vigodet, his successor, endeavoured to strike terror by measures of pure barbarity. By his order a body of cavalry scoured the countryside, slaying all those suspected of Artiguenian leanings, and exposing the quartered portions of their bodies at prominent places by the roadside. Each patriot, moreover, carried a price upon his head. It is not to be wondered at that the Uruguayan forces made reprisals, and that corpses replaced prisoners of war.

A renewed campaign waged by the Buenos Aires forces against the Spaniards was the signal for the abandonment of the settlement at Ayui. Once again the Royalists were shut up within the walls of Montevideo, and at the beginning of 1813 Artigas, with his men, marched down from the north to take part in the siege. The Uruguayan came now as an assured ruler of his own people; the Buenos Aires commanders regarded him as a unit in a greater system. The result was the inevitable quarrel, and a year from the inception of the operations Artigas took the most decisive step in his career. He gave no warning of his move. The evening before had witnessed his particular portion of the field covered with horses and men. The next morning saw the ground bare and deserted: Artigas and his army were already many leagues away.

MONTEVIDEO AND THE CERRO HILL.

"AFTER CATTLE."

To face p. 88.

From that moment Artigas became virtual king of a torn and struggling realm. The Buenos Aires authorities, incensed at his defection, placed a price of six thousand dollars on his head, continuing meanwhile the siege of Montevideo. Artigas retaliated by a formal declaration of war upon the central Government. The hostile ramifications were now sufficiently involved to satisfy the most warlike spirit. Artigas was fighting the Buenos Airens and Portuguese, and was only prevented from coming to close grips with the Spaniards by the fact that the intervening Buenos Aires armies had already taken that task upon themselves. As it was, the influence of the national hero spread out to the west with an amazing rapidity, passing beyond the Uruguay River, and holding good upon the remote side of the great Paraná stream itself. In a very short while his dominions in Argentine territory assumed an extent four times greater than that of his native country. The provinces of Entre Rios, Corrientes, Santa Fé, and Córdoba welcomed his new tricolour standard with enthusiasm.

Thus Artigas was now ruler of 350,000 square miles, with the exception of the various odd points of vantage held by the remaining three contending powers.

The fall of Montevideo and the final ejection of the Spaniards from the soil was followed by the retirement of the Buenos Aires armies to their own country. Thus to Artigas's realm was added the necessary complement of a capital and some seagoing ships that served as the nucleus of a national navy. The ex-smuggler was now at the zenith of his power. It is at this point that he affords by far the most interesting picture, since the amazing medley of sentiments for which his character was responsible were now given full play. Caring nothing for pomp and ceremony, he sent Otorgues to rule Montevideo, while his other chiefs assumed control of the various districts throughout the provinces. He himself, true to his Gaucho upbringing, avoided all towns, and finally settled himself in the north-west of Uruguay. On a tableland by the banks of the great river, some score of miles to the south of Salto, he established a camp from which he directed the policy of the five provinces that owned to his rule.

In the neighbourhood of this encampment of Hervidero was another, in which were confined those prisoners whose offences were not considered worthy of immediate death. Serving as it did to cleanse doubtful minds of rebellion, it was christened by the euphuistic name of Purificacion. There is no doubt that the methods employed for this exalted purpose often ended fatally for the unfortunates experimented upon. The popular tales of the deeds done at both encampments are extraordinarily revolting. Two phrases of jocular slang then much in use throw a lurid light upon the callousness of the period. "To play the violin" referred to the cutting of a human throat; "to play the viola" signified the severance of a live man's body—both gruesomely accurate similes. Men are said to have been flung wholesale into the river, attached to stones, and a peculiarly agonising form of death was engineered in the sewing up of a living victim in the hide of a freshly killed bullock, which was then exposed to the sun. The result was shrinkage, and suffocation for the miserable wretch within the reeking covering, an ending that was dubbed "the waistcoat" by a touch of similar humour. Numerous evidences of individuality, moreover, were evident in the various forms of punishment. Thus a certain Colonel Perugorria, who lay under a charge of treason, was, until his execution, chained to a post, as though he were a dog, by means of an iron collar round his neck, to which the steel links were attached.

Many of Artigas's supporters roundly deny the perpetration of these horrors; yet there is little doubt that many such acts were committed throughout the various provinces. To what extent they received the sanction of Artigas is far more uncertain. The probability is that he strongly discouraged wanton torture, although it lay beyond even such powers as his to hold back the Gaucho passions when they were fiercest and to prevent the merciless acts of revenge. Many eye-witnesses have related that he exhibited emotion and pity at the sight of a humanely conducted execution.

Indeed, there is no reason to suppose that Artigas, for all his errors and limitations, was not a true believer in the very lofty sentiments he used to express. One of the many examples of these is to be met with in his letter to the local authorities of Montevideo, when in 1815 they endowed him with the title of Captain-General, with the addition of that of "Protector and Patron of the Liberty of the Nation." Artigas, refusing the honour, which, nevertheless, remained attached to him, says: "Titles are the phantoms of States, and the glory of upholding liberty suffices for your illustrious corporation. Let us teach our countrymen to be virtuous. For this reason I have retained until now the rank of a simple citizen ... the day will come when men will act from a sense of duty, and when they will devote their best interests to the honour of their fellow-men."

The simplicity of Artigas was innate and genuine. One of his own nationality, on a visit to Hervidera, describes the costume of the dreaded leader. On that occasion Artigas was content with the plain costume of a countryman—plain blue jacket and pantaloons, white stockings, and a skin cloak, all rather shabby. The paraphernalia of a meal was of similar quality, and in addition lamentably scanty. Broth, a stew of meat, and roast beef were served on a couple of pewter dishes with broken edges; a single cup took the place of non-existent wine-glasses; no more than three earthenware plates could be mustered, and, since the seating accommodation was restricted to three chairs and a hide box, the majority of the guests had perforce to stand. Such were the clothes and household goods of the lord of five provinces, whose armies were battling with Portuguese Peninsular War veterans and with Argentine battalions, whose vessels had borne his flag to Europe to harass hostile vessels off the coasts of Portugal itself, who made treaties with England and other powers, and whose name was all but worshipped by a hundred thousand people!

J. P. Robertson, an English chronicler of the period, gives an interesting account of a meeting with Artigas. Assaulted and robbed by a band of the noted chief's adherents, he boldly set out for Purificacion to claim redress. His words deserve quotation at some length. "I came to the Protector's headquarters," he says, "of the so-called town of Purificacion. And there (I pray you do not turn sceptic on my hands) what do you think I saw? Why, the most excellent Protector of half the New World, seated on a bullock's skull, at a fire kindled on the mud floor of his hut, eating beef off a spit, and drinking gin out of a cow horn! He was surrounded by a dozen officers in weather beaten attire, in similar positions, and similarly occupied with their chief. All were smoking, all gabbling. The Protector was dictating to two secretaries, who occupied, at one deal table, the only two dilapidated rush bottom chairs in the hovel. To complete the singular incongruity of the scene, the floor of the one apartment of the mud hut (to be sure it was a pretty large one) in which the general, his staff, and secretaries, were assembled, was strewn with pompous envelopes from all the Provinces (some of them distant some 1,500 miles from that centre of operations) addressed to 'His Excellency the Protector.' At the door stood the reeking horses of couriers arriving every half hour, and the fresh ones of those departing as often.... His Excellency the Protector, seated on his bullock's skull, smoking, eating, drinking, dictating, talking, dispatched in succession the various matters brought under his notice with that calm, or deliberate, but uninterrupted nonchalance, which brought most practically home to me the truth of the axiom, 'Stop a little that we may get on the faster.'... He received me, not only with cordiality, but with what surprised me more, comparatively gentlemanlike manners, and really good breeding.... The Protector's business was prolonged from morning till evening, and so were his meals; for, as one courier arrived another was dispatched, and as one officer rose up from the fire at which the meat was spitted another took his place."

The General politely took his visitor the round of his hide huts and mud hovels, where the horses stood saddled and bridled day and night, and where the tattered soldiery waited in readiness for the emergencies that arose so frequently. When Robertson submitted his financial claim, Artigas remained as amiable as before. "'You see,' said the General with great candour and nonchalance, 'how we live here; and it is as much as we can do, in these hard times, to compass beef, aguardiente, and cigars. To pay you 6,000 dollars just now is as much beyond my power, as it would be to pay you 60,000 or 600,000. Look here,' said he, and so saying, he lifted up the lid of an old military chest, and pointed to a canvas bag at the bottom of it. 'There,' he continued, 'is my whole stock of cash; it amounts to 300 dollars; and where the next supply is to come from I am as little aware as you are.'" Notwithstanding this, Robertson then and there obtained some trading concessions that, he says, repaid him the amount of his claim many times over.

Surely this picture reveals Artigas more truly than all the long-winded polemics that have raged about the famous Uruguayan. It is given by one whose sympathies were against the aims of the Gaucho chief, and who has proved himself no lenient critic. Yet the description fits no mere cut-throat and plunderer. On the contrary, it reveals a virile personality, a thinker and worker of a disposition that goes far to explain the adoration accorded him by his troops. Artigas, at the hands of the visitor who had sufficient cause for his ridicule, comes to light as a *man*—contemptuous of poverty, misery, and sordid surroundings so long as his goal remained as clear and distinct as it ever was to his sight.

The picture is not without its pathetic side. It shows Artigas in the heyday of his power, yet even then hard put to it to supply his men with clothes and the common necessities of life. Imagine the calm force and philosophy of a being capable of governing more than a third of a million square miles of territory with the assistance of a treasury of three hundred dollars! Nevertheless, these *opéra bouffe* conditions represented the highest point of material prosperity to which Artigas ever attained. For five years he ruled thus, grappling desperately with the invading Brazilian armies, and resisting the efforts of the Buenos Aires forces to regain control of the four Argentine provinces that had espoused his cause.

With a prosperity thus frugally marked, it is easy to conceive the circumstances of the adversity that was to come. To their credit be it said that the Uruguayans faltered not in the least in the face of the ultimate doom that must have appeared inevitable. As their ranks became steadily thinned, the invading hordes of Portuguese soldiers swelled in numbers, while the Buenos Aires attacks on the river provinces became yet more determined. Yet, wanting in everything, its more capable and intelligent officers prisoners of war, the Uruguayans fought on to the very end—gaunt, haggard men who gave back blow for blow, though their courage was often sustained by no other means than the chewing of strips of hide. One of the officers of a regiment of lancers, once the pride of the army, describes the condition of the men in the last days of the struggle. At reveille, on a chilly winter's morning, each trooper would supplement the loin-cloth that alone remained to him by a whole cowhide. Thus when their backs were turned as they retired to their quarters, the number of men could only be judged by the quantity of moving cowhides!

Even then the final hour might have been indefinitely postponed but for the revolt of Ramirez, one of Artigas's own chieftains. After a homeric struggle, Ramirez obtained the victory over his old leader, and pursued him relentlessly through the provinces of Corrientes and Misiones. It was by this incessant chase alone that the victor retained his superiority. For such was the popularity of Artigas that a few days' halt sufficed for a number of fresh Gauchos and Indians to join him. When he had escaped from his penultimate defeat, accompanied by only twelve men, his pursuer lost touch with him for a week. At the end of that time the veteran had collected over nine hundred men, and was besieging Cambay, one of Ramirez's strongholds. A division was sent off post-haste to the spot, and it was here that the old warrior fought his last fight. Artigas, leaving most of his men dead upon the field, fled northwards and passed into Paraguay.

The later years of Artigas present the strangest contrast to his early life. Received and sheltered after some hesitation by Francia, the dreaded tyrant of Paraguay, he was first allotted a dwelling in the north of the country, and was afterwards permitted to dwell in the neighbourhood of Asuncion, the capital. Here he lived in complete retirement and peace until his death occurred, at the advanced age of eighty-three. Both his time and the small pension allowed him by the Paraguayan Government were spent in relieving the wants of his neighbours, by whom he was regarded with affection and veneration. The keynote to the true Artigas undoubtedly lies in these last years, when in humble tranquillity he had leisure at length to practise the benevolence and charity that he had so often preached from a corpse-surrounded pulpit. Difficult as it is to withdraw the personality of Artigas from the sea of blood that flooded his age, he was surely a product of an anarchical period rather than of anarchy itself.

CHAPTER VII

HISTORY

The Spanish colonies as nations—The first-fruits of freedom—Uruguay beneath the heel of Portugal—The advent of a second liberator—Juan Antonio Lavalleja—The forming of the league of the "thirty-three"—Opening of the campaign—The patriot force—Rank and its distribution—The crossing of the River Plate—Commencement of operations in Uruguay—A first success—Spread of the movement—Rivera embraces the patriot cause—The march upon Montevideo—A daring siege—How the army of occupation was deceived—Timely reinforcements—Lavalleja establishes an independent government—Incident at the opening of the Senate—Argentina comes to the assistance of Uruguay—Beginning of the rivalry between Rivera and Lavalleja—Dissension in the Uruguayan army—Temporary disgrace of Rivera—His acquittal—Lavalleja declares himself dictator—Uruguay's independence acknowledged by Argentina and Brazil—The national authorities enter Montevideo.

The end of the year 1824 witnessed the extinction of the last vestige of the power of Spain in South America. With one solitary exception, each former Spanish colony had now raised itself to the status of a nation. It is true that in the majority of cases the inhabitants of these countries suffered not only the wildest of anarchy, but in addition a degree of despotism that had been unknown during the Spanish régime, for all the selfishness of the Peninsula Government. Yet since the flock of tyrants that rose up, each like a grim phoenix, from the ashes of the Spanish Dominion were conceived of the tortured countries themselves, the South Americans took such small comfort as they might from a dim reflection that in their own hands lay the possibility of the improvement in the rulers born from their own bone.

Of these States thus freed from any other despotism but of their own making Uruguay formed the sole exception. For years she had remained beneath the heel of Portugal, writhing uneasily, but unable to remove the weight of the foreign occupation. When the time came for the full independence of the rest, however, Uruguay's longing to acquire their State was no longer to be repressed, even at the cost of the expulsion of the second European power that had fixed upon the land.

The man whose name stands out as the liberator of Uruguay for the second time is Juan Antonio Lavalleja. Ceding place only to Artigas as a national hero, Lavalleja had fought in many actions against the Spaniards, and had distinguished himself not a little in the original revolutionary wars. Alternate military and civil occupations have nearly always fallen to the lot of South American public men, and Lavalleja formed no exception to the rule. At the time when the victory of Ayacucho in Peru crowned the entire campaign against the Spaniards he held the comparatively humble and prosaic post of manager of a meat-curing factory in the neighbourhood of Buenos Aires.

The rejoicings that the victory of Ayacucho aroused in the capital of Argentina stirred to the depth both Lavalleja and a company of fellow-exiles from the Banda Oriental. A meeting of these patriots was held on the spot, the result of which was an enthusiastic determination to place their own country upon the same footing as the rest. Doubtless many hundreds of similar gatherings had already been effected—and concluded by vapourings of thin air. But the spirit of these men who had thus come together was of another kind. Having sworn solemnly to free their country, action followed hotfoot on the heels of words. A couple of their number were sent at once to Uruguay to prepare the minds of a trusted few, while the rest made preparations for the expedition that was to follow.

The mission of the two deputies proved successful. They returned to Buenos Aires, the bearers of many promises of support and co-operation. Nothing now remained but to take the first irrevocable step in the campaign that was to bloom out from this very humble seed.

"Treinta y Tres" has now developed into a proper name in the Banda Oriental; for the number of men who started out from Buenos Aires for the sake of Uruguay was thirty-three. The name has now been locally immortalised. Among the infinite variety of objects that it endows may be counted a province, a town, innumerable plazas and streets, and a brand of cigarettes.

There is certainly nothing that is intrinsically humorous in the adventures of these noble men who set out for their patriotic purpose in the face of such terrible risks. Yet as a specimen of the constitution of the armies of the South American factions at this period a survey of the grades held by the small gathering is illuminating. In the first place the diminutive expedition had for its Commander-in-Chief Colonel Juan Antonio Lavalleja, who had beneath him three majors and four captains. These in turn were supported by three lieutenants, an ensign, a sergeant, a corporal, and a guide. The remaining eighteen constituted the rank and file of the force—in fact, the Army proper.

The little expedition so overwhelmingly officered set out from Buenos Aires, proceeding northward along the Argentine shore. Reaching a point where the river had become comparatively narrow, they embarked in small boats, and launched out on the Uruguay at dead of night. A gale obliged them to seek refuge on a friendly island, and caused a day's delay. But the next evening they embarked once more, and reached in safety the beach of La Agraciada on their native shore. There they unfurled their chosen tricoloured banner, and swore once again to attain liberty or death.

The expedition was now actually on the scene of its mission, and shortly after daybreak it began its march to the north. During the course of a few hours they collected *en route* reinforcements of forty able-bodied and armed Orientales.

Proceeding steadily onwards, the gallant little army, officers and all, found itself in the neighbourhood of the small town of Dolores, better known formerly as San Salvador. This was held by a garrison of eighty men in the service of Brazil. Determined to inflict a first decisive blow, Lavalleja led his men onwards to the attack. The moment chanced to be especially propitious, since the officers and principal men in the town had attended a dance on the previous night. So great had been the delights of the *baile* that the principal men had found it necessary to continue their repose long into the morning—a circumstance that is not unknown even to this day.

Had it not been for an error on the part of the patriot guide the town would undoubtedly have been captured by surprise and taken almost without a blow. As it was, the official chanced to mistake the situation of a ford in an intervening small river. This necessitated a lengthy march along the banks ere a place suitable for the passage was found, and the presence of the small company with the tricoloured flag was discovered with amazement by the inhabitants.

Thus ere Lavalleja's expedition had succeeded in crossing the stream there had been moments of wild bustle in Dolores. Officers sprang out of bed to gird on their swords in haste; soldiers ran to assemble with uniforms even more than usually awry, while the municipal officers doubtless ran to and fro in aimless confusion. Nevertheless by the time that the turmoil was at an end the garrison had had an opportunity to muster, and to sally out against the advancing band that had not yet gained the town.

Since the Portuguese forces were under the command of an Oriental, Colonel Julián Laguna, a parley took place ere the two forces met. In the end, Laguna deciding to remain staunch to the foreign cause, the thirty-three and their allies charged, routing the enemy completely. Thus in the course of their first victory they won not only the town of Dolores itself, but a number of Uruguayan volunteers who joined them from out of the beaten force.

The thirty-three with their companions, delaying a very short while in the captured town, continued their march. A more pressing danger now menaced them. General Rivera, the Oriental who, having so distinguished himself in the former wars against the Portuguese, had entered the latter service when the Uruguayan cause became lost, was sent out with a force of seventy men to annihilate the daring aggressors. Here, again, when numbers and rank are compared, it will be seen that the regular forces of the country were more or less on a par with the thirty-three in their generosity in the matter of titles.

Nevertheless, however it was commanded, the thirty-three were destined to gain yet further support from the force detached against them. On his near approach to the devoted band, Rivera's patriotic instincts overcame all other considerations. At a meeting contrived between him and Lavalleja the pair embraced, and Rivera forsook the Brazilian service on the spot to join the cause of his country. The addition to their ranks of the famous fighter and his men was naturally greeted with enthusiasm by the patriots, who advanced filled with renewed confidence. On the other hand, the news of the defection created no little consternation among the Brazilians, who set a price upon the heads of both Rivera and Lavalleja, valuing the former at five hundred dollars more than the fifteen hundred offered for Lavalleja, although the latter remained the actual commander of the expedition.

The thirty-three had now abandoned their cautious north-west fringing of the coast. With their numbers increasing as they went, they struck for the south-east, making boldly for Montevideo itself, and defeating the various Portuguese forces that strove to oppose them.

Arrived at length at San José, some three score miles distant from Montevideo, Lavalleja determined on an especially daring move that proved his appreciation of the value of prestige. From there he sent all his prisoners with a strong guard under Rivera to Durazno, and at Canelones, farther on, he detached another party to obtain recruits from the neighbourhood of Maldonado. He himself, accompanied now by no more than a hundred men, continued in supreme unconcern his march to Montevideo. Arriving upon the outskirts of the spot, he encamped on the Cerrito de la Victoria, whence, employing a colossal piece of bluff, he set himself to besiege the city.

It is surely not often that a hundred men have sat down to invest a fortified town garrisoned by nearly two thousand soldiers. Yet it was in the amazing effrontery of the proceeding that success lay. On the very next day a strong force of the enemy, numbering over fifteen hundred men with four guns, sallied out from Montevideo. The hundred besiegers must doubtless have thought that all was lost; but, continuing the grim farce to the end, they opened fire to the best of their ability upon the advancing columns. The result more than fulfilled their most sanguine expectations. Convinced that the furious fusillade emanated from a powerful army, the Portuguese columns retired into the town, while the hundred men sat down again to continue the siege of Montevideo.

But their number did not now long remain at this ridiculously inadequate total. By twos and tens and even by hundreds the Orientales escaped from the city, flocking to the tricolour banner until the patriot army had swollen to a degree that rendered it formidable in fact as well as in fancy. So successful, moreover, had proved Rivera's mission in the Campo that in a few days almost the whole of Uruguay was in arms against the enemy's forces in its midst.

The work of the thirty-three had been extraordinarily rapid. So successful, indeed, had been the campaign that, in the place of disputing against another's authority, the moment had arrived for setting up their own, against which it should be treason to contend.

In order to effect this Lavalleja withdrew personally from the siege of Montevideo, and established an independent government at the town of Florida to the north of the capital. Moved by a truly lofty sense of patriotism, he handed over his leadership to the new authorities, who responded by creating him General-in-Chief of the Army of Liberation, and by endowing Rivera with the rank of Inspector-General. On this occasion the titles conveyed some material significance, since the Uruguayan Army now amounted to two thousand five hundred men.

The opening of this new Senate was attended by a dramatic incident. In order to be present at the assembly it was necessary for Lavalleja to leave the front of hostilities and to ride through rain and mud to Florida.

Ere entering the Hall of Assembly he was met by several ladies, amongst whom was the wife of Rivera, who begged him to change his dripping costume before he proceeded with the official business. "Thank you, señoras," replied Lavalleja, "I will attend to that as soon as our country has its government." Within a few minutes the consummation had been achieved, and Lavalleja was in dry clothes. The story affords only one more instance of the numerous inevitable satellites that attend the passage of a notable name through the ages; but here the ingenuous simplicity of the tale is almost sufficient in itself to vouch for its truth. At this point, properly speaking, ends the story of the thirty-three. Beneath the national edifice that they had built up the minor members of the devoted band had already become lost to view. The control of affairs was now vested in a Senate and Corporations, and Argentina, hastening to recognise the existence of the independent Government, sent her armies to its assistance, stipulating that in exchange for the alliance Uruguay should become one of the provinces of the River Plate.

With the survival of the first perils, moreover, the cohesion of the leaders of the famous thirty-three passed away. During the course of the final battles against the Portuguese a rivalry sprang into existence between Lavalleja and Rivera that gradually deepened into a jealous antagonism that has left its mark of bitterness upon the country to this day.

With the growing certainty of the success of the cause, and, consequently, of the honours and power in store for the chosen few among the patriot ranks dissension and suspicion became rampant. One of the more immediate outcomes of this regrettable state was the falling under suspicion of Rivera. Accused of opening up negotiations with the Portuguese, he was sent to Buenos Aires for trial. Acquitted by President Rivadavia of traitorous intent, he was, nevertheless, held in prison owing to his outspoken federal views, which were in direct opposition to the unitarian doctrines of Argentina. After a while, however, he escaped from captivity, and, collecting an army, completely re-established his reputation by invading and conquering the Misiones districts that were then in the power of the Portuguese. Although the territory was in the end ceded back again, the invasion was of material effect in concluding the war.

When, moreover, after the rout of the Portuguese fleet by the Argentine Admiral Brown, and the series of victories that culminated in the battle of Ituzaingo, it became evident that the expulsion of the Portuguese from Uruguayan soil was now inevitable within a very short time, Lavalleja did not wait for any definite conclusion of peace. In October of 1827, when, as a matter of fact, the terms of an armistice were still in dispute, he deposed the national Junta, and without further ado declared himself Dictator of his country. This office he held until July of the following year, when he voluntarily resigned from the post.

August witnessed a formal acknowledgment of the independence of Uruguay by both Argentina and Brazil, and in November a provisional Government was established. On May 1, 1829, the national authorities, amidst no little pomp and ceremony, made a formal entry into Montevideo, and Uruguay was at last definitely left to the care of its own rulers.

CHAPTER VIII

HISTORY—*continued*

Foreign war succeeded by internal chaos—Warriors as statesmen—The dictatorship of Lavalleja—His methods—The first open breach between Lavalleja and Rivera—A temporary reconciliation—Establishment of the Constitution of Uruguay—Lavalleja and Rivera candidates for the President's chair—Differences in the temperaments of the two—Rivera is elected first President of Uruguay—Jealousies and intrigue—Attack upon Rivera—Narrow escape of the President—Lavalleja's party temporarily occupy Montevideo—Defeat of the insurgent general—His flight into Brazil—Intervention of the Argentine Dictator Rosas—His support of Lavalleja—Combined forces beaten by Rivera—Lavalleja's second attempt proves unsuccessful—General Oribe succeeds Rivera as President—Lavalleja's party again in the ascendant—Rivera heads a revolution—Civil war—Intervention of France—Resignation of Oribe—Rivera elected President—His alliance with the French and Corrientines—Declaration of war against Rosas—Defeat of the latter—On the withdrawal of the French Rosas resumes the aggressive—Severe defeat of Rivera and his allies of the littoral provinces—Oribe besieges Montevideo—The services of Garibaldi—The Uruguayan forces decimated—Further incidents of the war—The power of Rosas broken by Brazil, Uruguay, and Entre-Rios.

For the purpose of a self-contained romance with a popular ending, the adventures of the leaders of the thirty-three should end at the moment when the liberation of the Banda Oriental became a dawning certainty, but history has an unfortunate knack of continuing where fiction ceases. The fiercest enemy of a hero is longevity.

In this case the phase is especially lamentable, since although daring deeds of arms persisted, the feats were wrought, not in a joint cause against a common enemy, but amidst a turbulent confusion of sudden alliances and yet more rapid breaches between friends and neighbours that rendered impossible speculation whence the tide of battle would flow next.

The three names that stood out from the very midst of the chaos of events were those of Lavalleja, Rivera, and Oribe. Since the three had fought shoulder to shoulder for their country's redemption this prominence was only fitting and just. Yet the rôle of each of the three differed widely now from his previous methods. Cohesion had departed with the enemy's forces: not so the tale of the battlefields, that multiplied until they stained the soil of the country a deeper red than ever before.

The first few months of complete independence gave no inkling of what was to come. After one or two politicians had held interim offices, General Rondeau, who had rendered great services to Uruguay, was made Governor. A disagreement, however, arose between him and the constitutional assembly. As a result he resigned his post, and departed to Buenos Aires, shaking the dust of the Banda Oriental from his feet.

Lavalleja was now invested with the chief office of the land. Alas for the difference between the striver after liberty and the sitter in the goddess's chair! Viewed from the lofty pedestal, freedom became distant far below and lost to sight. In short, Lavalleja became a dictator of the most arbitrary type from the very beginning of his authority. He muzzled the Press, such as it was, disbanded various battalions suspected of loyalty to his private interests, and then turned upon Rivera, his old comrade-in-arms. Not satisfied with depriving the latter of his office of Commandant-General, Lavalleja raised an army, and, intent upon destruction, marched against the man whom he feared as his most dangerous rival.

The despotic Governor was not mistaken in his estimate of Rivera's power. Indeed, the result of a battle would have been extremely doubtful, had the two forces come into conflict. But the strenuous efforts of several peaceful commissions ended in a reconciliation between the leaders—a mere loose patching up of differences, it is true, but one that served for the time being. In the meanwhile the Constitution of independent Uruguay was established and sworn to, the event being greeted by the populace with wild enthusiasm.

The new State was, of course, endowed with a President, whose chair remained to be occupied. As was inevitable, the two candidates for the high post were Generals Lavalleja and Rivera. Both were, perhaps, almost equally secure in the admiration of the nation. Nevertheless, the distinctions between the temperaments of the two were marked. Rivera was a democrat, a friend of the populace, whom he captivated by his intimacy and easy manner. Lavalleja's tendencies were, by comparison, aristocratic; yet it is doubtful whether he lost much in influence from his loftier pose.

The first legislative act of the National Assembly came as a bitter blow to Lavalleja. In October of 1830 that body elected as President General Rivera. As a nation Uruguay had now blossomed out into a full-blown Constitution. But the youthful constitutional flower was destined to suffer an almost continuous winter of frosts. It was beyond the limits of Lavalleja's forbearance to sit quietly by and to see his rival comfortably installed in the coveted chair of state. It was not long ere the machinery of plots was set in motion. The first attempt proved all but successful. Rivera, accompanied only by a few men, chanced to be in the small town of Durazno, suspecting nothing, when a force of five hundred of his enemies descended suddenly upon the place. Their object was the capture of the President, who only escaped by leaping through a window and by swimming across the River Yi. A rising of the Charrúa Indians was the next material fruit of the campaign of intrigue; but the rebellion served no other end than the practical extirpation of the remnant of the aboriginal race that had survived until then.

Very shortly after this a revolutionary movement was instigated in Montevideo itself. Headed by Colonel Garzon, who held in his pocket a commander-in-chief's commission from Lavalleja, the rising was temporarily successful. The National Assembly, intimidated, had already confirmed the appointment of Lavalleja as President, when Perez, the Vice-President, resisted, and the rest, encouraged by his example, made a firm stand. As a result, Lavalleja himself made his appearance in Montevideo, and, with his followers, occupied the municipal buildings. After an exchange of shots, however, he and his band were forced to retire.

During the course of these events Rivera had been absent from the town. On receiving the news he hastened back from the country, and, placing himself at the head of an army, set out in strenuous pursuit of Lavalleja. The latter was overtaken at Tupambay. A battle ended in the shattering of his company, and, closely pursued by the President, Lavalleja fled across the northern border and sought shelter in Brazil.

In the meanwhile the famous Rosas had come to power in Argentina, and the policy of this dictator was destined to awaken very material echoes in Uruguay. Lending support to Lavalleja, he sent a force of three hundred men across the river. In order to create a diversion, these captured the town of Melo from the Government party. Their triumph was fleeting. Beaten shortly afterwards by Rivera in person, the invading force fled to Brazil.

But the end of the tide of invasion had not yet come. At the beginning of 1834 Lavalleja, aided by further contingents furnished by Rosas, descended once more from the north into his native country. On this occasion the events of his former attempt were repeated with equally disastrous results to himself. Beaten once again, he sought Brazil, the sheltering spot of all the atoms of Uruguayan turbulence.

A little after this the four years of Rivera's term of office expired. It was now the turn of another of the thirty-three, General Manuel Oribe, to enter the arena. Oribe was a warrior as well seasoned as the others. He had fought strenuously under Artigas's standard; but at the coming of the crisis, declaring that he could no longer serve under such a tyrant, he joined the Buenos Aires cause. Later, he had formed one of the most prominent members of the thirty-three. Becoming embroiled in the disputes of the period, he had found himself in opposition to Rivera, although he had to thank the President for promotion in rank.

In March of 1835 General Manuel Oribe was created the second constitutional President of the Republic. One of his first cares was to undermine the weighty influence of Rivera, in whose power he saw a menace to his own office. The new President began the campaign by summoning back to their country all those *Lavallejistas* who had been living in forced exile in Brazil and Argentina. Then, in order to deliver a death-blow to a rival's prestige, he deprived the late President of his rank of commandant-general.

Exasperated beyond endurance at this latter move, Rivera immediately made his appeal to the only authority that was understood at the period—that of arms. The insurrection attained almost immediately to formidable proportions. Indeed, there is no doubt that the malcontent cause would have been successful almost immediately had not Rosas intervened. As it was, the Dictator sent over from Argentina to the assistance of the Government five hundred troops, under the command of Lavalleja, who had thrown in his lot with Oribe against his arch-rival.

As a preliminary to the actual hostilities Oribe sent forth a thunderous proclamation, in which Rivera was branded as a traitor to his country. The first battle ended in favour of the Government, the forces of the rebellion leaving over two hundred dead upon the field. The chief historical importance of the contest, however, lies in the fact that on this occasion were used for the first time the red and the white colours that distinguished the respective forces of Rivera and Oribe and that have ever since remained the emblems of bitter strife.

The fortune of war varied for a while. After numerous indecisive skirmishes, Rivera won an action at Yucutuja, while a month later Oribe was successful in a battle on the banks of the River Yi. Then followed the decisive battle of Palmar, from which the Government forces emerged no longer as an army, but merely as a scattering of fugitive stragglers.

In the meanwhile foreign influence, in addition to the lot of war, had veered in favour of the revolution. The arbitrary methods of Rosas, extended to foreigners resident within the land, had caused him to become embroiled with France. Thus the northern power, in addition to the institution of a blockade of Buenos Aires port, was only too glad of the opportunity of frustrating the plans of the Argentine despot in Uruguay. Allying their forces with those of the revolutionists, they captured the island of Martin Garcia from the Government troops, and were preparing further active measures of aggression when Oribe realised the hopelessness of his plight. Adopting the sole course that was left him, he resigned his office of President, and sailed for Buenos Aires, accompanied by his late ministers, and a considerable following of private friends.

Rivera's road to the return of power was now clear. In November of 1838 he made a triumphal entry into Montevideo, and in due course the National Assembly elected him President for the second time. One of the first acts of the new chief of the State was the avenging of Rosas' late interference in favour of his rival. Allying himself with the French Government and the Province of Corrientes, he declared war—not against the worthy Argentine nation, as was carefully explained in the proclamation, but against the "tyrant of the immortal people of South America."

Rosas was never slow in responding to a challenge of the kind. Scarcely had the declaration of hostilities been made when he sent an army of six thousand men to invade Uruguay. Rivera, his forces strengthened by a thousand French volunteers, marched to meet the enemy, and at Cagancha he obtained a signal victory, the Argentine troops being defeated with heavy loss, and thus forced to abandon their campaign in Uruguay.

It seemed as though the event had put the seal upon Uruguay's success. But the fortunes of the period were as erratic as the period was turbulent. Very shortly after the Battle of Cagancha the differences between Rosas and the French were settled, with the result that an armistice was effected. With the raising of the blockade of Buenos Aires and the departure of the French troops from the country, it was the turn of Rosas to laugh, for his enemy now stood before him single-handed.

On this occasion the first aggressive steps were taken by the naval forces. In 1841 the Argentine fleet, under Admiral Brown, made a practical end to Uruguayan sea power. Some minor vessels that were subsequently collected were given in charge of the Italian Garibaldi, and the famous guerilla leader carried on with them a war of privateering, without, however, meeting with any material success.

In a desperate attempt to stem the formidable tide of Rosas's power, the three provinces of Corrientes, Entre Rios, and Santa Fé allied themselves with Uruguay. From the joint States Rivera raised an army of seven thousand men. But even this heroic effort did not suffice. Boldly marching through Entre Rios towards Buenos Aires, Rivera found himself brought to an abrupt halt by the unexpected appearance before him of his old enemy, Oribe, at the head of an imposing army of fourteen thousand men. The ensuing battle, fiercely fought, ended in an overwhelming victory for the superior forces, nearly a thousand of Rivera's men being massacred in cold blood on the conclusion of the fight.

The beaten President retired from Entre Rios with the remnants of his army, while Oribe likewise crossed the Uruguay River, and marched leisurely southwards from Salto towards Montevideo. In due time his armies arrived before the capital, which they forthwith proceeded to invest, thus commencing the great siege of the place that endured for nine years.

The circumstances of the beleaguering are too numerous and complicated to bear recapitulation here. One of the most notable features of the earlier days was a proclamation issued by Oribe to the effect that he would spare no foreigners whose sympathies lay with the "rebels," as he termed the Government of Rivera—or rather of Joaquín Suárez, who had taken the defeated President's post in Montevideo. The result of the proclamation was exactly the reverse of that anticipated by Oribe, since the foreigners responded by raising legions of their own and by flocking to the active defence of the town. The capital, however, was closely invested by sea as well as by land, Garibaldi's flotilla finding itself unable to make any headway against Admiral Brown's blockading fleet.

In the meanwhile Rivera had not been idle. With the amazing recuperative power that was characteristic of so many of the noted leaders of the period he had scraped together from the countryside a force of nearly four thousand men. With these he harassed the rear of the besieging force to such effect that the Buenos Aires Government, in order to leave the blockade undisturbed, raised a fresh army, and sent it, under the command of General Urquiza, to cope with the unexpected source of danger.

Urquiza came up with Rivera at India Muerta, and the result was fatal to the Uruguayan force. The end of a desperate conflict saw nearly a thousand of Rivera's men lying dead upon the Campo. In accordance with the drastically conclusive methods of the age, the number of prisoners was small by comparison. As to the surviving remnant, it was scattered to the four winds on the face of the downlands.

The terrible defeat of India Muerta deprived Rivera of his military prestige and Uruguay of her last hope of aggressive warfare. Cooped up in Montevideo, the Government appealed in despair for foreign intervention. England and France, viewing the policy of Rosas with dislike, complied with the request. But in the end their interference proved futile, although the combined European forces went the length of blockading the Argentine ports, and of defeating Rosas's troops on the banks of the Paraná.

Rivera in the meanwhile had fallen upon evil days. His last defeat had involved him in straits that went beyond even the loss of men and power. The fatal day won for him, unjustly enough as it proved, the active suspicion of his own people. Doubtful of his loyalty, the Montevideo Government applied to Brazil for his banishment to Rio de Janeiro. The petition was acceded to; but the Uruguayan leader seemed a veritable human phoenix in his ability to spring undismayed from the ashes of each successive disaster. With the ultimate object of taking an active part once again in his country's defence, he succeeded in getting himself appointed by Montevideo as Minister Plenipotentiary to Paraguay.

Rivera, however, had no intention of proceeding to take up his office. Once free of Brazil, he sailed boldly down the river to Montevideo, and raised the popular opinion of the capital so much in his favour that, after a short period of disturbance in the beleaguered city, he was once again endowed with trust and command. He took himself forthwith to the Campo, where he resumed his warlike operations with varied success.

Nevertheless, it was many years ere this particular period of Uruguay's strenuous vicissitudes came to an end. The year 1851 marked one of the numerous dawns in the fortunes of the land. Then an alliance was concluded between Uruguay and Brazil, while the famous General Urquiza, revolting against the Buenos Aires tyrant, brought the forces of Entre Rios to join the league that was now formed against Rosas. The result was the Battle of Monte Caseros, in which the combined forces made an end to the dictator's power, and caused him to flee to Europe.

The soil of Uruguay was once again free from hostile troops. During the fleeting period of peace that followed, it is necessary to take leave of two of the three Orientales who had ridden to such purpose on the breath of the whirlwind. A little more than two years after the Battle of Monte Caseras, Lavalleja died at Montevideo. In harness to the end, the liberator of his country ended his career just as he had once again been elected to take a share in its government. Three short months later Rivera followed his old comrade and enemy to the land where the cavalry lance is unknown and where no gunshot crashes echo.

CHAPTER IX

HISTORY—*continued*

Condition of Uruguay at the conclusion of the war against Rosas—Measures for the relief of poverty—Juan Francesco Giro elected President—The arising of antagonistic elements—Giro resigns in favour of Bernardo Berro—A revolution ends in the formation of a triumvirate—On the death of Lavalleja and Rivera, Flores becomes Dictator—Rebellion against his rule—Brazil sends an army to the assistance of General Flores—Further revolutionary movements—Manuel Basilio Bustamente succeeds Flores—The policy of General César Diaz—His exile and return at the head of an army—Defeat and death of Diaz—Two interim Presidents—Continuous civil war—General Flores enters the Republic in command of a strong force and is declared Dictator—The Paraguayan war—Causes of its outbreak—The policy and military strength of Paraguay—Strategic errors—Uruguay's share in the campaign—Flores returns to Montevideo from the seat of war—His assassination—General Lorenzo Batlle elected President—The continuance of political unrest—Various presidents and dictators—The Government of the present day—Don José Batlle y Ordoñez—Doctor Claudio Williman—The Uruguayan battle-fields in tabular form—Progress of the land.

With the Battle of Monte Caseros and the fall of Rosas the range of episode enters comparatively modern times. Although the war had ended successfully for the Uruguayan cause, its conclusion left the country in an utterly impoverished and desolate condition. Through the terrible stress of events in a land of such infinite natural resources the population was roofless, and in many districts actually at the point of starvation—an unheard of situation for such a country. As for the treasury, it was virtually empty, and the harassed Government found itself under the necessity of seeking for loans from without its frontiers on any terms that it could obtain.

On the 1st of March, 1852, Don Juan Francisco Giro was elected as the fourth constitutional President of Uruguay. The newly elected chief of the State made desperate efforts towards ameliorating the financial condition of the country, but political complications were destined to work against success from the very start. A fortnight after he had assumed power the Uruguayan army that had borne a brilliant share in the victory of Monte Caseros returned home from Buenos Aires. Its commander, General César Diaz, was acclaimed as a popular hero, and was promptly created Minister for War and Marine, although his sympathies were directly opposed to the Government.

It was not long ere the antagonistic elements that now surrounded him led to the resignation of Giro, who in October delegated his authority to Don Bernardo Berro. The latter, however, was able no more than his predecessor to restrain the tide of partizanship, and in July of 1853 an open revolution broke out, headed by General Diaz and Colonel Palleja. The outbreak occurred during a review in the centre of Montevideo, and, dramatically conceived, proved definitely successful within the course of a few minutes. In the first instance Berro was forced merely to appoint a fresh set of ministers, whose views were hostile to his own; but very shortly afterwards the President was obliged to vacate his post in haste, and to take refuge in the French legation.

At the end of September, 1853, a triumvirate was formed of Generals Lavalleja, Rivera, and Colonel Flores. The deaths of both the former occurred ere the new regime could be adopted in practice, and thus the survivor, Colonel Venancio Flores, was elected to complete the term of the presidency that Giro had vacated. He had scarcely taken charge of the reins of government, however, when his authority was rebelled against, this time by the party who had lately been in power. Leaving General César Diaz in charge of the Government, Flores himself headed a successful campaign against the revolutionists, at the end of which his military rank was raised to that of General.

The unrest did not long remain quelled. Indeed, so threatening did the situation become that Flores appealed to the Brazilians for aid. In response the northern republic sent an army of four thousand men, who occupied the principal cities of Uruguay. The result, as may be imagined, was a yet more marked seething of discontent. In 1855, despite the presence of the foreign troops, the Colorado, or red party, now definitely formed, revolted, and by force of arms obtained possession of the capital for a while.

The success of the revolutionists was short-lived. General Oribe and many other members of the Blanco, or white, group, came to the assistance of Flores. In the end a compromise was effected. The revolutionists retired; Flores resigned his post, and Don Manuel Basilio Bustamente was elected as temporary President. At this stage of Uruguayan history, however, space does not permit a detailed description of the various revolutions that followed the one upon the heels of the other, and that were separated by intervals of merely a few weeks or months.

An event of striking importance, however, occurred in 1858, during the presidentship of Don Gabriel A. Pereira. The latter had been opposed by

General César Diaz, who had stood as an unsuccessful candidate for the office, and the inevitable jealousies soon became embittered once more to the point of active explosion. The policy of Diaz was now to incorporate the Banda Oriental with the Argentine Provinces, and thus to form a single country that should be known as the United States of La Plata.

On the discovery of his plan Diaz was exiled to Buenos Aires, and with him many of the more prominent members of the Colorado party. Diaz, however, soon made his way back across the river, and, collecting an army of eight hundred men, marched upon Montevideo, his forces swelling in numbers as he went. Unsuccessful in its attempt upon the capital, the revolutionist army retired, and, after an indecisive battle or two, met with total defeat at Cagancha. Diaz was taken prisoner in this action, and was shot in company with fifty of his followers.

The remainder of Pereira's term of office passed in comparative tranquillity. He was succeeded in 1860 by another representative of his own party, Don Bernardo Berro, who was elected in constitutional fashion. Three years later, however, General Flores entered the arena of politics once more. The pretext under which hostilities broke out was slight enough in itself. A refusal on the part of the Government to permit the celebration of the anniversary of the Battle of Quinteros had enraged the Colorados, and Flores, espousing their cause, led an army into the field. A lengthy series of battles ensued, in the majority of which Flores was successful. While the war was still raging, Berro, having completed his term, was succeeded as President by Don Atanasio Aguirre. Flores, however, having now obtained the active support of Brazil, was carrying all before him, and in February of 1865 he entered Montevideo in triumph, and was proclaimed provisional Governor and then Dictator of the Republic.

In recapitulating the history of Uruguay at this period the incessancy of the stream of warlike events is amazing. Scarcely had Flores seated himself upon what was virtually the throne of his dictatorship when an event of international importance, the Paraguayan war, occurred that was destined to convulse three republics and an empire.

The pretext on which war was declared was the armed intervention of Brazil in the affairs of the Banda Oriental, and the support lent to Flores by the Brazilian army—an interference that Francisco Solano Lopez, the tyrannical Dictator of Paraguay, took upon himself to resent hotly. Yet, even had not this particular bone of contention come into being, the war was undoubtedly inevitable. Paraguay's distrust of Brazil, and the latter's dread of the really formidable military forces that the inland republic had gathered together, had piled up a situation that only the faintest flame was required to set ablaze.

The military strength of Paraguay at this period was considerable. With an army of eighty thousand men of wild courage, backed by an adequate number of cannon, she might well have bidden defiance to any other single republic of South America. But her strength was exceeded by her confidence. Desirous of sweeping all before him, Lopez divided his forces, and dispatched an army to the north in order to invade Brazil, while another corps was told off to strike in a south-easterly direction. In order to effect this latter move it was necessary to obtain Argentina's consent to cross her province of Corrientes. This permission, which would have involved a breach of neutrality, was, not unnaturally, refused. Incensed at this check to his plans, Lopez declared war upon Argentina, and occupied the province of Argentina by force of arms. In the meanwhile Flores, in return for the support he had received from Brazil, threw in the lot of the Banda Oriental with that of the northern empire.

Thus Paraguay found herself face to face with the allied powers of Brazil, Argentina, and Uruguay, and a struggle ensued that cost the lives of tens of thousands ere the death of Lopez ended the long and desperate fight, at the conclusion of which Paraguay stood all but bereft of her adult manhood. Flores assumed command of the Uruguayan forces that took part in the campaign, and the Oriental division distinguished itself on numerous occasions in the course of the arduous conflict.

Fifteen months after the beginning of the war Flores found it necessary to return to Montevideo, where, in spite of the foreign campaign, symptoms of internal unrest had again become evident. Here in 1868 he met with the fate that had passed him by in the course of the Paraguayan war. Learning that a *coup d'état* had suddenly come about, and that a body of men had taken the Government House by assault, Flores without delay started out in his carriage to gain the scene of action. This move, as a matter of fact, had been foreseen by the conspirators, and a broken-down wagon blocked one of the streets through which he had to pass. As the General's carriage came to a halt in front of the obstruction, a group of men rushed out from the neighbouring doorways, and a minute later the body of Flores, mortally wounded by gunshots and knives, was left lying in the roadway.

This tragedy, however, was of little material assistance to the Blanco party. Indeed, the sole result, so far as they were concerned, was the execution of one or two of their leaders. The power remained with the party of the dead Flores, and General Lorenzo Batlle was elected President, ruling with no little determination despite the frequent revolutionary movements that continued to occur. On various occasions, it is true, the situation of the Government became critical enough, and in 1870 the capital itself was besieged by the insurrectionists; but in the end Batlle prevailed, and the insurrectionists were repulsed, at all events for the time being.

Beyond these warlike episodes much of importance occurred during the rule of this President, which lasted until 1872. Two distinct catastrophes marked the years 1868 and 1869. The former was darkened by a terrible visitation of cholera, while during the latter a financial crisis arose that caused the ruin of many thousands of Oriental families. Nevertheless, the year 1869 is to be marked in white among the milestones of Uruguay's progress; for it was then that the railway was inaugurated, and a line completed between Montevideo and Canelones that marked the first falling into line of the Republic with the more advanced countries.

The next President, Doctor José Ellauri, failed to complete his term of office. In January of 1875 a military revolution forced him to take hasty refuge in a Brazilian warship that was lying in the port of Montevideo, while Don Pedro Varela was acclaimed by the army as chief of state. Raised to power at the point of the bayonet, Varela found it necessary to sustain his post by the same force. Although his armies succeeded in suppressing the numerous popular risings, the dissatisfaction in the end became so general and a condition of monetary crisis so pronounced that Varela was forced to resign.

LAGO DEL PRADO: MONTEVIDEO.

THE PRADO: MONTEVIDEO.

To face p. 124.

Colonel Latorre next assumed power as Dictator. His handling of this dangerously powerful office was liberal, and after three years of office he was elected in 1879 as constitutional President of the Republic. Almost immediately after this, however, the political situation became too complicated for his patience, and he vacated his post, declaring, it is said, that the Uruguayans were ungovernable as a race. Doctor Francisco Vidal, who succeeded him, was replaced in 1882 by General Santos. Although no marked internal disturbances occurred during the presidentship of this latter, the Blanco party were making strenuous efforts just outside the frontiers of the Republic to organise a revolutionary campaign on a serious scale. In 1886, when his office was completed, Santos caused Vidal to be elected once more, meaning to succeed him again, as he had already done on a previous occasion.

No sooner had Vidal occupied the presidential chair than the threatened revolution broke out. General Santos, at the head of the Government forces, effectually suppressed the rising, whereupon Vidal resigned in his favour. A governmental crisis ensued; the Ministry resigned in a body, and Santos was wounded in the course of an attempt upon his life. Efforts towards the keeping of the national peace were now made on both sides, and by means of strenuous endeavour a mixed Ministry was formed. Known by the title of "the Ministry of Conciliation," the new Government was acclaimed with enthusiastic rejoicings throughout Uruguay. Shortly after its formation Santos proceeded to Europe in order to obtain a complete recovery from his wound, and General Tajes was elected President of the Republic.

During Tajes's term of office and that of his successor, Doctor Julio Herrera y Obes, matters remained fairly quiet. In 1894 Don Juan Idiarte Borda became chief of state by election, and three years later a revolution on the part of the Blanco party broke out afresh. At the end of six months' fighting Borda was assassinated in the streets of Montevideo, and the tragic event was followed by the patching up of a temporary peace.

Don Juan Lindolfo Cuestas, who next assumed control of the Government, was successful in bringing about a treaty with the Blanco party, and in September of 1897 the revolutionists laid down their arms. We now arrive at a period that is practically that of the present day. In 1903 Don José Batlle y Ordoñez was elected President. For the first year of his rule he had to contend with further risings of the Blanco party, in the course of which numerous battles were fought. In the end the Government forces were signally successful, and in September of 1904 peace was signed and a general amnesty declared.

In 1907 Doctor Claudio Williman succeeded Señor Batlle. The first years of his tenure of office passed in tranquillity; but at the end of 1910 the Blancos became active once more, and various actions were contested ere the Government troops once more obtained the mastery of the situation in January of 1911.

Having thus brought this rough sketch of Uruguayan history to its conclusion at the present day, it must be admitted that the trend revealed throughout is distinctly warlike. Indeed, the battles that have reddened the soil of the Banda Oriental since its first colonisation are amazingly numerous. I have compiled a list of some 120, and were minor skirmishes included a volume would be needed to contain the list. It is, indeed, the militant portion of history that must necessarily stand out chiefly in a cursory survey such as this. The progress of industry, education, science, and art by the side of the roar of strife is necessarily a silent one. Its course has been none the less forceful for all that; and universities, schools, national institutions of every kind, portworks, and the general paraphernalia of commerce testify to the fact that Uruguay has not permitted her numerous internal struggles to divert the nation from its true forward march. In at least one sense the situation renders tribute to the virile qualities of the Uruguayan. For there are surely few nations that can exhibit a battle-roll such as this, and yet at the same time produce convincing evidence of prosperity and progress. With a proper manipulation of the great national energies, and their devotion to the pursuits of peace alone—tendencies that are becoming each year more marked—the prospects of the Banda Oriental would excel even the present fair promise of her future.

CHAPTER X

URUGUAYAN MANNERS AND CUSTOMS

The temperament of the Oriental—Some merits of the race—The Spanish Main as treated in fiction—Distinction between the villains in print and in actual life—Civility as a national trait—Courtesy of officials—The Uruguayan as a sturdy democrat—A land of equality—Some local mannerisms—Banquets and general hospitality—Some practical methods of enjoying life—Simplicity versus ostentation—Some consequences of prosperity—The cost of living—Questions of ways and means—European education and its results—Some evidences of national pride—The physique of the Oriental—Sports and games—Football—The science of bull-fighting—Eloquence and the oratorical art—Uruguayan ladies—Local charm of the sex—South American institutions—Methods by which they have been improved—The advantages of experiments—The Uruguayan army and navy—Some characteristics of the police—Honesty of the nation—Politics and temperament.

Life in Uruguay is perhaps best described by the German word *gemüthlich*, an untranslatable adjective that savours in its birthplace just a little of light beer, easy-chairs, cigar smoke, steaming coffee, and an atmosphere of *camaraderie*. After which it is necessary to come to an abrupt halt in this task of translation, since the danger of dragging in a foreign word becomes evident when it is necessary to introduce another in order to explain it. In any case, this good-fellowship of the Uruguayan is of a far lighter order than the Teutonic, and is only remotely concerned with the material matters of life. Like the majority of the races of Iberian descent, the Oriental is essentially sober in his tastes, and frequently of an ascetic temperament. Such traits are inborn and natural, and by no means the result of a campaign of schooling and self-repression. He has not, for instance, found it necessary to undergo an outward treatment of badges and blue ribbons nor to devote himself to a special era of self-protection from the like of which the chastened Anglo-Saxon is only just emerging.

For generations the Spanish Main has afforded a lucrative field to the writers of pure sensationalism—if the word be allowed. Their choice has undoubtedly been a wise one, and a judicious compound of fair creoles, satanic dons, swashbuckling pirates, and heroes of the tenderest age has proved an almost inexhaustible gold-mine of really lurid fiction. Yet it cannot be said that this fervid literature has led to a complete understanding of the South American character by the British youth. As to the popular and stirring villainies, I will not attempt to deny that in the past deeds have been enacted that were as terrible as those which have shuddered in print between gaudy paper covers. There were many beyond, infinitely worse, and altogether unthinkable. But the perpetrators of these were seldom enough of the stereotyped temperament as portrayed by the blood-and-thunder authors. Alas for the double-dyed deceit that lurked between the terrific drunken orgies! The real chief organisers of such colossal outrages as have obtained went about their business with a directness that was worthy of a better cause, and reddened the pages of history with a strictly methodical and painstaking industry. Moreover, they were as sober as an infant of eight at a Band of Hope festival.

But all this has very little to do with the present-day dwellers in Uruguay, and their habits and customs. The atmosphere of the country is essentially one of civility. If you would learn the temperament of a nation, mark the behaviour of its humbler public functionaries! In fact, one of the first steps that a student of national character should take is merely to ask a policeman the first question that enters the mind. In order to apply the severest test the query should be a crassly foolish one. In France may be expected vivacious expostulation, in Germany an explosion of imperative military sounds, in Holland a placid non-comprehension, in Portugal a pathetic eagerness to satisfy at all costs—I have tried all these, and more beyond than would stand inclusion here without the risk of wearying. The Uruguayan policeman, in his uniform of British pattern, is essentially courteous, while the manners of the tram conductors, railway guards, and those other genii of transit in whose hands the fate of the traveller lies are equally to be commended.

THE PRINCIPAL PLAZA: MONTEVIDEO.

THE HARBOUR: MONTEVIDEO.

To face p. 130.

The absence of sycophancy that is characteristic of nearly all South American Republics is especially marked in Uruguay. A sturdy democracy is evident here even amongst those whose menial service is of the nature to evoke professional obsequiousness in other parts of the world. The waiter, for instance, will serve with brisk attention, but at the end of the repast he will as often as not pocket the customary tip as a matter of course that is unworthy of comment, to say nothing of thanksgiving. At the same time, it is certain that he would bear no grudge against a well-acquainted patron who had omitted the ceremony altogether. At a genuine Uruguayan hotel the returning guest who has been fortunate enough to win the esteem of the hall porter will find his hand cordially grasped in greeting by that official. The Banda Oriental is a country of discrimination and individuality where personality counts and where popularity is a very material asset. Such a land as this is undoubtedly a home of opportunity.

The hospitality of the higher classes is proverbial. Indeed, reputable conviviality of all kinds is at a premium. In Montevideo the occasions for the giving of banquets are numberless. Thus if a man has achieved something in particular it is necessary that a banquet should mark the event, if he has expressed his intention of achieving anything in particular, a banquet forms the appropriate prelude to the work, and if he has failed to do anything in particular, there is nothing like one of these selfsame banquets to console him for the disappointment.

It is, in fact, much to the Uruguayan's credit that he contrives to extract a vast deal of enjoyment from life in a comparatively homely and unostentatious manner. The race meetings here, for instance, are most pleasant functions, although the horses are not burdened with the responsibility of those tremendous stakes that prevail in some other parts. The theatres, too, although they obtain the services of excellent companies, are moderate in their charges—moderate considering the usual scale that prevails in South America, that is to say.

The advent of a prosperity, however, that now seems more definite than ever before has produced a similar effect upon household expenditure as in the neighbouring countries. The cost of living has risen by leaps and bounds during the past two or three years—a fact that salaried foreigners resident in the country have found out to their somewhat acute inconvenience. In the Campo, naturally enough, this phenomenon of ways and means has not occurred. When live stock and acres are numbered only by the thousand such annoying matters as house-rent and the butcher's bill fail to carry any significance. Nevertheless, in Montevideo the former has practically doubled itself within the last half-dozen years, and all similar items have followed suit as a matter of course. But the rise in the price of land signifies prosperity, and is at all events welcome enough to those directly interested in the soil.

South America, taken as a whole, is a continent whose inhabitants are not a little addicted to ostentation. The phase is natural enough in view of the conditions that obtain in so many of the Republics. In the case of the pastoral countries, even in quite modern times the broad lands had lain comparatively valueless until the introduction of the freezing process for meat and the opening up of the great wheat and maize areas sent up the price of the soil by leaps and bounds. Yet even prior to this era a certain amount of prosperity had prevailed, and young South Americans had become accustomed up to a certain point to wend their way for educational purposes to France and to England, and thus to assimilate European ideas with those that prevailed at the time in the republics of the south.

The sudden advent of overflowing wealth thus found them to a great extent prepared to introduce the most high-flown of modern ideas into the life of their own country. No doubt the very consciousness of these riches that, head for head, undoubtedly far surpass that of the dwellers in the old continent, caused the South Americans to fling aside the last vestige of pastoral simplicity and to make the roots of this great wealth of theirs bud out into residential palaces and entertainments of a rather fabulous order. Since they had shown clearly enough that their material gains had surpassed those of Europe, what more natural than that they should endeavour to prove with equal conclusiveness their ability to outshine the continent of their ancestors in the ornamentation and luxuries that follow automatically in the footsteps of fortune! Surely the trait is nothing beyond the proof of a healthy rivalry.

The Uruguayan is curiously free from all evidence of this ostentation. The life he leads is well supplied with comforts, but its tendency is simple. Thus, although a very fair number of well-turned-out carriages and motor-cars exist in Montevideo, they are seldom to be seen parading to and fro in imposing processions along an avenue or street specially adapted for the purpose, as is the case in many other cities. Rather less rigorous tenets, moreover, obtain in the case of the costume of the male city dwellers, and the whole atmosphere of the country, in fact, is one of plain comfort that has little concern with outward display. Uruguay, for the present, at all events, has retained its democracy. Whether it will continue to do so when the national wealth has become more consolidated is another matter.

The physique of the Uruguayan men is of a distinctly high order. Well-set-up and fresh-complexioned, they represent a favourable testimonial to the climate of the country. In all equestrian exercises they are, as may be imagined, past masters, and they have proved themselves apt pupils at sports and games of all kinds. As is general throughout almost the length and breadth of South America, football is much in vogue here, although, owing merely to the scarcity of the population, the ubiquitous game is less played in the country districts than is the case in Argentina.

The art of bull-fighting still obtains in Uruguay, notably at Colonia, on the banks of the river, where a large new edifice has been erected for the benefit of this, I think, regrettable sport. *Espadas* from Spain frequently come out to perform here; but with the exception of Colonia, that attracts the tourist class from abroad, the haunts of bull-fighting lead only a precarious existence in the Republic.

The Oriental is undoubtedly a man of deeds; but in his case the tendency to action is not effected at the expense of speech. He is, indeed, a born orator, and on the slightest provocation will burst forth into a stream of eloquence that can be quite indefinitely continued. In any case, it is pleasant enough to listen to the resounding periods in which the customary lofty sentiments are couched, but it is as well to bear in mind that the oratorical effort may mean very much—or very little.

Uruguay, more especially its capital, is well-found in the matter of femininity. Indeed, ever since it became a full-blown city Montevideo has been celebrated for its pretty women. This fortunate state of affairs has now become a well-recognised fact, in which the masculine portion of the community takes an even greater pride than does the sex more directly involved. Should a patriotic Montevidean be engaged in conversation with an interested foreigner, the chances are that it will not be long ere the confident question is asked: "And our señoritas, what is your opinion of them?"

In such a case there can be only one opinion—or expression of opinion. Conscience may be salved by the reflection that it is as difficult to find a woman without some stray claim to beauty as it is to light upon a dame of sixty without a grey hair. In both cases the feature may be hard to see. If so, it must be taken for granted. In the case of the Montevidean señorita no such feat of the imagination is necessary. To the far-famed graces of her sisters throughout South America she adds the freshness of complexion and the liveliness of temperament that are characteristic of the land.

Indeed, to conceive these lighter virtues, added to the natural Spanish stateliness, is to picture a very bewitching feminine consummation. Much has been written concerning the señoritas of Uruguay, and yet not a line too much. Their own kith and kin have sung their praises with all the tremendous hyperbole of which the Spanish tongue is capable. White hands, bright eyes, raven hair, and a corresponding remainder of features that resemble all pleasant things from a dove to the moon—the collection of local prose and verse on the subject is justifiably enormous.

The Montevidean lady has now, of course, become essentially modern. She rides in a motor-car, plays the piano instead of the guitar, and has exchanged the old order in general for the new. Yet the same vivacity, courage, and good looks remain—which is an excellent and beneficial thing for Montevideo and its inhabitants. Indeed, the beach of Poçitos or the sands of Ramirez shorn of their female adornment would be too terrible a disaster to contemplate even on the part of the most hardened Oriental. And at this point it is advisable to forsake for the present the more intimate affairs of the people, leaving the last word to the ladies, as, indeed, is only fitting—and frequently inevitable.

The majority of South American Republics—or rather of those in the lower half of the continent—are keenly alive to the benefits of many of the European methods and institutions. Although each of these countries possesses a strong individuality of its own, the generality of these younger nations have almost invariably shown themselves eager to graft to their system foreign methods of organisation that have stood the test of time and that have not been found wanting.

Indeed, in matters of practical progress the citizen of the more enlightened South American Republics is blessed with an unusually open mind. This condition has naturally borne fruit in experiments, and it is this very tendency to receptiveness that has frequently laid these States open to accusations of irresponsibility. Often enough the charge has proved entirely unjust, since it was based on nothing beyond a too fervent outbreak into an experimental region from which it was hoped to extract remedies and innovations that should tend to the betterment of the Republic.

The direction of the public services affords striking instances of the kind. The navy, army, and police of the more progressive of the republics are usually modelled on European patterns. The navy is usually conducted on the English system, the army follows German methods, and the police copies as closely as possible the time-honoured principles of what is undoubtedly the finest force in the world, the English constabulary. Uruguay follows this procedure only in part. The kit of the troops here is of the French, rather than the German, pattern; and although the naval uniforms throughout the civilised world are all more or less alike, that of the Uruguayan does not resemble the British as closely as do some others, notably that of the Chilian. The costume of the Oriental police, however, helmet and all, is almost exactly the counterpart of the British, although it boasts the additional adornment of a sword and of spats.

The work of the Uruguayan police, moreover, is to be commended for a lack of officiousness and fussy methods. They are little concerned with larceny, and with the similar forms of petty dishonesty, for the nation, as a whole, is endowed with a strict sense of the sacredness of property. The trait is to a large extent inherent in all the nations of the River Plate; but in this instance it may well be that it has become even more accentuated by the drastic methods of General Artigas at the beginning of the nineteenth century, whose abhorrence of theft and whose exemplary castigation of the crime may well have left an impression that has endured for almost a century.

I have already referred to the sobriety of the Uruguayan. Perhaps for the reason that he is of a more openly jovial temperament he is slightly more addicted to looking upon his native wine when it is red than is the Argentine or Paraguayan. But the cases where this occurs are isolated enough. Indeed, in the matter of sobriety the Uruguayan can easily allow points to almost every European nation. The majority of crimes that occur to the east of the River Plate are neither those brought about by dishonesty nor drink. They are far more frequently the result of differences of opinion and of old-standing feuds that are avenged by the knife and revolver, for the Uruguayan, though courteous to a degree, is quick to resent offence, more especially when the umbrage given is brought about in the course of a political discussion.

CHAPTER XI

ABORIGINAL TRIBES

The population of Uruguay prior to the Spanish conquest—Principal tribes—Paucity of information concerning the early aboriginal life—The Charrúas—Warlike characteristics of the race—Territory of the tribe—Stature and physique—Features—The occupations of war and hunting—Temperament mannerisms—A people on the nethermost rung of the social ladder—Absence of laws and penalties—Medicine-men—A crude remedy—The simplicity of the marriage ceremony—Morality at a low ebb—The prevalence of social equality—Method of settling private disputes—The Charrúas as warriors—Tactics employed in warfare—Some grim signals of victory—Treatment of the prisoners of war—Absence of a settled plan of campaign—Arms of the Charrúas—Primitive Indian weapons—Household implements—Burial rites—The mutilation of the living out of respect for the dead—Some savage ceremonies—Absence of religion—A lowly existence—Desolate dwellings—Change of customs effected by the introduction of horses—Indian appreciation of cattle—Improvement in the weapons of the tribe—Formidable cavalry—The end of the Charrúas—Other Uruguayan tribes—The Yaros—Bohanes—Chanas—Guenoas—Minuanes—Arachanes.

At the time of the Spanish Conquest the territory which now constitutes the Republic of Uruguay was peopled by about four thousand Indians. These, however, did not form a single nation, but were divided off into a number of tribes. The most important of these were the Charrúas, Yaros, Bohanes, Chanas, and Guenoas. Each of these groups possessed its own territory, and each was wont to exist in a state of continued hostility with its neighbours.

Nothing is known of the history of these folk previous to the arrival of the Spaniard, and even during the earlier periods of the conquest information is scanty enough, since contact between native and European was confined almost entirely to warlike occasions, and since, even when opportunity offered, the early colonists were neither sufficiently adapted nor especially educated for the purpose.

The Charrúas constituted the leading tribe of these aboriginal people. They owed this ascendancy to their warlike spirit, and to their comparatively large numbers. It was they who murdered Juan Diaz de Solis, the discoverer of the Rio de la Plata, together with many of his companions, and it was they, moreover, who offered the most strenuous resistance to the colonising attempts of the Spaniards.

The Charrúas, to the number of a couple of thousand, inhabited the coast of the River Plate, and carried on a semi-nomadic existence between Maldonado and the mouth of the River Uruguay, occupying a region that extended inland for about ninety miles, its inner frontiers running parallel with the coast-line. The stature of these natives attained to middle height; they were robust, well built, and usually free from that tendency to obesity which is the characteristic of the Guarani Indians. As a race they were distinguished by rather large heads, wide mouths, and flat noses. Their skin was unusually dark, and in colour approached the complexion of the negro more nearly than that of any other South American race. Peculiarly adapted to resist hunger and fatigue, they were agile and swift of foot as became those who existed principally on the deer and ostriches that they hunted. It is said that their health was such that many attained to a very advanced age.

The character of these Indiana was essentially warlike and turbulent, and they were remarkable for their passion for revenge and deceit. Of a taciturn and apathetic temperament, they refused to submit to discipline of any kind. They were, moreover, peculiarly averse to outward display of any emotion. A laugh, for instance, would be noiseless, signalled merely by a half-opening of the lips; conversation was carried on in a low and unmodulated tone of voice, and a true Charrúa would run a considerable distance to gain a comrade's side rather than be under the necessity of shouting openly to him. The sole occasions on which the exercise of patience would seem to have come naturally to the race were those of hunting and of scouting. A child of nature, with the faculties of hearing and sight marvellously developed, the Charrúa became reticent and morose when brought into contact with civilisation.

ANCIENT STONES EMPLOYED FOR NUT-CRUSHING.

To face p. 140.

In social ethics these dwellers on the coast ranked low; indeed, their place was amongst the lowest in the scale of tribes. Division either of labour or of the spoils of war was unknown. Each hunted and fought for his own hand alone, while the wife constructed a few rude utensils and performed the duties of a slave. Their system knew neither laws, punishments, nor rewards, and the only services that were wont to be recompensed in any way were those of the medicine-men, whose natural cunning was doubtless as superior to that of the rest as is the case elsewhere. Nevertheless, these leeches seem to have been acquainted with only one remedy. This was to suck with might and main at that portion of the body beneath the surface of which an inward pain was complained of. The marriage ceremony was confined to the obtaining of the consent of the bride's parents. The state of wedlock, however, was considered of some importance in the man, as it conferred on him the right to go to war, and to take part in the councils of the tribe.

Morality, as understood by the more advanced sections of humanity, was at a low ebb. Wedlock was permitted an unnaturally liberal range and licence. Not only was polygamy general, but marriages between brothers and sisters were permitted, although it is related that their occurrence was rather rare. Cases of monogamy, however, were not unknown, and, whenever the opportunity offered, a wife would desert a multi-spoused husband in order to take up her abode with a man who was willing to accept her as his only wife. Conjugal faithlessness was held to be an excusable failing; indeed, on the arrival of the Spaniards, the men would frequently offer their wives to the Europeans in return for some material advantage.

Some evidence of that social equality that is so strongly a characteristic of the tribes of the River Plate is to be met with among the Charrúas. Such chiefs as existed were almost altogether lacking in real power or authority. A leader, as a matter of fact, was elected by the people merely in order to act in cases of emergency, and his chieftainship, held on sufferance, was liable to be taken from him on the coming to the front of a man held more suitable for the post. It is a little curious to find that in so fierce a race private quarrels were not adjusted by means of the crude arms of war that they possessed. These disputes were fought out with the fists, and after a satisfactory exchange of blows the matter was ended for good and all.

Notwithstanding this sensible method of settling their individual differences, the Charrúas were merciless in the wars waged against neighbouring tribes or Spaniards. On the first outbreak of hostilities they were wont to hide their women and children in the woods, after which spies were immediately sent out to locate the position of the enemy. This determined, it was usual to hold a council of war in the evening, and to make a surprise attack at the first glimmerings of dawn. The method of their onslaught was one calculated to terrify. Dashing out of the semi-obscurity, they would make a furious charge, uttering loud cries, the fierceness of which was supposed to be accentuated by means of the warriors striking themselves continually on the mouth.

Women and young children captured in their attacks were taken back as prisoners to the rude encampments of the conquerors, where they afterwards received complete liberty, and became incorporated with the tribe. No quarter, however, was shown to the men of the beaten force. It is said by some of the early European adventurers who came into contact with this fierce race that they were not only wont to scalp their fallen enemies, but that each was accustomed to cut an incision in his own body for every dead foeman whose body lay to the credit of his prowess or cunning. Some doubt, nevertheless, is thrown upon the existence of these habits, although they are affirmed by three rather notable authorities, Barco, Lozano, and Azara. Fortunately for the Spaniards, who discovered in the Charrúas by far the most dreaded enemies that it was their lot to encounter in this part of South America, these Indians were easily turned from a settled purpose or plan of campaign. Thus they would lose many opportunities of pushing home success, halting in an advance in order to celebrate a first victory, and remaining on the ground for the purpose of marking the occasion at length.

The fact that these rude savages should have obtained victories over the Spaniards by means of the crude arms that were known to them speaks wonders for their bravery. Their choice of warlike implements was no whit greater than that enjoyed by the lake-dwellers of the Stone Age. Arrows, spears, clubs, and maces—all these were made up of stone heads and wooden shafts. That which might be termed the characteristic native weapon was the *bolas*, the pair of stone balls attached to ostrich sinews or to some other contrivance of the kind. These—as remains the case to the present day in other lands—were employed as slings, and, for the purpose of entangling an enemy, were the most dreaded implements of all.

For the purposes of peace as well as for those of war the sole materials available to the Charrúa for the fashioning of implements were stone, wood, bone, and clay. Thus the household equipment was wont to be confined to the most primitive types of knives, saws, punches, hammers, axes, mortars, pestles, and roughly baked pottery. It is certain that they used canoes, since they used to cross over to the islands facing Maldonado, but nothing is known concerning the particular build of these humble craft.

Waged under such circumstances existence knew little glamour. Yet even here certain ceremonial institutions obtained. The women, for example, on attaining to adult age were accustomed to tattoo three stripes upon their faces as a signal of the fact, while the men wore a certain kind of headgear to bear a similar significance. On the death of a male, the warrior was buried with his arms, usually on the summit of a small hill. Later, when the luxury of domestic animals became known, the rites grew more elaborate, and the dead man's horse was usually sacrificed on the grave.

In any case the occasion of a man's death was marked by self-mutilation on the part of his wives and female relatives. These would commence by cutting their fingers, weeping bitterly all the while, and afterwards would take the spear of their deceased relative, and with it would prick themselves in various parts of the body and more especially in the arms, which were frequently pierced through and through. Azara was privileged to witness a number of these painful ceremonies, which must have been carried out with conscientious zeal, since he remarks that of all the adult women that he saw none was without mutilated fingers and numerous scars on the body.

These methods of accentuating sorrow, however, were light when compared with the tortures that adult sons were wont to inflict upon themselves on the loss of their father. It was their duty first of all to hide themselves, fasting, in their huts for two days. This effected, it was customary to point a number of sticks and to transfix the arms with these from the wrist to the shoulder, with an interval of not more than an inch between each. In this porcupine-like condition they proceeded either to a wood or to a hill, bearing in their hands sharpened stakes. By means of these each would dig out a hole in the earth sufficiently deep to cover him to the height of the breast, and in this custom demanded him to remain during a whole night. On the next day the mourners rose up from their uncomfortable holes, and met together in a special hut that was set apart for the ceremonial purposes. Here they pulled the sticks from their arms, and remained for a fortnight, partaking of only the scantiest nourishment. After which they were at liberty to rejoin their comrades, and to resume the comparatively even tenor of their normal existence.

The Charrúas afford one of the rare instances of a race who knew no religion. They neither worshipped a benevolent divinity nor endeavoured to propitiate a malignant spirit. They were, nevertheless, superstitious up to a certain point, and dreaded to leave their huts during the night. There is no doubt that some vague belief in an after-existence must have been implanted in their lowly minds. Although they do not seem ever to have referred openly to the belief, the sole fact of the burial of the dead man's arms in the same grave as the corpse is sufficient proof of their supposition that the weapons would be needed in some half-imagined and dim place beyond. But neither priest nor magician was in their midst to stimulate their wonderings on the point.

The highest degree of science or intellect, as a matter of fact, was represented by the medicine-men with their simple and mistakenly practical remedy. The race had no acquaintance with either music, games, dancing, or with ordinary conversation as understood amongst more civilised beings. In matters of personal adornment the Charrúas were equally unsophisticated. A few ostrich feathers in the hair constituted the beginning and the end of the men's costume; the sole garment of the women was a loin-cloth. Of too dull a temperament to discover even the simplest pleasures that the majority of races contrive to extract from their existence, the sole luxury in which these folk indulged was the bathing in the streams of the country. But this recreation was limited to the midsummer months: during all the other periods of the year they refrained entirely from ablutions.

The point as to whether these benighted Indians were cannibals has never been definitely cleared up. The charge of eating human flesh has been brought against the tribe by a certain number of authorities. It is stated, for instance, that the body of Juan Diaz de Solis, the discoverer of the River Plate and one of the first victims of these warriors, was consumed by the attacking party after his murder. But the evidence is not clear in either this case or in any other of the kind, although it is likely enough that they partook of the taste that was shared by various tribes who inhabited the country to the north. Their ordinary food, in any case, was the flesh of the deer and ostrich, as well as fish. Their meals were frequently demolished in a raw condition, doubtless of necessity, although they understood the means of producing fire by the friction of wood. Vegetable food was unknown to them, but they contrived to produce an intoxicating liquor from the fermentation of wasps' honey mixed with water.

A glance at the more intimate domestic life of these wild possessors of so many strictly negative attributes may well complete a rather desolate picture. The home of the Charrúa was on a par with the remainder of his few belongings. A few branches, stuck into the earth and bent towards a common centre, constituted the foundation; one or two deer-skins placed on top of these formed the superstructure. These dwellings, as a matter of fact, were no more crude than those of the Patagonian natives, and little more so than the huts of the Chaco Indians to the north-west, although the structures of both these latter were—and still remain—thatched with grasses and vegetation in the place of skins. In the case of the Charrúa the inner accommodation was limited to a few square feet; but the confined space sufficed to hold an ordinary member, although if the human units increased unduly, a second hut was erected by the side of the first. For furniture, there were the few crude household implements already mentioned, the weapons of the men, and the deer-skin or two spread upon the ground to serve as couches.

It was in this manner that the Charrúas were accustomed to live when the Spaniards, much to the rage of the original inhabitants, landed upon their shores. From that time onwards their method of existence underwent a change. With the introduction of horses they adopted the habit of riding, and soon became extraordinarily proficient in all equestrian arts, although their natural fleetness of foot suffered inevitably during the process. The cattle that now roamed the Campo in great numbers afforded them ample and easily obtained meals. Indeed, although they may have had some legitimate cause for grievance, the material benefits that the influx from Europe accorded the Indians were enormous.

Yet the hatred with which these fierce warriors of the Campo regarded the white intruders tended with time to increase rather than diminish. As a foe the Indian was far more formidable now than at the time of the first encounters. Behold him on horseback, careering like the wind across the pastures, armed with a deadly iron-tipped lance some fourteen feet in length! For he had obtained the means now to fight the *conquistadores* with their own weapons, and even his arrows were pointed with metal, although he still retained the homely stone in the case of his ever efficient *bolas*. Thus he remained, immutably fierce, alternately winning and losing the endless fights, but never conquered nor enslaved for three centuries. At the end of that period, in 1832, came the end of his race, and the small remnant was practically annihilated. The fate of the last four of the Charrúas is pathetically humorous, as illustrating what unsuspected ends a wild community may be made to serve. Two men and two women, the sole survivors of the unconquered warrior tribe, were sent across the ocean to Paris, where they were placed on exhibition, and doubtless proved a profitable investment.

Having concluded with the Charrúas, the remaining aboriginal tribes of Uruguay demand very little space by comparison. There were, nevertheless, half a dozen minor groups that inhabited the other portion of the land that is now Uruguay.

The Yaros Indians occupied a small district on the south-western coast of the country, and were a warlike race whose customs and manner of existence much resembled those of the Charrúas. With this latter race they were on terms of hostility, and only allied themselves with their aboriginal neighbours for the occasional purpose of a joint attack upon the Spaniards. At the beginning of the eighteenth century they were to all intents and purposes exterminated by the more powerful Charrúas, the few survivors joining the ranks of their conquerors.

Little is known of the Bohanes, who occupied the coastal territory to the north of the Yaros. They were likewise enemies of the Charrúas, and in the end suffered partial extermination at the hands of the latter tribe. It is said that a certain number escaped into Paraguay and became absorbed amongst the Guarani inhabitants of the north. It appears certain that, although this insignificant group could not number much more than a hundred families, their language differed entirely from the tongues of the neighbouring tribes.

NATIVE "BOLEADORAS."

To face p. 148.

The Chanas were island-dwellers whose character contrasted rather remarkably with that of the inhabitants of the mainland. When first met with they were occupying the islands in the River Uruguay to the north of the point where the Rio Negro joins the principal stream. A race of peaceable and rather timid folk, they suffered not a little at the hands of the more warlike tribes. Thus, when the Spaniards occupied their native islands, the Yaros endeavoured to obtain a footing on the western coast-line; but, driven from here by the Charrúas, they found shelter in a collection of islets to the south of those that had formed their first abode. They were more or less expert fishers and watermen, and possessed a language of their own. Many of their customs were akin to those of the Guarani Indians. Thus when the bodies of their dead had been buried for a sufficiently long time to lose all flesh, the skeletons would be dug up, painted with grease and ochre, and then entered once again in company with their ancestors. In the case of a dead child it was their custom to place the body in a large earthenware urn which they filled with earth and ochre, covering up the vessel with burnt clay.

The Chanas lent themselves readily to civilisation. Towards the middle of the seventeenth century they became converted to Christianity, and in the beginning the Jesuit mission station of Soriano was peopled almost entirely by members of this tribe. Of an intelligence and temperament infinitely superior to that of the remaining tribes, they mingled freely with the Spaniards after a while, and adopted European manners and customs. The race disappeared eventually merely from the force of absorption by marriage with their civilised neighbours.

The Guenoas existed in the north-western portion of the country, leading a semi-nomadic life. They were to be distinguished from the Indians who dwelt to the south of their territory in that they were amenable to discipline in their natural state. At their head were recognised chiefs, or caciques, who appear to have exercised no little authority. They were endowed, moreover, with a certain amount of superstitious belief, and witch-doctors were to be found among them. They had also learned the art of signalling from a distance by means of bonfires. Although a warlike race, they were far more susceptible than the Charrúas to outside influence. A portion of the tribe eventually found refuge in the Jesuit missions, and the majority of the males took service in the Spanish and Portuguese armies.

The Minuanes occupied a territory to the east of the Guenoas, and in physical appearance, manners, and customs closely resembled the Charrúas, to such an extent, indeed, that the two tribes have frequently been confused by writers. An error of the kind is natural enough, since the two groups were wont to bind themselves in hard-and-fast alliance in order to combat the Spaniards. The Minuanes, however, were a trifle more advanced in some respects than their southern allies. They were accustomed, for instance, to wear loin-cloths, with the frequent addition of a skin flung across the shoulders. Moreover, their hostility towards Europeans was undoubtedly less deep-seated, since the Jesuits succeeded in incorporating them for a while in one of their missions. The majority, it is true, soon returned to their own wild life, but a certain number remained.

The last tribe to be noticed is that of the Arachanes, a people of Guarani origin who lived on the east coast between the ocean and the great Lake Merim. Practically nothing is known of these folk. They were dispersed and exterminated at the commencement of the seventeenth century by the Brazilian mamelukes in the course of their raids from San Paulo.

CHAPTER XII

MONTEVIDEO

Population—Attributes of the city—Situation of the Uruguayan capital—The Cerro—A comparison between the capitals of Argentina and Uruguay—The atmosphere of Montevideo—A city of restful activity—Comparatively recent foundation—Its origin an afterthought—Montevideo in 1727—Homely erections—Progress of the town—Advance effected within the last thirty years—The Uruguayan capital at the beginning of the nineteenth century—Some chronicles of the period—The ubiquity of meat—Dogs and their food—Some curious account of the prevalence of rats—The streets of old Montevideo—Their perils and humours—A comparison between the butchers' bills of the past and of the present—Some unusual uses for sheep—Methods in which the skulls and horns of cattle were employed—Modern Montevideo—The National Museum—An admirable institution—Theatres—Critical Montevidean audiences—Afternoon tea establishments—The Club Uruguay—The English Club—British community in the capital—Its enterprise and philanthropy—The *Montevideo Times*—A feat in editorship—Hotels—Cabs and public vehicles—The cost of driving.

It may come as a surprise to many to learn that Montevideo, the capital of Uruguay, possesses a population of almost four hundred thousand inhabitants. By no means one of those centres that are remarkable only for population, it holds almost every conceivable attribute of a modern city—from boulevards and imposing public buildings to plazas, statuary, and a remarkably extensive tramway service.

Montevideo is situated at a peculiarly advantageous point on the Uruguayan shore. No student of geography, it is true, could point out the exact limits of so immense a stream as the La Plata. Yet for all practical purposes the capital of the Republic sits just beside this very phenomenon. Thus it may be said that the eastern side of the town faces the ocean, while the southern looks upon the River Plate. To enter more fully into the geographical details of the spot, the chief commercial and governmental districts cover a peninsula that juts well out into the waters, thus forming the eastern extremity of the semicircular bay of the actual port. Upon the ocean side of the peninsula the shore recedes abruptly northwards for a short space, and it is here that lie the pleasant inlets that are not a little famed as pleasure resorts.

At the riverward extremity of the port bay is a landmark that is indelibly associated with Montevideo, whether viewed from sea or land. The famous Cerro is a conical hill, surmounted by a fort that dominates all the surrounding landscape. But of the Cerro, since for various reasons it is a place of importance, more later. The capital itself claims the right to prior notice, and to the rendering of a few introductory facts.

Since the distance between the chief town of either republic only just exceeds a hundred miles, a comparison between Montevideo and Buenos Aires is almost inevitable. Indeed, it has become something of a hobby on the part of the Oriental who has visited the Argentine city, and vice versâ. Fortunately, the comparison can be made without the engendering of bad blood, since to a great extent that which the one town lacks is possessed by the other. Thus, in the first place Montevideo, although astonishingly thriving, is without the hastening crowds and feverish hustle of the city across the waters. Again, although its sheltered bay is yearly accommodating more and larger vessels, the Oriental town is innocent of those many miles of docks teeming throughout with steamers. Yet, on the other hand, it possesses its rocks and shining sands of pleasure that draw the Argentines themselves in shoals across the river.

Indeed, the atmosphere of Montevideo is restful, and at the same time free from the slightest taint of stagnation. Even the more modest thoroughfares are comparatively broad, while the many new avenues are spacious and well planned to a degree. Perhaps the keynote to the town in these respects may be found in the fact that, although the absolute dominion of the priests has long been a thing of the past, the sound of the cathedral and church bells is audible above the hum of the traffic. Even in the ears of the most ardent Protestant the effect is not without its soothing and tranquillising properties.

It is true that there have been some who, deceived by its peaceful appearance, have altogether underrated the actual activity of the city. As a matter of fact, the progress of Montevideo deserves far wider recognition than it has obtained. The town represents something of a babe even amongst the roll of comparatively youthful South American cities. Its foundation, in 1726, indeed, was due to an afterthought, following an expulsion of Portuguese who had landed at the solitary spot and fortified it in the course of one of their later expeditions. Thus Colonia had long afforded a bone of contention between the two nations, and even Maldonado had provided several battlefields ere the present capital was colonised or thought of.

In 1727 the panorama of Montevideo could not well have been an imposing one. At that time the place possessed no more than two buildings of stone, although it could count forty others of hide. But the erections of this homely and odorous material that in the colonial days were made to serve almost every conceivable purpose could have added very little to the æsthetic properties of the budding settlement. Once established, however, the city grew apace, and in due course the natural advantages of its position raised its status to that of the premier urban centre of the land.

But, although Montevideo flourished and increased for rather more than a century and a half, its leap into complete modernism has only been effected within the last thirty years. In this respect it has only followed the example of the important cities of the neighbouring republics. Thus, in 1807, when its ninetieth birthday was marked by the British occupation, the accounts of numerous foreign visitors to the place testify to its primitive state, although all agree that in the main the capital was a pleasant spot.

That the streets of the period were badly paved it is not surprising to hear, since, owing to many obstacles, the art of accurate paving is one of the very last that has filtered through to South America in general. On the other hand, it is admitted that the thoroughfares were well lit. Amongst the more disagreeable peculiarities were some for which the butcher's trade was responsible.

In a country of oxen the superabundance of meat was made only too evident. "Oftentimes," says an English chronicler of the period, "when a particular piece of meat is wanted, the animal is killed, and after cutting out the desired part, without taking off the skin, the remainder of the carcass is thrown to the dogs, or left to rot in the streets." After this the author proceeds to make a startling statement: "Almost every animal is fed on beef: from this circumstance pork and poultry bought casually in the market, and which has not been purposely fattened, are tinctured with a very ancient and beef-like taste." The first part of this piece of information is undoubtedly accurate; but to what extent the latter is the result of imagination or of fact it is perhaps best not to investigate too closely. According to this theory, some of the plainest of joints must have contained in themselves the elements of several courses, with a species of menagerie meal as a consequence!

In any case, it is well known that the effect of this abundant meat diet upon the prowling dogs of the town was to render them savage and dangerous to the casual passer-by, who frequently had to defend himself as best he might from their attacks. The extraordinary prevalence of rats from similar causes is confirmed by other authors, Uruguayan as well as English. The brothers Robertson, who are responsible for such an excellent description of Paraguay at that period, have some curious experiences to relate concerning this visitation. Both received much hospitality at the hands of their Uruguayan friends. "The only drawback," writes one of them, "upon the delightful way in which I now spent my evenings was the necessity of returning home through long, narrow streets so infested with voracious rats as to make it perilous sometimes to face them. There was no police in the town, excepted that provided by the showers of rain, which, at intervals, carried off the heaps of filth from the streets. Around the offal of carrion, vegetables, and stale fruit which in large masses accumulated there, the rats absolutely mustered in legions. If I attempted to pass near these formidable banditti, or to interrupt their meals and orgies, they gnashed their teeth upon me like so many evening [ravening?] wolves ... sometimes I fought my way straight home with my stick; at others I was forced to fly down some cross and narrow path or street, leaving the rats undisturbed masters of the field."

No doubt had a militant vegetarian of the period found his way to Montevideo he might have pointed out many object-lessons in favour of a lesser carnal devotion. On the other hand, it is lamentable that the cheap value at which carcasses were then held has not continued to prevail to this day. To the small population of a hundred years ago meat seemed to grow as easily as grass-blades, and the uses to which it was wont to be put seem astonishing enough in an era of butchers' bills and shilling steaks.

Since until comparatively recent years in the River Plate Provinces mutton has been held unworthy of even a beggar's acceptance, the carcasses of the sheep suffered the most ignominious end of all. Amongst the other means they were made to serve, the animals were driven to the brick-kilns, slaughtered upon the spot, and their bodies flung into the ovens to feed the fires. As for the cattle, their skulls and horns were everywhere. Prepared by the foregoing for revelations of general utility, it is not surprising to read that houses as well as fence-lines were frequently constructed from such tragic material.

Such reminiscences of the past, however, have drawn the trail too far aside from the modern city of Montevideo, where dogs are subject to police regulations, and the rat is scarce, and meat as dear as elsewhere. As for the town itself, it has sprung up afresh, and renewed itself yet once again since the colonial days. Indeed, the sole buildings of importance that remain from the time of the Spanish dominion are the cathedral and Government palace.

SOLIS THEATRE AND NATIONAL MUSEUM.

THE CERRO FORT.

To face p. 156.

The national museum at Montevideo is both well represented and amply stocked. It is a place into which the average foreigner enters with sufficient rarity, which is rather lamentable, since a very varied local education is to be derived from its contents. Uruguayan art, natural history, geology, literature, and historical objects all find a place here. The collection of primitive Indian utensils, and of *bolas*, the round stones of the slings, is unique. It is said that in the case of the latter, which have been brought together from all districts, almost every species of stone that exists in the country is to be met.

The historical objects here, moreover, are of great interest to one who has followed the fluctuating fortunes of the country. The early uniforms and weapons of the Spaniards, the costumes and long lances of the first struggling national forces, and a host of other exhibits of the kind are assisted by a considerable collection of contemporary local pictures and drawings. Many of the earlier specimens of these are exceedingly crude, but none the less valuable for that, since the battle scenes are depicted with much the same rough vigour that doubtless characterised their actual raging.

In the gallery devoted to Uruguayan painters there is at least one picture that is remarkable for its power and realism, the work of a famous modern artist, representing a scene in the great plague visitation that the capital suffered. It is a little curious that in the rooms where hang the specimens of European art the biblical paintings of some of the old Italian masters should be hung side by side with modern productions of the lightest and most Gallic tendency; but it is quite possible that this may have been done with intention in support of the propaganda against the influence of Church and religion that has now become so marked throughout South America. In any case, the custom is one that does not obtain in Montevideo alone. The taxidermic portion of the museum is exceedingly well contrived, and the entire institution, with its competent staff, under the direction of Professor José Arechavaleta, is worthy of all praise.

With social institutions of all kinds Montevideo is amply provided. The theatres are well constructed, well patronised, and frequently visited by some of the most efficient companies in existence. It is true that, owing to the difference in the size of the two towns, Montevideo usually obtains the tail-end of a visit the most part of which has been spent in Buenos Aires. But such matters of precedence do not in the least affect the merits of the various performances. Both actors and musicians here, moreover, have to deal with an audience that is at least as critical as any that its larger neighbour can provide.

One of the evidences of Montevideo's modernity is to be found in its afternoon-tea establishments. Unfortunately, the name of the principal one of these places has escaped me, so that it must receive its meed of praise in an anonymous fashion. It is certainly one of the daintiest specimens of its kind that can be conceived both as regards decoration and the objects of light sustenance that justify its existence. As a teashop it is a jewel with an appropriate pendant—a tiny coal-black negro boy official at the door, whose gorgeous full-dress porter's uniform renders him a much-admired toy of humanity.

The chief and most imposing of the capital's clubs is the Club Uruguay that looks out upon the Plaza Matriz, the main square. The premises here are spacious and imposing, and the club is quite of the first order. The membership is confined almost entirely to the Uruguayans of the better classes, although it includes a small number of resident foreigners. The English Club is situated on the opposite side of the same square, and is an extremely cosy and well-managed institution that sustains to the full all the traditions of the English clubs abroad.

The English community in the capital is fairly numerous, and is in closer touch with its Uruguayan neighbours than is the case with the majority of such bodies in other South American countries. The enterprise and philanthropy of the colony are evident in many directions. It has long possessed a school and a hospital of its own; but subscriptions have now been raised for the erection of a larger and more modern hospital building, to be situated in pleasant surroundings on the outskirts of the town. A great part of the credit for this, as for many other similar undertakings, is undoubtedly due to Mr. R.J. Kennedy, the British Minister.

The English Colony is represented journalistically by a daily paper, the *Montevideo Times*, a sheet of comparatively modest dimensions that is very ably edited and conducted. Indeed, the record of Mr. W.H. Denstone, the editor, must be almost unique in the history of journalism all the world over. For a period that, I believe, exceeds twenty years the production, in journalese language, has been "put to bed" beneath his personal supervision, and not a number has appeared the matter of which has not come directly from his hands. As a testimony, not only to industry but to a climate that permits such an unbroken spell of labour, surely the feat is one to be cordially acclaimed in Fleet Street!

The Montevideo hotels, although there is much to be said in their favour, are comparatively modest in size, and somewhat lacking in those most modern attributes that characterise many in other large towns of South America, and even those in the pleasure resorts on the outskirts of the Uruguayan capital itself. The best known is the Lanata, situated in the Plaza Matriz. But I cannot recommend the Lanata with any genuine degree of enthusiasm. The Palacio Florida, a new hotel in the Calle Florida, is, I think, the most confidently to be recommended of any in the capital. The tariff here is strictly moderate, the service good, and the place is blessed with the distinct advantage of a very pleasant lounge on each floor.

In many respects Montevideo, although its scale of expenses is rising rapidly, still remains a place of cheaper existence than Buenos Aires. But not in the matter of its cabs and public vehicles. The hooded victoria of the Argentine capital is frequently replaced here by the landau, and on a provocation that may not have exceeded half a mile the piratical driver will endeavour to extract a dollar—the equivalent of four shillings and twopence—from his victimised passenger. The reason for this ambitious scale of charges no doubt lies in the fact that the Montevidean is very little addicted to driving in cabs, of which vehicles, indeed, the very excellent tramway service of the city renders him more or less independent. Thus, as the solvent person is said to bear the burden of the tailor's bad debts, the economies of those who ride in Montevidean tramcars are visited upon the pockets of those others who patronise the cabs.

CHAPTER XIII

Montevideo—*continued*

The surroundings of the capital—Pleasant resorts—The Prado—A well-endowed park—Colón—Aspects of the suburbs—Some charming quintas—A wealth of flowers and vegetation—European and tropical blossoms side by side—Orchards and their fruits—The cottages of the peasants—An itinerant merchant—School-children—Methods of education in Uruguay—The choice of a career—Equestrian pupils—The tramway route—Aspect of the village of Colón—Imposing eucalyptus avenues—A country of blue gum—Some characteristics of the place—Flowers and trees—Country houses—The Tea Garden Restaurant—Meals amidst pleasant surrounding—An enterprising establishment—Lunch and its reward—Poçitos and Ramirez—Bathing-places of the Atlantic—Blue waters compared with yellow—Sand and rock—Villa del Cerro—The steam ferry across the bay—A town of mixed buildings—Dwelling-places and their materials—The ubiquitous football—Aspects of the Cerro—Turf and rock—A picturesque fort—Panorama from the summit of the hill—The guardian of the river mouth—The last and the first of the mountains.

The Uruguayan's appreciation of pleasant Nature is made abundantly clear in the surroundings of the capital. The city, as a matter of fact, is set about with quite an exceptional number of pleasant resorts both inland and upon the shore. Of the former the Prado park and the pleasure suburb of Colón are the best known. The Prado is reached within half an hour from the centre of the city by means of tramway-car. Situated on the outskirts of the town, the park is very large and genuinely beautiful. Groves of trees shading grassy slopes, beds of flowers glowing by the sides of ponds and small lakes, walks, drives, and sheltered seats—the place possesses all these commendable attributes, and many beyond.

The Montevidean is very proud of the Prado, and he has sufficient reason for his pride. He has taken a portion of the rolling country, and has made of the mounds and hills the fairest garden imaginable. The place would be remarkable if for nothing more than the great variety and number of its trees, both Northern and subtropical. But here this fine collection forms merely the background for the less lofty palms, bamboos, and all the host of the quainter growths, to say nothing of the flowering shrubs and the land and water blossoms. One may roam for miles in and out of the Prado vegetation, only to find that it continues to present fresh aspects and beauties all the while.

The expedition to Colón is a slightly more serious one, since, the spot being situated some eight miles from the centre of the town, the journey by tramcar occupies an hour or so. As much that is typical of the outskirts of Montevideo is revealed by the excursion, it may be as well to describe it with some detail.

THE BEACH AT PARQUE URBANO.

THE SAN JOSE ROAD BRIDGE.

To face p. 162.

It is only when once fairly launched upon a journey of the kind that the true extent of Montevideo and the length of its plane-shaded avenues proper become evident. Nevertheless, as the car mounts and dips with the undulation of the land, the unbroken streets of houses come to an end at length, giving way to the first *quintas*—the villas set within their own grounds. The aspect of these alone would suffice to convince the passing stranger of the real wealth of the capital. Of all styles of architecture, from that of the bungalow to the more intricate structure of many pinnacles and eaves, many of them are extremely imposing in size and luxurious to a degree. A moral to the new-comer in Montevideo should certainly be: Own a quinta in the suburbs; or, if you cannot, get to know the owner of a quinta in the suburbs, and stay with him!

But if you would see these surroundings of Montevideo at their very best, it is necessary to journey there in October—the October of the Southern hemisphere, when the sap of the plants is rising to counterbalance its fall in the North. The quintas then are positive haunts of delight—nothing less. Their frontiers are frequently marked by blossoming may, honeysuckle, and rose-hedges, while bougainvillæa, wistaria, and countless other creepers blaze from the walls of the houses themselves.

As for the gardens, they have overflowed into an ordered riot of flower. The most favoured nooks of Madeira, the *Midi* of France, and Portugal would find it hard to hold their own in the matter of blossoms with this far Southern land. Undoubtedly, one of the most fascinating features here is the mingling of the hardy and homely plants with the exotic. Thus great banks of sweet-scented stock will spread themselves beneath the broad-leaved palms, while the bamboo spears will prick up lightly by the ivy-covered trunk of a Northern tree—a tree whose parasite is to be marked and cherished, for ivy is, in general, as rare in South America as holly, to say nothing of plum-pudding, though it is abundant here. Spreading bushes of lilac mingle their scent with the magnolia, orange, myrtle, and mimosa, until the crowded air seems almost to throb beneath the simultaneous weight of the odours. Then down upon the ground, again, are periwinkles, pansies, and marigolds, rubbing petals with arum-lilies, carnations, hedges of pink geranium, clumps of tree-marguerites, and wide borders of cineraria. From time to time the suggestions of the North are strangely compelling. Thus, when the heavy flower-cones of the horse-chestnut stand out boldly next to the snow-white circles of the elder-tree, with a grove of oaks as a background, it is with something akin to a shock that the succeeding clumps of paraiso and eucalyptus-trees, and the fleshy leaves of the aloe and prickly-pear bring the traveller back to reality and the land of warm sunshine.

But it is time to make an end to this long list of mere growths and blossoms. The others must be left to the imagination, from the green fig-bulbs to the peach-blossom and guelder-roses. Let it suffice to say that a number of these gardens are many acres in extent, and that you may distribute all these flowers—and the far larger number that remain unchronicled—in any order that you will.

As the open country appears in the wider gaps left between the remoter quintas, and the space between the halting-places of the tram is correspondingly lengthened, the speed of a car becomes accelerated to a marked degree. The cottages that now appear at intervals at the side of the road are trim and spotlessly white. They are, almost without exception, shaded by the native ombú-tree, and are surrounded with trelliswork of vines and with fig-trees, while near by are fields of broad beans and the extensive vineyards of commerce.

Along the road a rider is proceeding leisurely, a large wooden pannier jutting out from either side of his saddle. This bulky gear, that lends such a swollen appearance to the advancing combination of man and horse, denotes a travelling merchant of humble status. What he carries within the pair of boxes there is no outward evidence to tell. Their contents may be anything from vegetables or chickens to scissors, knives, or sweetstuffs. Since, however, he has now drawn rein by the side of one of the white cottages, his wares almost certainly do not comprise the first two, for the market for such lies within Montevideo proper. By the time, however, that the lids of the panniers have been raised and the bargaining has commenced the car has sped far onwards, and has dropped him from sight. Thus the business of the travelling merchant—like that of the majority of passers-by—remains but half understood.

But here, at all events, comes a group of riders of another kind, whose purpose is clear. Half a dozen small boys and bareheaded girls, mounted upon disproportionately tall ponies, are jogging along on their way to school. Uruguay prides itself, with no little reason, upon the efficiency of its system of education, and the humblest hut now sends forth its human mites to absorb the three R's and to be instilled with patriotically optimistic versions of their country's past. These rudiments mastered, they need not necessarily halt in their scholastic career, since, according to the laws of the land, a professorship is open eventually to the most lowly student who persists for sufficient time. And Uruguay is undoubtedly a nest of opportunities. An embryo statesman or learned doctor may be represented by each of the urchins who are now plodding onwards with serious intent through the dust!

In the meanwhile the car has won its way fairly out into the open country, always green, smiling, and thickly shot with the pink of peach-blossoms. The rails have now drawn well away from the centre of the road, and are separated from the actual highway by a grassy space. Stirred by the importance of possessing a track all to itself, the car is undoubtedly aspiring to the rank of a railway train, and goes rushing at a really formidable pace upon its verdure-embedded lines. Swaying over the shoulders of the land, past plantations, lanes, and hedges, it plunges onwards in grim earnest to the terminus of the line at Colón itself.

The actual village of Colón gives little indication of the nature of the district. The railway-station, shops, and houses are all pleasantly situated, it is true, and the restaurants and pleasure-gardens are unusually numerous. The attractions of the place, however, lie well outside the central nucleus of buildings. From this some remarkably imposing eucalyptus avenues lead outwards into the favourite haunts of the Montevidean when on pleasure bent.

Undoubtedly the most salient feature of Colón is the eucalyptus. Indeed, the place primarily consists of mile upon mile of these stately avenues, fringed by blue gums of an immense size. Bordering these magnificent highways, that cross each other at right angles, are country houses here and there that are reproductions of those in the suburbs of Montevideo. In between the avenues, again, are clumps and small forests of eucalyptus, whose tops soar high up in tremendously lofty waves, that enclose vineyards, peach-orchards, and olive-tree plantations.

Here and there are lanes walled in by mounting hedges of honeysuckle and rose, while many of the private grounds are guarded by the impassable lines of aloe. Add to this basis all the other trees, shrubs, and flowers that have already been passed on the outward journey, and you have the main attributes of Colón.

EUCALYPTUS AVENUE: COLÓN.

To face p. 166.

Since the topic of the inner man appeals at least as much to the Uruguayan as to any other mortal, there are some very pleasant restaurants set in the midst of this land of eucalyptus. Perhaps the best and prettiest of these is one known by the very English name of the Tea Garden Restaurant. One of the chief peculiarities of the place is that tea is actually partaken of there from time to time, as the modern Oriental is beginning to accord this cosmopolitan beverage a recognised place by the side of coffee and his own native Yerba Maté.

At the Tea Garden Restaurant it is possible to lunch by the side of a lake, with ripening grape-bunches above to throw their reflections in the soup, and with the falling petals of orange-blossom floating daintily past the steaming cutlets, while the music of the ducks blends admirably with the clatter of the table weapons. With really good cooking and attentive service added to these side attractions, what more could one want!

But the proprietors of the restaurant are nothing if not enterprising. They give the wayfarer something even beyond an excellent meal. At the end of the repast each guest is presented with a ticket that entitles him to a free cab-ride to the tramway terminus. The idea is admirable. Nothing is wanting but the cabs! At all events, when I had concluded lunch there the surface of the fine avenue was innocent of any vehicle, and continued so until the walk to the car was accomplished. But the courtesy of the offer had been effectual, and a certain sense of obligation remained.

The bathing-places of Poçitos and Ramirez are akin in many respects to these inland resorts. By the side of the sea here are fewer blossoms and rather smaller eucalyptus groves, but a greater number of open-air restaurants and one or two quite imposing hotels. Indeed, Ramirez, the nearer of the two, is endowed with a really fine casino, that faces the shoreward end of the pier, and that has by its side the spacious and well-timbered public park.

Poçitos occupies the next bay, and is notable for its lengthy esplanade and for the very pleasant houses that give upon the semicircular sweep. This bay, moreover, is the first that has, so to speak, turned its back upon the river and has faced the open ocean. As a token, the waters are tinged with a definite blue, and the air holds a genuine sting of salt that rapidly dies away when passing up-stream away from here. To the Buenos Airen, who enthusiastically patronises the place, Poçitos is delightful, if for no other reason than the sense of contrast to his own surroundings that it affords him. Not that he has any reason to grumble at the river frontier of the rich alluvial soil, from out of which his fortunes have been built. But here, in place of the soft, stoneless mud, is bright sand, and genuine rocks, piled liberally all over the shore, that shelter crabs, and pools that hold fish of the varieties that refuse to breathe in any other but guaranteed salt water. So it is that the summer season sees the long rows of tents and bathing machines crowded and overflowing with the Uruguayans and the host of visitors from across the river.

Both Ramirez and Poçitos are within the range of the ubiquitous tramcar. But this very efficient service, not content with its excursion of half a dozen miles and more on the ocean side of Montevideo, runs in the opposite direction completely round the port bay, and performs the yet more important journey to Villa del Cerro, the small town that lies at the foot of the hill that is so closely associated with Montevideo and its affairs. A far shorter route to this latter place, however, is by the busy little steam ferry that puffs straight across the bay, and that starts faithfully at every hour, as promised by the timetable, although, if that hour coincides with the one specified, the event may be accepted as a fortunate accident.

Its most patriotic inhabitant could not claim loveliness for Villa del Cerro. The existence of the spot is mainly due to the presence of some neighbouring *saladeros*, or meat-curing factories, and thus the small town presents the aspects of the more humble industrial centres. There are two or three regular streets, it is true, that contain a few houses with some faint pretensions to importance. Upon the balconies of these the local señoritas are wont to gather of an evening. They are obviously a little starved in such matters as romance, and a little fearful lest their eye language should lose its eloquence through too long a disuse. Thus the advent of any passing stranger whatever suffices to cause a certain flutter and excitement in the balconies above.

Outside these main streets the pattern of the town has been left much to the discretion of its most lowly inhabitants. Buildings composed of unexpected material sprout up from the earth in unexpected places. Earth, boards, tin, and fragments of stone are amongst the commonest of these, although there are a certain number, stiffened by bricks, whose comparatively commonplace exterior looks smug and respectable by the side of the rest.

Mounting upwards, the architecture of the outskirts comes as something of a relief, since its simplicity is crude and absolute to the point of excluding any jarring possibilities.

The ranchos here are composed of nothing beyond loose fragments of rock piled one on top of the other, with an odd hole here and there that serves for window or door, frequently for both.

At one point in the midst of these primitive stone dwellings a small group of scantily clothed boys are playing football, the implement of their game being an old sheepskin rolled into the nearest imitation to a globe to which its folds will consent and held together roughly with string—one more instance of the spreading triumph of football, that wonderful game that seems to conquer its surroundings and to implant itself firmly throughout the world entire.

The turf slopes of the Cerro itself are all about one now. From the distance they had appeared of an unbroken green, but when actually approached the broken patches of bare rock upon their surface become evident. The last of the stone shanties are not only contrived upon one of these, but constructed from the very site upon which they repose. The result is a difficulty to distinguish between the natural rock and the habitable flakes.

The short turf of the wind-swept Cerro is innocent of blossoms save for the ubiquitous verbena, a few stunted tobacco flowers, and some other lowly blooms. Upon the very summit, where the rock breaks out boldly and piles itself in jagged heaps, is a picturesque fort, from the midst of whose walls of solid masonry rises the dome of the light that guides the ships into the harbour below.

The panorama that opens itself out from this point is not a little remarkable. On the one side lies the bay of Montevideo, thickly dotted with its steamers and sailing vessels, with the towers and streets of the capital spreading far inland upon the opposite shore. Beyond this, again, are the undulations of the hills, the coastline, and the ocean that shines brilliantly, although it is only dimly blue. On the other hand stretches the River Plate, whose waters are deepening their yellow as they extend towards the landless horizon, beneath which lies Buenos Aires and Argentina.

The Cerro guards the entrance to the great river. It is the first true hill upon its banks—and the last, for over a thousand miles. For the next of its kind signals the approach to Asuncion—beyond Argentina and far beyond the Banda Oriental—in far-away Paraguay. And much water flows between the tropical heat of Asuncion and the cool freshness of this Cerro. Therefore the place is worthy of mark as the southernmost of the two widely separated sentinel hills that guard such different climes.

CHAPTER XIV

FROM MONTEVIDEO TO THE NORTHERN FRONTIER

Leaving Montevideo—General aspects of the Campo—The Rio Negro as a line of demarcation—Growing exuberance of the scenery—*Flor morala*—Blue lupin—Camp flowers—A sparsely populated countryside—Absence of homesteads—A soft landscape—Humble ranchos—Cattle and horses—Iguanas and ostriches—Deer—Cardoso—Influence of climate and marriage upon the colonists—A cheese-making centre—A country of table-lands—A Campo load—Some characteristics of the way—A group of riders—Some contrasts—A country of rocks—Stone walls—Crude homesteads—Kerosene tins as building material—"Camp" stations—The carpets of blossom—Piedra Sola—Tambores—Landscape and nomenclature—Increase in the height of the table-lands—Scenes at a country station—Aspects of the inhabitants—Some matters of complexion—The train and its transformation—Influence of the country upon the carriages—Northern passengers—Metropolitan and local costume—Some questions of clothes and figure—Relations between mistresses and maids—Democratic households—A patriarchal atmosphere—Things as they seem, and as they are—Conversation no guide to profession.

A journey from south to north through the heart of Uruguay reveals an infinitely greater variety of landscape and humanity than is suspected by the dwellers in the better known littoral districts of the land. It is true that for the purpose the employment of the homely and convenient railway train is essential. Although it has been my good fortune to drive for day after day and for league upon league through lesser areas of the Uruguayan Campo, to cover such a lengthy stretch as this by means of coach and horses is only possible for him who can afford the supreme luxury of ignoring time.

The first portion of the journey, moreover, although far from wearisome in the circumstances, is effected across a landscape almost every league of which presents the exact replica of its neighbours. Once clear of the woods, fields, vineyards, orchards, and flowers that lie so pleasantly to the landward side of Montevideo, the rolling grass waves of the Campo come to stretch themselves from horizon to horizon, rising and dipping with a ceaseless regularity of sweep until it becomes difficult to believe that the entire world itself is not composed of these smiling folds of land.

It is not until nearly three hundred kilometres have been traversed, and the train has rumbled over the long bridge that spans the Rio Negro that the first symptoms of a changing scenery become evident. The undulations have become less regular, and the hill-tops are soaring higher into the sky-line. Indeed, the tendency throughout is towards an exuberance that has been hitherto lacking. Thus not only the outbreaks of stone that scar the hill-faces at intervals are bolder in character now, but the wealth of field flowers, too, has grown in extent and brilliance.

A broad, glowing bank of the purple *flor morala* lines the railway track on either hand, pricking across the landscape in twin unbroken bands of colour. Where the loftier flower ceases, the red, white, and mauve of the verbena clings closely to the turf. At longer intervals sprout clumps of blue lupin blossom, while the white mallows, harebells, and tobacco flowers lurk thickly in between the groves of thistle, and large yellow marguerites and daisies mingle with a variegated host of blooms.

The countryside is as sparsely populated as elsewhere. League upon league of the great rolling sweeps of the land spread their panorama unflecked by a single homestead. So far as the mere picturesque is concerned, the result is admirable. The soft, dreamy landscape is at its very best when unburdened by human habitation. Yet in such cases the picturesque becomes a luxury won at the expense of the practical. Undoubtedly from the green background of the pastures should shine out the white walls of estancia-houses and ranchos. The time is now probably near enough when such will actually be the case; but in the meanwhile the land waits in complacent patience, sprouting out its grassy covering with contemptuous ease.

Yet it must not be imagined that the landscape, however lonely, is altogether deserted. Now and then may be discerned the clump of trees that stand out like islands from the sea to shelter the dwellings of the owners of these great areas of soil. At long intervals, too, springs up a hedge of tall cactus that flanks the humble rancho, whose tin roof, as often as not, is held down in its place by means of small boulders—a feature of architecture that recalls the châlets of Switzerland, although it is certain enough that the respective buildings have nothing else in common.

Here and there graze the dumb supporters of the homesteads—herds of cattle, troops of horses, and flocks of sheep. These districts of the centre have not yet attained to the standard of breeding that characterises the lands that fringe the great rivers to the south and west. Thus, the cattle, although sufficiently fat and sleek, lack the finish of the more aristocratic Hereford. Shaggy of coat, long of horn, and exhibiting an utter lack of restraint in the strangely varied colour scheme of their bodies, they are essentially of the *criollo*, or native, order.

In the neighbourhood of these licensed occupiers of the pastures are others whose existence is more precarious. These are hares who race away at the advent of a train, and iguanas whose long tails stream behind them as they depart in a flurry. As for the ostriches, they have obviously come to the conclusion that their life is too short and their neck too long for any excitement of the kind. They are plainly bored by the advent of this noisy invention of man, and regard it languidly from the height of the two long legs that repose in a supercilious attitude.

On through the undulating Campo, where the rain pools lie like dew ponds upon an English South Down, and where the banks of the intermittent streams of the cañadas thread in and out of the green grass for all the world like the bodies of black snakes. A company of deer are feeding peacefully in the distance, intermingled with the bulky members of a herd of cattle with whom the wild creatures have condescended to associate for the time being.

The train has pulled up at Cardoso now, the centre of a district that is considerably more populous than the majority. The place was once the site of a German colony, and indeed the sole reasons why it does not remain so to this day must be laid at the doors of climate, surroundings, intermarriage, and the influence of all three. As it is, chastened by the all-powerful atmosphere of the spot, Teutonic features, customs, and language have already become modified almost to the extinction of the original type.

The phenomenon affords only one more of the innumerable instances of the tremendous power of absorption that is latent in the South American continent. In contrast to the mutability of all things intrinsically human, the industry of the community remains the same as when the first colonists, strangers and foreigners, introduced it to the spot. Cheese-making is still the staple trade of Cardoso, and the district is not a little famed for the art.

This particular neighbourhood, however, is to be noted for something of more enduring importance than cheese. It is here, indeed, that the soil of the land, after many tentative swellings, each more ambitious than the last, takes upon itself to change its outline in a determined and conclusive fashion. The universal, gentle swell of the undulations has given way to steeper walls of green surmounted by curiously level, flat surfaces. Thus the face of the Campo is now dotted, so far as the eye can reach, with a collection of tablelands, each separate and differing slightly from the rest in the details of its pattern, but each marvellously distinct and clearly cut. The feature is characteristic of central northern Uruguay, and is continued well beyond the frontier into Brazil.

Obeying the sociable instinct that so frequently links the railway line with the highway in these parts of the world, the main road runs close alongside the locomotive track. Where it goes the dark, rich soil gleams moistly in every dip, and each cup in the land holds its pool, for heavy rains have preceded the brilliant sunshine of the day.

For many leagues the broad surface of the way has been broken by nothing beyond the inevitable attributes of such thoroughfares—the occasional pathetic heap that stands for the dead body of a horse or cow, or the bleaching framework of bones that gleam out sharply after the vultures' and caranchos' feast. But here at length comes a body of riders, half a dozen Gauchos, enveloped in ponchos of various patterns, who are pricking onwards at the easy canter that renders the conquest of any space whatever a question of mere time.

Thudding over the hill-tops, splashing through the mud-holes below, the progress of the grim, silent centaurs is as inevitable and certain as the presence of the knives at their belts or the maté-bowl slung by the saddles. Then the train has sped ahead, dragging after it a world of its own as remote from the atmosphere that surrounds the six diminishing horsemen as is the clank of the engine from the light jingling of the silvered bridles.

The crop of stone upon the land has become more prolific. The rock has come to adorn the sides of the table-lands more especially, breaking out with precision at the spot where each slope of the green eminences starts out abruptly from the level, after which it continues, unbroken, to the summit. The material, however, has been made to serve for purposes of utility, and here and there are corrals and walls of loosely piled stones, a novel sight to one who is working his way upwards from the south.

The scarce ranchos, however, continue on much the same pattern that has characterised them throughout the journey. The crudeness of many of these is scarcely to be excelled in any part of the world. To imagine an edifice composed of the lids and sides of kerosene tins, roofed and finished off at the odd corners by straggling tufts of reed, is to picture the abode of by no means the most humble settler.

One or two are embellished, it is true, by a rough trellis work from which the vine-leaves hang thickly, while others are decorated by nothing beyond a variety of multi-coloured garments that hang out in the sunshine to dry. Clustered together, the modest homesteads would appear sordid and mean. As it is, the open solitudes of which each stands as the human centre lend it a certain dignity that is not in the least concerned with the pattern of the structure itself.

The train has halted at a couple of small "Camp" stations, and has puffed onwards again, leaving the respective brick buildings, with their scatter of outhouses, to sink back into the lethargy that the passenger train disturbs but for a few minutes every other day. In the neighbourhood of Achar, the latter of these halts, the surrounding country has broken out into an exceptional blaze of flower. The purple of the flor morala stains hillsides entire; the scarlet verbena glows in spreading patches that from a distance might well be mistaken for poppy-fields, while all about are other flower carpets of yellow, blue, and white.

The wealth of blossom continues unbroken as far as Piedra Sola, or Solitary Stone—a spot aptly named from a curious square block of rock that reposes upon the top of a mound in so monumental a fashion that it is difficult to believe that it is the work of Nature rather than of human beings—and beyond it, adorning a country that grows ever bolder until Tambores is reached.

All the attributes in these primitive parts savour of Nature and of its simplicity. The very nomenclature is affected by this influence. Thus no historical significance is to be looked for in the name of Tambores—drums. The origin of the word lies in the surrounding table-lands that have grown loftier and more accentuated here than their brethren to the south, and whose shape resembles not a little the instruments of war.

Tambores is a place of comparative importance. It is true that no architectural beauties are to be looked for at the spot, since the quaint collection of edifices that are scattered in the neighbourhood of the station are almost without exception the tin and reed structures common to the district. Such rare exceptions as exist, moreover, hold out merely minor claims to aristocracy in the shape of an entire sheet or two of corrugated iron. Yet these modest precincts guard a really important cattle and wool centre, and even now many hundreds of bales are lying in readiness in their wagons, while cattle stamp impatiently in the trucks that will bear them southwards to Montevideo.

Passing to and fro by the honeysuckle hedge that flanks the platform is a motley collection of folk. The majority of the men are in sad-coloured ponchos, and in *bombachos* that frequent staining has imbued with an earthy hue. In addition to the railway officials, beshawled women, children, dogs, and hens complete the gathering. A feature that is especially noticeable here is the number of dusky complexions that have come to assert themselves in the midst of the fresh-coloured Uruguayan faces. Quite distinct from the swarthiness of the Indian, the tint here savours undoubtedly of the African.

It becomes, moreover, steadily more marked as the Brazilian frontier is approached.

Indeed, the evidence of variety is everywhere. Even the conventional aspect of the train itself and of its passengers has undergone no little alteration since the start. As it pulled out from Montevideo the train was undoubtedly a model of its kind that took no little pride in its well-ordered level line of day coaches, and sleeping and restaurant cars.

Once well out into the country, however, the democratic influence of the land has overcome its patrician make-up. A passenger coach or two has dropped away at one station; some trucks and goods-vans have been added at another, until its appearance has become as heterogeneous as that of a Uruguayan volunteer soldier in a revolution. In fact, the farther from the capital it gets and the nearer to its destination, the more *négligé* and doubtless practical does its appearance become. Like to a man who starts out for a walk on a hot summer's day, it is metaphorically trudging along bareheaded, with its coat slung over its shoulder.

In the case of the passengers the same may be said without the apology of metaphor. It is in the occupants of the first-class coaches that the transformation is most evident. Many of the men remain in at least portions of the same clothes of metropolitan cut that served them in Montevideo. But ponchos have now been brought out and donned to hide what lies beneath— ponchos of fine texture, these, that stand quite apart from the meaner drapings of the *peon*, but nevertheless essentially national and of the land.

As for the women, the few who have remained constant to the train since the beginning of the journey remain in much the same trim as when they first entered the carriage. The persistence may be due to the vanity that is alleged by man to be inherent in woman, or merely to the laudable desire of giving the country cousin an object-lesson in costume.

It must be admitted that the garments of these latter tend to comfort somewhat at the expense of appearances. The loosest of blouses, wraps, and skirts are wont to make up a figure in which a waist may at times be suspected, and even occasionally hoped for, but is never seen. Decidedly the procedure savours of rigid honesty on the part of the country cousin. For frankly to promise nothing is surely more admirable than the transient advertisement achieved by the manufacture of merely temporary space in the position rightfully sought for by superfluous material.

Many of these country ladies with the honest and unaccentuated figures are accompanied by their maids, these latter for the most part negresses. The bond between mistress and maid is very close here. Indeed, in Northern Uruguay such episodes as a "month's warning," a demand for an extra "night out," the right to "followers," and all other similar bones of contention that arise in more populous centres between employer and employed are unknown.

Here the maid, whether she be negress, mottled, or white, obtains an assured, if minor, footing in the family circle. Not only her love affairs but her appetite will call forth the ready sympathy of her mistress. Seated together, their meals will be shared in common, as indeed is occurring in the case of sandwiches and wine in the railway carriage even now. To complete the patriarchial atmosphere, the railway guard has joined one of the groups in question in order to assist, purely platonically, at the impromptu meal, and his manner is equally courteous towards señora and maid.

It is certain that he who travels in the remoter parts must put aside all preconceived notions of degree and appearances. Close by is seated a group of young men who are discussing the opera in Montevideo with critical fervour. After a while the conversation, as is inevitable, turns upon politics, and the arguments and views are bandied to and fro with the eloquence common to the race.

But there is original philosophy here, whether sound or otherwise. Schemes for alleviating the lot of the humble worker follow hard upon the heels of topics of municipal reform, parliamentary procedure, and the vexed and intricate question of where the Uruguayan-Argentine frontier floats in the broad dividing river. The phrases are wonderfully apt, the proposals astonishingly daring. During a pause in the political discussion one of the debaters explains his own walk in life. He is a jeweller's assistant. Another is head waiter in a Montevidean hotel. These products of the land are undoubtedly bewildering. Each has been talking like a prime minister.

CHAPTER XV

FROM MONTEVIDEO TO THE NORTHERN FRONTIER

—continued

A remarkable transformation in Nature—The Valley of Eden—The gateway of the garden—An abrupt descent—From bare plain to sub-tropical forest—Picturesque scenery—Eden station—Some curiosities of nomenclature—Beggary as a profession—The charity of the Latin lands—The cliffs of the valley—Varied aspects of the vegetation—The everlasting sweet pea—Some characteristics of the mountains—A land of tobacco—Negro cultivators—Appearance and dwellings of the colonial population—Some ethics of climate and customs—Tacuarembo—A centre of importance—A picturesque town—Scenes at the station—Some specimens of local humanity—A dandy of the Campo—The northern landscape—The African population—Nature and the hut—The tunnel of Bañada de Rocha—Paso del Cerro—On the Brazilian border—Rivera—A frontier town—Santa Ana—The Brazilian sister township—A comparison between the two—View from a neighbouring hill—The rival claims to beauty of the Uruguayan and Brazilian towns.

Tambores has been left behind, and the train is speeding once again through the undulations and table-lands of the pastures. Although the new-comer is unaware of the fact, the climax of the journey is drawing near, and one of the most remarkable transformations in Nature is about to reveal itself with the suddenness of a pantomimic stage-shifting.

That the stranger to the land should remain unaware of what lies before him is not surprising. The rolling downs have encompassed him in unbroken sequence from the moment that the outermost suburb of Montevideo was left behind. They are about him now, sinking and rising until their smooth green sweeps upwards in long waves against the blue horizon. Never was a fresher, blowier country, with its every inch open and bare to the sunlight and breeze. It is difficult to imagine such a land rubbing shoulders with a landscape less frank and guileless. Its only fitting boundaries are white cliffs, and, beyond them, the wide ocean.

Yet if Nature aspired to human ideals of consistency the hills would go hopping to many a queer tune. After all, it is best to leave it to arrange its surprises in its own way. The first symptom of a coming change is afforded by the appearance of a growth that has remained a stranger to the landscape until now. Rock plants, with thick, heavy, silver leaves and snowy blossoms rise up thickly of a sudden to whiten the ground. Then without warning the train is speeding downwards through the rock walls of a cutting that seems to have opened out from the ground at the call of an Open Sesame steam-whistle. Two or three hundred yards of a steep descent that makes a precipice out of the stone side on either hand, then a rapid widening of the barrier to the view—and the thing is done! The train has entered the Valley of Eden.

Just as Adam in his fig-leaf gasped in dismay at his eviction from the garden, so does the modern traveller in boots and buttons exclaim in surprise as he passes through the stone gateway of this later Eden. The two or three hundred yards have made an incredible memory of the open downland. In its place are rugged cliffs to right and left, at the base of which dense sub-tropical forest sends its waves upwards to cling to the stone sides as far as they may.

In the centre of the valley is a stream that goes rippling over its rocky bed, overhung with a curtain of flowering trees that hold strange nests within their branches, and the festoons of the lianas that plunge thickly downwards towards the earth. The scene, in fact, holds all the enthusiastic variety of the sub-tropics. Nothing is wanting to the picture. The rock, leaves, flowers, palms, and the vivid patches of smooth green by the edge of the stream have as accessories the turkey-buzzards and black vultures carving their lazy circles above, and the brilliant host of butterflies beneath that float airily to and fro as though to outflash even the wonderful feathers of the local woodpecker.

The train, as though itself entirely taken aback by these new aspects of Nature, has been proceeding at little beyond human walking pace. Now it has drawn up by the side of a modest building and a few surrounding huts that are almost smothered in the verdure. Eden station! The sight of the place is far less incongruous than the sound. As a matter of fact the valley itself is well named. No spot could better endow with its glamour the simple life that endures until the inevitable boredom leads to the death of innocence. Nevertheless, the railway company should reserve special accommodation for the garden. Let the traveller proceed to Margate or Southend as he likes. But a third-class ticket to Eden! The thing is inconceivable, yet it is done every day.

The advent of the train, however, affords a harvest to at least one inhabitant of this secluded and fair corner. An aged negro, who was undoubtedly born a slave across the Brazilian frontier, is slowly hobbling the length of the train collecting toll from the passengers as he goes. In South America are two professions that stand apart from all the rest. Failing the status of a millionaire, become a beggar by all means! As regards a profitable occupation, not one of the intermediate walks of life can equal the extremes at the social poles. That of politician is perhaps nearest akin to both; but, intrinsically, the phrase is transitory, since a rapid absorption at one end or the other is practically inevitable.

The aged negro is collecting his dues with grave complacency. A general dealer in receipts, his profits are by no means restricted to mere cash. Business in centavos is amazingly brisk; but so are the transactions in cigarettes, cigars, fruit, and morsels of food. Ere the train starts the benignity has grown deep upon the old man's face. When the place is lonely and still once more he will totter back to his tiny reed hut, with its insignificant patch of maize, and will smoke, and eat, and drink, in senile enjoyment of the lengthy holiday that separates his tri-weekly half-hours of work. He may thank the God of beggars that he was born in a Latin land.

The train is moving onwards once again, and the bold grey cliffs and bluffs recede as the valley widens. Although the first full beauty of the scene has lost by the expansion, the wealth of colour remains. The forest trees for the most part are flecked with brilliant yellow, while the surface of the swamps that now cover the centre of the valley are thickly spangled with the pure white of their own broad blossoms.

OXEN DRAWING RAILWAY COACH.

BEFORE THE FAIR: TACUAREMBÓ.

To face p. 186.

But an attempt to describe the various growths would be the task of a botanist. One alone must be described for its striking propensities if for nothing beyond. In all directions are bushes of glowing mauve flower—or, at least, so they appear at the first glimpse to the eye. The sight is not a little amazing, since many of the shrubs, a dozen feet in height, are covered from top to bottom with an unbroken coat of petals. A nearer inspection solves the mystery some while after. The flower itself is a parasite, an everlasting sweet pea, that goes the length of concealing from sight the bush on which it depends.

In the meanwhile the valley has widened until the well-defined cliffs that hemmed in its beginning have disappeared altogether. But the country remains entirely distinct from the open Campo that preceded the gate of Eden. There is pasture here, it is true, but it is pasture broken and intersected by woodland, river courses, ravines, and mountains. It is curious to remark that among the latter, although many are bold and lofty, there is not a peak to be met with. In obedience to what appears to be a hard-and-fast law of the hills, the top of each is shorn evenly across, leaving a flat and level summit.

The country is one of tobacco now as well as of maize, and the aspect of the cultivators coincides to a great extent with the popular notions of the *mise en scène* of the tobacco-fields. The population of the tiny mud huts that decorate the land is almost entirely negro, and the inevitable piccaninny is much in evidence, having apparently escaped in shoals from the London music-hall stage. The costume of the younger boys, however, would scarcely pass muster in a more conventional neighbourhood. The sole garment of many of the younger ones consists of a shirt, and a very frayed one at that—a costume that is eminently suitable to the palm-tree, but criminal beneath the oak.

The next halt is at a place of importance, one of the chief features, in fact, of the Far North. Tacuarembo numbers a population of almost eight thousand, which, although the figure may not impress the outer world, renders the spot something of an urban giant in the neighbourhood. As though to compensate for its lack of imposing buildings, Tacuarembo is exceedingly picturesque. With its avenues of tall trees, and its houses peering everywhere from beneath the shade of an unusual richness of vegetation, the place is sufficiently delightful and striking in its own fashion.

The station itself gives the keynote to the aspects of the place. Within half a dozen yards of where the white steam goes hissing upwards from the engine the green young peaches hang in thick clusters from their branches. To their side is a hedge of blossoming roses that continues until the flowery architecture changes abruptly to a wall of golden honeysuckle. At the rear of this, surrounding the outer yard of the place, are poplars and eucalyptus, while the heavy scent of the purple paraiso-tree overpowers the fainter colours of the mimosa.

A dozen or so of the local "coches" are waiting in the shade of all these and in that of the vines that clamber upwards by their side. They are crude affairs, whose lack of paint and polish is more than counteracted by the dictatorial attitudes of the brigand-like drivers who lounge at ease upon the boxes. It must be admitted that the manners of these latter are far less formidable than their appearance. Indeed, they smile far more graciously than the corresponding metropolitan tyrants of South America as they drive off one by one, bearing away their patrons beneath the shady avenues.

The majority of folk, however, remain for some while to chat together, since in these parts the railway station is an accepted centre of sociability. The queer medley of the crowd possesses its own charm. A group of officers in dark uniforms and red kepis rub shoulders with Gauchos and peones in dark clothes and black or blue *bombachos*. Beyond is a knot of women in the homely and loose costume of the district, bare-headed, and with hair drawn tightly back to be wound into a plain knot at the back of the head. An elaborate dandy, dressed ostentatiously in the favourite black from head to foot, is extracting a few centavos from the pockets of his shining velvet waistcoat with which to endow a couple of dissolute-looking beggars who have drawn near.

Although the jet-black faces of the negroes and the browner tints of the half-castes are much in evidence, the countenances of the true Uruguayans remain remarkably fair and fresh. Indeed, the features of many are unusually handsome, and curiously untouched by the stress of heat and climate.

Perhaps the most striking of all in the neighbourhood is the tall figure of one who has detached himself from a group of friends, and is walking toward where a line of tethered horses is waiting. Like the other who has been distributing alms to the beggar, he is clad from head to foot in black. Nevertheless, the aspects of the two are as different as night and day. The one is a walker of the streets, this latter a true lord of the Campo. Unmistakably a landed proprietor of no little consideration, his costume affects the Gaucho to a marked degree. With scarf wound negligently round his neck, loose jacket, and broad bombachos, the spotless black of the finest material is finished off by the light boots of the man whose life is spent in the saddle. In his hand the *rebenque*—the inevitable riding-whip—glistens with its silver carving, a work of art.

None could deny the coquetry of his appearance; but this is the stern coquetry of the warrior and hunter, as a glance at his grave, rather hawklike features will confirm. A strikingly handsome figure of a man, he stalks with assured tread, raising his sombrero with a simple gesture to acquaintances, until he reaches the spot where the line of horses are tethered. His mount is a magnificent bay, whose leathers and bridle are silvered as thickly as they may be and yet remain flexible, while the saddle and stirrups are heavily coated with the same material. He has swung himself into the saddle now, and is riding away, forcing his horse with consummate ease into a series of curvets and caracoles that evoke admiration even from the numerous professional centaurs in the crowd. But the rider never once looks back as he swings away in the shade of the trees. The romantic figure is either unconscious of admiration or too accustomed to the tribute to be concerned. In any case, he is a product of the land, a veritable paladin.

To the north of Tacuarembo are grass hills overshadowed by the inevitable tall table-lands. Where the rock juts out from the side of these the fronds of many varieties of fern sprout thickly, and by their sides are clumps of evening primrose, everlasting pea, and a wealth of far more brilliant blossoms of the tropical order. In the hollows the vegetation of the wooded streams grows ever more luxurious, and here the flowers star the banks in the wildest riot of profusion.

Seeing that it is springtime, all this is as it should be. But there cannot be many parts of the world whose inhabitants are permitted such a striking reminder of the season as is the case just here. In the neighbourhood of one of these enchanting streams is a very humble mud hut. Its dwellers are pure Africans, and they are just without, enjoying a sun-bath with all the zest of the race.

But the interest of this particular spot is not concerned with them at all; it is centred upon the modest homestead itself. The mud walls have responded in an amazing fashion to the call of the year. Not content with a background of lichen and moss, they have flung out lengthy streamers of fern, from amidst which peer shyly the blossoms of various plants. Obedient to the impulse of spring, each of the four sides has garbed itself thus. In less exuberant parts the effect would be strained for with toil and achieved with triumph. But here the black inhabitants regard their eloquent house as a matter of course.

Just after leaving the small station of Bañada de Rocha is a tunnel. This fact may appear totally unworthy of mention—anywhere else but within the countries bordering on the River Plate. Here a tunnel is an object to be paused at, and to be inspected with not a little curiosity. Although it is possible that some minor burrowings may exist, to the best of my belief the three republics of Argentina, Uruguay, and Paraguay can count no more than two regular tunnels between them. The wonderful shaft bored through the heart of the Andes is one—the other is before us here at Bañada de Rocha. As the only specimen of its kind in Uruguay, therefore, it is not without distinction, and is worthy of at least a passing remark.

After passing through the tunnel the line drops down into a fairly wide plain, hemmed in by numerous low ranges of the inevitable flat-topped hills, while a few elevations of the same curious nature dot the country in the nearer neighbourhood of the track. In a short while, however, the more broken country has surged up all about once again, bearing upon its surface quaint rocky projections, some shaped exactly as tables, others in the form of sugar-loaves, while yet others resemble giant mushrooms sprouting cumbrously from the soil.

Ere reaching the station of Paso del Cerro a great grove of carolina-trees rises majestically, and in the grateful shadow of the branches a long line of bullock-wagons, each vehicle loaded with the wool for which the region is noted, goes winding its way towards the station in the stolid fashion of such processions. Paso del Cerro is delightfully situated, facing as it does a range of hills whose surface is dotted with ranches that appear picturesque enough in the distance. Beyond this point lofty cliffs of rock soar aloft, pressing near to the line. In the nooks and crannies of the great walls are dwarf trees of fantastic shapes that make pleasant breaks here and there in the bare rock of the surface.

A little farther on the colour of the soil begins to undergo a transformation, and soon the red sandstone—the colour that is typical of the same, as well as the more northern, latitudes in the surrounding republics—is stretching everywhere to join with the green in dominating the landscape. A few more wayside stations, and then Rivera and the Brazilian frontier are drawing near, while the mountain ranges that mark the Brazilian territory are already in sight.

Rivera is a town of no little local importance, small though its extent may be as it nestles in a hollow in the midst of the hills. The soft pink of its buildings and the red of its roads and hillsides contrast delightfully with the green foliage and brilliant flowers with which the spot is so liberally endowed. Rivera, moreover, is a place that can lay claim to some quite notable characteristics of its own. It possesses, for instance, a magnificent avenue, the Sarandi, that stretches for over a mile, shaded by trees for all its length, from off the central portion of which lies the pretty little plaza.

FRONTIER STONE AT RIVERA.

TUNNEL AT BAÑADA DE ROCHA.

To face p. 192.

The best view of both the town and of the surrounding country is to be obtained from the solitary hill near by that marks the boundary between the two republics, and that bears upon its summit an old and battered boundary-stone. Viewed from here the panorama is fascinating. To the north, and immediately below, lies Santa Ana, the Brazilian sister-township of Rivera, that sends out its buildings almost to join walls with those of the Uruguayan. Santa Ana itself presents a picturesque enough prospect with its white houses and luxuriant gardens, its wide, unpaved, shadeless streets, its rambling barracks, and its red-bricked bullring. As a background to this bright, sunlit picture, and one that throws it into strong relief, rise range upon range of the dark hills with their shaven summits, starting up abruptly in the first instance from the confines of the town itself, and fading away gradually into the misty distance of the province of Rio Grande. Skirting the base of the hill to the east is a short avenue devoid of buildings that serves as the frontier line, and marks with no little emphasis where one town ends and the other begins. The significance of the spot is accentuated by the sight of the sentry-boxes of the frontier guards and custom officials. To the south, reclining in its own hollow, lies Rivera, with its shady avenues and its conspicuous round-towered church.

The aspects of the two towns are curiously different, considering the fact that from their absolute propinquity they form to all intents and purposes a single city. In the first place the difference in the tint of each is marked. The general colour of the Rivera houses is red, while that of Santa Ana is pure white. The distinction is merely the result of differing national customs. The houses of both places are constructed of precisely similar stone, but the Brazilian prefers to face his walls with plaster. *Autres pays, autres moeurs*; but it is seldom that the contrast may be viewed from so near at hand. The architecture, moreover, of the Santa Ana buildings is of a much squarer and older design than that of those in the Uruguayan town. The former city, as a matter of fact, is considerably more ancient than the latter, to which not only the growing timber but the buildings as well bear witness. In Santa Ana the trees, although not nearly so numerous, have attained to far grander proportions than has been the case with those across the border.

If one should not judge humanity from outward appearance, the procedure is even less wise in dealing with a collection of human habitations. Feminine powder and rouge are as mere toys in the matter of guile compared with the alluring scenic effect that a city is capable of producing by means of bricks and mortar. Judged from the summit of the hill without, Santa Ana presents an even more inviting appearance than that of Rivera. Once within the walls the aspects of the situation alter abruptly. Santa Ana possesses one spot of beauty, it is true. Its luxuriant and shady plaza where the date-palms flourish is an oasis of delight set in the midst of sordid surroundings and dusty heat. With this exception, it must be admitted that the place is shadeless, dirty, and evil-smelling.

The streets of Rivera, on the contrary, are clean, well paved, and sheltered from the rays of the sun by the innumerable green branches that stretch so pleasantly above. The townsfolk, moreover, differ less from those of Montevideo than might be imagined, although the heat of the climate has been responsible for a rather sallower and swarthier type.

CHAPTER XVI

HERE AND THERE IN URUGUAY

Uruguayan roads—A comparison with those of Argentina—The benefits of stone—Some fine metalled highways—The road to San José—On the way to Pando—The journey as effected by motor-car—A smiling landscape—Distant sand-dunes—A spotless range—The mountains of Minas—The town of Pando—A typical minor urban centre—The ending of the macadamised road—The track beyond—An abrupt change in the order of going—The bumps of the Campo—Piriapolis—A budding pleasure resort—Completeness of the enterprise—Eucalyptus forests—A vehicular wreck by the way—Unsuccessful Samaritans—The work of Señor Piria—The Castillo—An imposing home—View from the spot—The Pan de Azucar—A landscape of mountain, valley, forest, and sea—Architecture of the Castillo—Piriapolis Bay—A centre of future bathing—Preparations already effected—The hotel and casino—A wonderful feat of private enterprise—Afforestation—Encouragement of the industry by the Uruguayan Government—The work of Mr. Henry Burnett—The transformation of arid soil into fertile land—Commercial success of the venture—The Maldonado sand-dunes—Fulgurites—A curiosity of the sands—Discoveries by Mr. C. E. R. Rowland.

A feature that is not a little remarked upon by those who have entered Uruguay from the stoneless Pampa of Argentina is the excellence of the roads that surround Montevideo, and of several, indeed, that penetrate for a considerable distance inland. The highway to the town of San José, for instance, that extends for ninety-six kilometres is macadamised throughout its length, and is, moreover, excellently constructed and sustained.

The benefits of convenient deposits of stone are strikingly emphasised here. Now that a start has been made, there is no reason why efficient roads of the kind should not pierce the countryside in all directions. For, notwithstanding the natural fertility of its soil, there is scarcely a corner throughout the whole length and breadth of the Republic that is not seamed to a smaller or larger extent with these layers of useful stone, the eruption of which frequently marks the surface itself of the land.

The road to San José, as a matter of fact, is by no means the only important one of its kind. There are various similar specimens, equally well constructed if of less imposing length. A very admirable road leads from the capital to the small town of Pando in the neighbouring province of Canelones. The journey by motor-car is an easy one, and renders an admirable insight into the nature of the country in this particular district.

Curiously enough, the least smooth portion of this highway is represented by a mile or so of its length on the outskirts of Montevideo itself. This point once passed, however, the undulations in the surface of the road die away, and the broad grey thoroughfare stretches with remarkable smoothness over hill and dale. The car can snort along at the utmost speed its power will permit, since the grey band opens out ahead with a refreshing openness that is totally devoid of secrecy, and only at the lengthiest intervals is its surface darkened by the form of a rider or of a lumbering country cart.

The progress is of the switchback order, with long-drawn-out rises and falls that are effected with alternate exuberance and strainings, while on either hand the fields, verdure, and masses of fruit blossom speed by in very pleasant sequence. For a spring shower has laid the dust, and when the Oriental landscape smiles, its countenance is supremely fascinating. As though to add just the tinge of sombreness that is requisite for the accentuation of the delightful scene, a dark forest of eucalyptus stands out here and there by the way, the massive serried trunks and branches painting the landscape with a heavy splash of gloom.

For the first few leagues the aspect of the country—although the great variety of its attributes preserves it entirely from the taint of mere monotony—remains much the same. After a while, however, the skyline to the right becomes lightened in a rather remarkable fashion. The foreground is a medley of green, brown, and purple—rendered respectively by the hills, trees, orchards, and a patch or two of ploughed soil. At the back of these rich colours a range of very lofty snow-white sand-dunes has risen up. The gleaming barrier marks the frontier-line of the land; upon its farther side, invisible, of course, from inland, are the breakers of the South Atlantic Ocean. Indeed, the effect of this spotless range, when viewed from the shoreward side, is doubly curious, since the verdant landscape that leads right up to them gives no other indication of the propinquity of the sea.

To the north-east elevations of quite another kind have been slowly rising upwards from the horizon as the car speeds along. As the town of Pando itself is more nearly approached, the distant mountains of Minas have swollen into view to assert themselves in a fashion that is not to be overlooked. Great rounded masses piled in dim purple against the horizon, their aspect presents a sharp contrast to that of the dunes close by. The latter are shadowless things, clear-cut and wanting in depth for all their purity; the inland mountains are deep and secretive, with an outline that confounds itself mysteriously with the sky.

The town of Pando itself is remarkable for little in the way of commercial or industrial development beyond forming the centre of a very flourishing agricultural district. The place possesses a quaint red-brick church, the walls of which are adorned with a curious number of balconies. With this exception the buildings are unpretentious; but almost every one is lent its own particular charm by the wealth of gardens and shade-trees with which the spot is endowed. Pando, indeed, is one of those very pleasant minor urban centres with which Uruguay is so plentifully besprinkled, with its delightful surroundings of orchards, vineyards, and cultivated land planted here and there with eucalyptus forests and with groves of other trees. In the near neighbourhood of the town runs a typical Uruguayan stream, its banks thickly lined with verdure, more especially with the weeping willows whose branches droop downwards in a thick green curtain over the water's edge.

EUCALYPTUS FOREST: PIRIAPOLIS.

THE CASTILLO: PIRIAPOLIS.

To face p. 198

It is at this placid rural centre that the macadamised road ends. There is no mistaking the terminus of the metalled highway. One turn of the wheels of the car has left the smooth, hard surface behind—and then begins quite another order of going. The progress of an automobile over a representative local road of the country partakes of many elements, amongst others of those of steeplechasing, toboganning, and of the switchback railways common to those centres less well provided with natural forms of excitement. The mounds and valleys of the way provide an unbroken succession of surprises to which the car responds by lurching and dipping wildly, although the dexterity of the driver keeps it staggering upon its four wheels. Nevertheless, a very little of this goes a long—or an incredibly short—way. So after a while the nose of the car is turned—a manoeuvre that demands as much caution as putting a small boat about in a gale—and the vehicle bumps its way back again through the smiling outskirts of Pando to come to rest, as it were, upon the hard, grey road again.

The sand-dunes of which a glimpse has been obtained at Piriapolis are characteristic of almost the entire length of the Uruguayan coast that gives upon the Atlantic Ocean. There are many spots along this open shore that are well worthy of a visit. Not the least of these is Piriapolis—a place that is in the act of making a very bold bid for popularity as a pleasure resort. Piriapolis is a spot of no little interest. Situated a little to the west of Maldonado on the southern coast that faces the open Atlantic, the place is a budding town, and is noteworthy as much for what it promises in the future as for its present aspects, interesting enough though they are. Piriapolis is remarkable in being a one-man place—by which no connection is implied with the one-horse epithet of tradition—in that it has emanated from the mind and pocket of a prominent Uruguayan, Señor Francisco Piria.

Piriapolis lies to the coastward side of the railway line that is being prolonged in the direction of Maldonado, and, as matters at present stand, it is necessary to board a construction train, and to proceed soberly along the unballasted track to the point where the coach, with its four horses abreast, waits in readiness to complete the journey. It must be admitted that the road that goes rising and falling over the hilly country is not good. The future will doubtless endow the district with a network of highways of quite another kind.

But Piriapolis is young. Hence the unfortunate wagon that is lit upon, shortly after the start, stuck hard and fast in the deep mud of a hollow. In the way of good Samaritans, horses are detached from the coach to assist in the struggle; but the tenacious mud clings in unyielding obstinacy to its wheeled prey. In the end the contest is abandoned for the time being; the lent horses return to their place in front of the coach, and the driver of the wagon departs gloomily to scour the neighbouring country in search of oxen.

As the coach proceeds, the way lies through a wild and mountainous country that bears not a little resemblance to portions of the South West of Ireland. But here in the place of the whitewashed Irish cabins are mud ranchos, almost every one of which reposes beneath the sheltering branches of its own particular unit or group of ombú-trees.

After a little more than an hour's drive the aspect of the country to the front changes abruptly, and presently the coach enters the cool shade of a great forest of eucalyptus and pine. It is difficult to conceive these stretches of giant trees as not having covered the soil for generations. Yet less than twenty years ago the face of this particular district was as bare as any of that of the surrounding country, since it is only eighteen years ago that Señor Piria planted the first sapling that went to form this present forest land.

Roads of a better order now prick their way the length of the woodland aisles, and after a while a lonely little store and post-office stand out from amidst the trees. A little beyond evidences of civilisation appear quite unexpectedly. A pair of fine wrought-iron gates are to the front. Once through these an avenue, adorned by statues at intervals of a few yards, leads to a square turreted building that is known as the *castillo*, or castle, of Señor Piria himself. The dwelling is a pleasant one, with its broad stone terraces that overlook pretty grounds, covered with semi-tropical trees, shrubs, and flowers, laid out after the Italian style.

The view obtained from the upper terrace here is decidedly beautiful. Beyond the gardens spread broad orchards and vineyards, and at the back of these again on one side is a belt of forest that covers the ground for seven miles and more until the edge of the sea itself is reached—a sparkling line of blue that is visible in the distance from here. On the opposite side rises a rugged hill of immense queer-shaped boulders, from the interstices of which grows a dense tangle of scrub.

By far the most conspicuous object, however, in the whole panorama is the aptly named Pan de Azucar, or Sugar Loaf Mountain, that rises to a height of some two thousand feet on the west of the castle. The hill is a bare mass of serrated rock, and represents one of the highest points in the Republic. It is the dominating feature in a landscape that affords a wonderful combination of mountain, valley, forest, and sea.

The architecture of the castillo itself is somewhat original. The ground floor is almost entirely occupied by the guests' bedrooms, apartments with great vaulted ceilings that open promiscuously the one into the other. The living apartments are on the first floor, and the walls of the central hall are hung with many old Italian paintings. Above this again is the square tower that stands as the summit of the house. I mention the architecture more particularly, since it is entirely unusual, the ordinary country houses of Uruguay being almost without exception constructed on a single floor.

The seven miles of eucalyptus forest that intervene between the castillo and the sea afford a delightful drive to the shore of Piriapolis Bay. This portion of the coast consists of a shelving sandy shore eminently suited for the purposes of bathing, and is backed by an imposing vista of forest and mountain. The hill immediately behind the bay, by the way, is locally known as the Sierra de los Ingleses, having been employed, it is said, for the purposes of smuggling in the old days by English sailors.

It is at this point that the future town and pleasure resort of Piriapolis is to be situated. Some considerable start in this direction has already been made, as will be evident when it is explained that a great hotel has already been constructed, and is now complete, and ready for the day when it shall be officially opened. The place is of quite a palatial order, and is provided with no less than 120 bedrooms, as well as with a magnificent dining-room and very spacious apartments and lounges. A broad terrace runs the entire length of the building on the seaward side, and the tide, when at its highest, reaches to within twenty yards of the hotel itself. A very useful addition to the place is a large vegetable and fruit garden that holds everything of the kind that is needed. The plants and trees flourish amazingly well here, although, curiously enough, their roots are planted in no more satisfying a soil than sand.

The enterprise, however, has not contented itself with the erection of the hotel. In the neighbourhood of this building is a small casino, destined to be employed for the purpose of games of chance, and almost the entire margin of the bay is dotted by little, square, four-roomed châlets. At some distance from the hotel a stone mole is in the course of construction, and it is here, of course, that the pleasure steamers will land their passengers when the place is once in the full swing of its active life.

THE PAN DE AZUCAR MOUNTAIN.

THE NEW HOTEL: PIRIAPOLIS.

To face p. 202.

At present the place stands empty—a prepared shell awaiting this influx. As a feat of private enterprise Piriapolis must take a high rank; for the difficulties of transport have added vastly to the labour of the undertaking. It is a beautiful spot, in any case, and the pleasure resort should meet with all the success it deserves.

The topic of Piriapolis brings us to the question of afforestation. On this portion of the coast the science is undoubtedly one of supreme importance, and one to which of late years a fitting amount of attention has been paid. The Government of Uruguay has very wisely done much towards the encouragement of tree-planting and the transformation of apparently arid areas to regions of genuine fertility.

As an instance of this liberal and progressive policy it may be mentioned that in 1909 Mr. Henry Burnett, the British Vice-Consul at Maldonado, was awarded a gold medal and a bonus of three thousand dollars for having been the first to plant a collection of over ten thousand maritime pines. The labour in the first instance of inducing these young trees to grow was arduous, and time after time the budding plantation was buried beneath the masses of driven sand. With the eventual survival, however, of the first screen the remainder of the task proved easy, and Mr. Burnett has now in his possession over one hundred thousand maritime pines.

Encouraged by this example, numerous other landholders of the district have succeeded in cultivating similar plantations, and the result has proved highly beneficial, not only in the transformation of the country but from the commercial point of view as well. For districts that until recently were absolutely worthless are now valued at anything from ten dollars to forty dollars the hectare.

A peculiar characteristic of these Maldonado sand-dunes is to be met with in the fulgurites that are found there—the vitrified sand-tubes caused by the action of lightning that are referred to by Darwin on the occasion of his visit to the spot. Similar phenomena obtain in a few other corners of the world, but those found here are by far the largest in size, some extending to no less than five feet in length. Owing, however, to their extremely fragile nature, it is impossible to extract these larger specimens in any fashion but in comparatively small fragments.

Mr. C. E. R. Rowland, the British Vice-Consul at Montevideo, has taken especial interest in these fulgurites of the Maldonado Sands. The British Museum contains some very fine specimens sent by him, and he has supplied the national museum at Montevideo with its first specimens of these curiosities. This same gentleman, by the way, quite recently discovered two distinct species of Uruguayan lizards that, sent for classification to the South Kensington Natural History Museum, were discovered to be of kinds that until then had been perfectly unknown. They remain in the museum to which they were sent, dignified by the name of their discoverer.

CHAPTER XVII

MERCEDES AND THE SWISS COLONY

The journey to Mercedes—The outskirts of Montevideo—Santa Lucia—A pleasant town—Native quince and gorse—San José—The terminus of a great highway—Some feats of engineering—The urban importance of San José—A modern flour mill—Mal Abrigo—Character of the soil—A country of boulders—Some animals of the Sierra de Mal Abrigo—The surroundings of Mercedes—A charmingly situated town—The terminus of the line—Some characteristics of Mercedes—Urban dwellings—The delights of the patio—The disadvantages of economy in space—Streets and plazas—The hospital—A well-equipped institution—View from the building—An island in Rio Negro—The Port of Mercedes—River craft—Some local scenes—An equine passenger—Formidable gutters—The industries of the town—The Hôtel Comercio—Colonia Suiza—Situation of the Swiss Colony—Uruguayan Campo dwellings—Method of construction—Simplicity of household removals—Aspect of deserted huts—The houses of the Swiss Colony—Habits in general of South American colonists—The range of nationalities—Liberty accorded—Population of the Colonia Suiza—Its industries—A dairy-farming community—An important butter factory—An instance of a rapid rise from poverty to riches.

The railway journey from Montevideo to the town of Mercedes, on the Rio Negro, is of ten hours' duration. The first portion of the run is, of course, through the pleasant suburbs of the capital that have already been sufficiently described. At Juanico, some forty kilometres distant from the starting-point, the denser plantations and orchards have already fallen away, and the country has definitely assumed its natural grazing character, broken into here and there by large areas of alfalfa. The place, as a matter of fact, is an important dairy centre, from which Montevideo obtains a considerable proportion of its butter, milk, and cheese.

Santa Lucia, the next halt, is another of those smiling Oriental towns embowered in gardens and orchards, and surrounded by tree-dotted pastures. Close to the confines of the town runs the Santa Lucia River, with its banks thickly bordered by willows and poplars that at one point give way to a wide avenue of the popular and gigantic eucalyptus. The spot is much patronised in the summer for the purpose of picnics; for—to his credit be it said—the Uruguayan is a great connoisseur of the *al fresco* and its charms.

On leaving Santa Lucia the railway line makes a sweeping bend, and then crosses the river by an iron bridge that proudly claims the distinction of being the longest on the system. Upon the farther side of the stream the country is brightened by the innumerable blossom sprays of the many wild quince-trees, and by the broad clumps of glowing gorse. Soon, however, the aspect of the landscape alters again, and the train is speeding once more through the open Campo of pasture-land and of wheat and barley fields.

San José, the next town of importance to be reached, is remarkable as being the terminus of a splendid macadamised road that runs a distance of ninety-six kilometres from Montevideo to this point. This excellent highway is constructed in a really imposing fashion, and is engineered with a lordly disregard of all obstacles. Just before reaching San José, for instance, it crosses the river in the neighbourhood of the town by a magnificent bridge no less than 360 metres in length. This work was commenced by an Uruguayan engineer in 1906, and was completed in 1909, at a cost of nearly two hundred thousand gold dollars. The Uruguayans take a vast amount of very just pride in this structure, which is probably one of the finest road bridges in existence. It forms a fitting conclusion, moreover, to the best road in lower South America.

The town of San José itself is fairly important from the point of view of population, since it numbers thirteen thousand inhabitants—a fact that places it in the first rank of the country towns of the Republic. Its chief church dominates all the remaining buildings, and affords a notable landmark for many miles around. With the exception of this, San José contains little of interest. It is, in fact, merely a typical "camp" town that serves the surrounding agricultural area. A most up-to-date mill that turns out daily twenty-one tons of flour is, however, worthy of remark, since from the moment that the wheat is dumped into the granary to that when it emerges as fine flour and is mechanically poured into sacks, the whole process is effected by machinery.

Beyond San José the line climbs gradually to the summit of a small sierra, whence a spreading panorama of the surrounding country is obtained. On leaving Mal Abrigo, the next station, the character of the landscape alters. The rich, black, vegetable soil has given way to a rocky surface. Huge boulders of all shapes are strewn everywhere as though flung by some giant upheaval into their tremendous confusion. In the intervals of these great rocks grow thorny trees and shrubs. Indeed, this Sierra de Mal Abrigo differs from anything that has gone before. Hares abound in the neighbourhood, and at the approach of the train great numbers of the animals speed away behind the sheltering boulders. The armadillo, too, is especially plentiful in this region, which seems to favour the partridge and martineta almost equally well.

Bizcocho is the last point of call before reaching Mercedes, from which it is distant some twenty kilometres. From here the ground—once again an open, treeless plain—slopes continuously as it descends towards the valley at the Rio Negro. At the near approach to Mercedes itself the country assumes the smiling aspect that seems the inevitable attribute of the environs of the Uruguayan towns. Gardens, orchards, streams, plantations, vineyards—all these flit past in rapid sequence, until the train pulls up at Mercedes station, the terminus of the line.

This terminus of the line is well defined in more senses than one. The station is situated on a bluff that hangs immediately over the Rio Negro. It is merely necessary to proceed to the end of the rails, just beyond the platform, in order to look sheer down upon the water of the river some hundred feet below. A thoughtful act on the part of the railway company to halt on the very brink, and thus to supply a panorama in the place where the rails can no longer travel!

MERCEDES: FROM ACROSS THE RIO NEGRO.

To face p. 208.

As a town Mercedes is attractive to a degree. The place can boast of no great size, it is true, since its population does not exceed ten thousand. Yet it is exceptionally fortunate both in its situation and in the style of its buildings.

The main portion of the city consists of some half-dozen streets running parallel to the river, crossed by a rather greater number of thoroughfares that lead directly from the water's edge. The houses are almost without exception of the older style of architecture—rather low, spreading buildings, each of which encloses one of those charming patios that, alas! are now growing steadily fewer with each year. Surely nothing is more delightful than this verdure-filled courtyard set in the midst of the house—the small stone-bound garden with its flowers, shrubs, and palms, on to which give all the lower rooms of the establishment! They would doubtless continue to exist for centuries were it not for the growing power and insistence of their chief enemy, economy of space!

The streets and plazas of Mercedes are fairly animated, for the town is the centre of considerable social life. The majority of folk here are of rather darker complexion than those of the capital, but the women are almost equally good-looking. *Coches* are plentiful in the town; each of the two-horsed buggies will seat six people with ease, and even then will speed along at an exhilarating pace, for the steeds of these public conveyances are both willing and well cared for.

The highest point of the town is occupied by the hospital. This, like so many other Uruguayan institutions of the kind, is a very fine establishment, well appointed, and provided with large, airy rooms and corridors. From the roof of this hospital is revealed a magnificent view of the town and its surroundings. The entire panorama is one not easily to be forgotten. So far as the river itself is concerned, it is possible from this point of vantage to follow its windings for miles in both directions. The river here, by the way, attains to very nearly a quarter of a mile in width—no despicable stretch of water even for a tributary of the mighty Uruguay.

In mid-stream just opposite Mercedes is an island—a gem of an island embowered in luxurious vegetation, and completely fringed by large weeping willows, whose drooping festoons of green all but touch the waters. In conformity with the utilitarian spirit of the age, a scheme is on foot for the construction of an hotel in this place, and surely no more alluring spot could be lit upon for the purpose—although the danger to the landscape from the erection of an unsuitable building would be very real.

Between this island and the buildings of the town is the port. Here the topsail schooners and the various river craft of all descriptions lie at anchor, including the small stern-wheel steamers that serve for the passenger traffic into the far interior of the land, and a few large barges piled high with the bones of cattle. Jutting out into the stream near here is a small mole, from which point a small motor-ferry is wont to ply to and fro, and thus give connection with the Fray Bentos road upon the opposite shore. Just to the left of this, anchored in mid-river, lies a large houseboat, which serves as the headquarters of the local rowing and swimming clubs.

It is, of course, in this neighbourhood that the river life is at its busiest. Upon the rocky shore are groups of women in bright-coloured dresses busily employed in washing household linen and various garments—a sight, as a matter of fact, that may be anticipated with certainty upon any populous Oriental river bank. The motor-ferry, too, has by no means the monopoly of transit, and numerous smaller craft are continually passing from one shore to the other. Their occupants are not necessarily limited to the human species. Here, for instance, is a horse being brought across in a small rowing boat. The animal appears quite unconcerned; he is doubtless accustomed to the aquatic excursions in so tiny a skiff.

Returning from the riverside, a peculiar characteristic of the Mercedes streets should attract the eye, or, failing this, stumblings will ensue of a certainty. On either side of the roadway is an immense gutter of over a yard in depth and width. These portentous channels serve to carry off the rainfall of the heavy storms that occur from time to time, and on a dark night constitute formidable obstacles in the path of an unwary foot-passenger.

Mercedes possesses a fairly important *saladero*, and, in addition, constitutes a centre of the charcoal-burning industry. A couple of hundred tons of this commodity is frequently shipped from the place in the course of a month. So far as hotels are concerned, the Comercio is distinctly to be recommended. The establishment is well above the average of those that the ordinary provincial town can boast, being clean, airy, and comfortable, and provided, moreover, with a very genial host.

Colonia Suiza is situated, some twenty miles inland from the coast, midway between Mercedes and Montevideo. In order to reach this very picturesque spot from the former town by rail it is necessary to hark back to Mal Abrigo, from which junction the run to the Swiss Colony is a short one. The country through which the journey is made is of the usual grazing order, sparsely populated, the ground being marked only here and there by a typical Uruguayan rancho.

The modest establishments of this particular district are worthy of special mention. Each is contrived from square blocks of turf, carefully cut, and placed one on top of the other with the grass edge downwards. The exterior of the walls is left without any attempt at facing or adornment, and thus presents a distinctly crude and peculiar appearance. The dwelling, however, is rendered snug and waterproof by being plastered from within. These walls are extremely well made, considering the fact that their composition is not assisted by any additional material. The roof is made of wood, cut in lengths, and thatched over with wood or straw.

Household removals on the Uruguayan campo are not necessarily matters of weighty thought, whose occurrence is to be anticipated with dread for many months beforehand. When the family who owns one of these mud ranches decides to move, the procedure is very simple. The roof, doors, and windows of the home are taken down and collected. After which it is merely necessary for the party to pack these along with them on horseback, until a suitable site is lit upon for a new erection of turf into which the portable finishing touches may be inserted. That effected, the owners are once more at home. As for the discarded dwelling, it remains much as before, save that it is minus roof, door, and windows.

Many of these skeleton huts are to be met with on the rolling face of the country. They possess this in common with birds' nests, that from a distance it is difficult to ascertain whether they are occupied or to let. If deserted, there is no reason why any chance family on the move should not take possession by no more formal means than that of affixing roof, door, and windows in the gaps that await them. Many of these ranchos, by the way, are surrounded by very pretty gardens, and hedged in by tall hedges of geranium and rose.

Once arrived at the Swiss Colony, however, the aspect of the dwellings becomes altogether changed. The houses here resemble strongly the châlets of the Swiss mountains, for, like the remaining colonies of the kind throughout the River Plate republics, the immigrants have introduced their own ways and fashions of living. Indeed, the existence of such bodies provides an ample testimonial of the conditions of freedom under which life is conducted in these countries.

RIO NEGRO BRIDGE.

ON THE RIO NEGRO.

To face p. 212.

The number and strange variety of these self-contained colonies in this part of the world is scarcely realised. They are, of course, totally distinct from the ordinary, scattered immigrant dwellers. When surveyed *en masse* the result is not a little extraordinary. In the three Spanish-speaking republics of Argentina, Uruguay, and Paraguay that, together with Southern Bolivia, formed the old River Plate provinces, exist distinct and important settlements of Swiss, Austrians, Poles, Australians, Welsh, Boers, and Jews, besides numerous lesser groups of many nationalities beyond.

Within the frontiers of each perfect liberty obtains to continue existence as it is led in the country from which the immigrants came, and thus each is provided with its own churches and institutions. In the case of the more recently founded it is almost as though a portion of the foreign land had been translated bodily to South American soil, while those of older standing have invariably yielded more or less to the influence of their surroundings. But the choice of remaining entirely aloof, or of assimilating the customs that prevail outside their own frontiers lies entirely in the hands of the immigrant communities. It is, of course, only natural that each section should carry on that particular branch of industry to which it has been accustomed in its country of origin.

The Colonia Suiza constitutes an important body, containing, as it does, no less than four thousand inhabitants. Here it is not surprising that the staple industry should be that of cheese manufacture and dairy produce. In addition to this a fair amount of agriculture is carried on. The soil of the district is well adapted to linseed, and numerous vineyards are responsible for the production of a local wine of very fair quality.

Consisting for the most part of small dairy farms, no regular township exists in the colony, although a small village has sprung into being in the neighbourhood of the railway station, and three hotels are distributed at wide intervals across the area occupied. The community, first established in 1862 by the arrival of seven Swiss families, is flourishing, and its members have clung to their national habits with more tenacity than is usual.

The largest and most important butter factory in the place produces in the springtime a daily quantity of no less than a ton of butter. Its proprietor, ere he emigrated, played the rôle of a small shopkeeper in his own country. His house was burned to the ground, but, fortunately for himself, the property was insured. He employed the money derived from this source for the purpose of the voyage to South America, and, arrived at the Colonia Suiza, he found employment in the carrying round of the milk. In a very short while he was employing others to perform this service for himself, and is now a wealthy man, thus affording one more example of those rapid rises from poverty to riches that are so characteristic of South America.

The general aspects of this colony are peculiarly agreeable. Situated in one of the most pleasant districts of a smiling land, it is well watered and timbered. The verdure of the place, moreover, is enhanced by the numerous green lanes that intersect it. Indeed, no more delightful situation could be imagined than that occupied by many of the châlets of Swiss design.

CHAPTER XVIII

COLONIA

An historical town—Rarity of ruins in the River Plate countries—Specimens at Colonia—Situation of the town—Past antagonism between the capitals of Argentina and Uruguay—Present aspect of Colonia compared with the former—A sleepy hollow—Periodical awakenings of the place—Impressions of the old town—Its colouring and compactness—Fortifications of the city of discord—A warlike history—Nations that have warred together at this spot—The reddest corner in a bloodstained land—Surroundings of the town—Crumbling masonry—A medley of old and new—A Colonia street—Old-time scenes of peace and war—Some pictures of the past—Cannon as road posts—The Plaza—An episode in the wars with Portugal—The eternity of romance—Real de San Carlo—A modern watering-place—Its buildings—The bullring—A gigantic pelota-court—Popularity of the spot—A miniature tramway—Attractions of Real de San Carlo—Vegetation on the sands—A curious colour scheme—Pleasant lanes—Buenos Aires as a supplier of tourists.

The small town of Colonia stands quite alone in many respects. Not as regards situation, climate, and a reputation as a pleasure resort. In all these three the spot is especially favoured; yet in each of these it possesses a number of formidable rivals along the Uruguayan coast. Excursionists flock to Colonia, it is true, but such flighty nomads are more concerned with beaches and bathing than with the subtler and deeper interests of the spot.

To the historian and to the antiquarian Colonia represents a gem. It must be admitted that the values of such treasures go strictly by comparison. Uruguay is rich in the amethyst and topaz, but poor in architectural ruins. Indeed, these romantic features are distressingly—or pleasingly—rare throughout all the lands that made up the provinces of the old River Plate. So far as I am aware, almost the sole examples of any real antiquity are to be met with in the Jesuit ruins of Paraguay and the Misiones Province, and in the few fragmentary Inca relics upon the Andes slopes. Beyond these there is Colonia. Therefore if the gem lack the full brilliance of some of the specimens that an older continent can produce, its importance must not be under-estimated, since it possesses the rare merit of being all but unique in its own country.

From the Uruguayan bank of the great river Colonia faces Buenos Aires. The one is not visible from the other, since almost forty miles separate the two cities—a distance that has frequently been found too short for the peace of mind of both. For, although they now sit on their respective banks in undisturbed peace, the past has only too many instances to show of how the pair opposed each other with an active hostility that worked its share in the building up of the warlike history of Colonia.

The present fate of Colonia is much akin to that of many of those spots that serve as the decayed shells of old-time battles and terrific alarums. In short, it is a sleepy hollow. There are certainly times when a large river steamer comes to rest for a while against its wooden jetty, and disgorges a crowd of tourists who wander aimlessly about the quaint streets. But such spells are short, since the interests of the spot can compare in the minds of very few of such visitors with the great bullring and pelota-court, recently erected some half-dozen miles up-stream, to which they are on their way. Thus the place has barely time to shake its old walls, and yawn with its blank windows, wondering at this sudden new life that has sprung up within it, when the spasm has passed away, and Colonia sinks back from its semi-conscious state into full slumber again.

The first impressions of the old town, when viewed from the river, present a rather strange medley of brown, yellow, grey, white, pink, and green. Thrown together as abruptly as this, the colour scheme doubtless sounds perplexing. Yet in reality the tints blend with consummate harmony. The brown is rendered by the rocks that hem in the little bays and inlets of the foreground, while the lichen that clings to the stone accounts for a strangely brilliant yellow. The grey is produced by the most important asset of the town, the ruined walls and battlements of the fortifications that pile themselves sullenly upon the rocks along the river bank, penetrating the waters at many points. The pink and white gleam very softly from the more modern houses in the background that mingle with the old, crumbling erections of grey, while at close intervals the verdure of trees and shrubs sprouts out thickly from amongst the masonry. To conclude with all this colour, so far as possible at one fell swoop, the town is dominated by a brilliant white lighthouse shaft and the twin red towers of a modern church.

Undoubtedly one of the most curious effects for which Colonia is responsible is that of its compactness. There is scarcely a town in Uruguay, or in Argentina either, whose outskirts do not straggle far away from the centre into the Campo. To one who has inevitably become accustomed to these architectural loose-ends the accurately defined boundaries of the riverside town are not a little striking. The reason is a very simple one. In the old days the city of discord was completely surrounded by fortifications and, since it has performed the feat—almost unique in the country—of failing to grow in extent since that time, its original abrupt boundaries have remained. The result, from an artistic point of view, is undoubtedly far more imposing than that produced by the stress of modern development.

Colonia is not a town to be skimmed over lightly. It is worthy of almost as careful a reconnoitring as it has frequently suffered in the past. For the place can boast of half a dozen regular sieges, and pitched battles, sallies, and skirmishes galore. Indians and Spaniards, Spaniards and Portuguese, Uruguayans and Spaniards, Uruguayans and Portuguese—all these have fought together here on countless occasions, and yet the list of the warring companies is not ended. The red ponchos of Urquiza's Gauchos have charged up to the grey walls, staining the brown earth crimson as they went; buccaneers of all nations have come and gone, and the scarlet of a British garrison has gleamed out against the background of stone. Colonia is the reddest spot of all in a sadly bloodstained land.

But, however much the aftermath of battles may brood, the aspect of the place is as fair as could be desired. Just opposite its site are the first green islands of the river, the oceanward outposts of the lengthy series that rest in the midst of the waters upstream. This shore of the mainland itself is picturesque in another fashion. Bright semicircles and crescents of sand fringe the rocks of the innumerable small bays. Upon the natural boulders, and ledges, and heaps of masonry above are clusters of green leaves starred with blossoms. Here and there a growth of more artificial kind is spread upon the stone; for the sole figures upon the foreshore are those of two washerwomen, busily engaged amongst the pools, whose variegated harvest is increasing in area as it is spread out to dry.

COLONIA: RUINED FORTRESS WALL.

A CAMPO GRAVEYARD.

To face page 218.

In places the surface of the old masonry is level and wide; in others it is necessary to leap from point to point just as it is in the case of the rocks below. Scrambling and walking thus for several hundred yards, the way lies past a collection of ruined houses, the massive walls of which prick upwards in gaunt desolation. Beyond these again is a narrow passage, paved principally by the chance falling of the masonry, that leads into one of the actual streets of the town.

The medley here is fascinating from the mere force of its quaintness. The first houses that flank the slender thoroughfare as it winds its way uphill are a few pink erections, fairly modern, with windows plainly barred, and open doorways, through which is visible the foliage that decorates the patio within. Side by side with these is a building of quite another type, an old grey house, stately and imposing, though now little beyond a shell of ruins. Its front is thickly set with the remnants of graceful balconies, and with broken shields and coats of arms. Upon the massive doorway is an ancient bronze knocker in the form of a human hand. But the hapless instrument has been silent now for many a generation, since at the back of the doorway itself is nothing beyond a confusion of tumbled stone into whose crevices the roots of the intruding shrubs and flowers have pressed themselves.

The street is quite deserted; the temptation to raise the bronze hand and bang out the echoes is almost irresistible. It is certain that one could arouse nothing beyond the ghosts of the past. Yet the answer to such an appeal might prove a little too intense for the modern tranquillity of mind. Confined to the days of peace, the vision would be well enough. The house, the walls, the patio, the fretwork of the balconies, the carving of the coats of arms—all these would be intact and hung about with humanity. In obedience to the most commonplace demands of the all-pervading romance, breeched men, whose long-draped cloaks hid the lace and buckles of their costume, would send out their voices and the tinklings of their guitars towards the señoritas, whose soft eyes glowed beneath a tremendous headgear, and who wore their filmy wrappings and short skirts with true Iberian grace.

Within the courtyard the negro slaves would lounge at their ease, while near them would repose the great guardian dogs of the house. Now and again would sound a heavy rumble from the street without that signified the advent of visitors in a cumbrous coach of state—an interruption that would still the notes of voice and guitar string, and that would excite the negro attendants into sudden life and the dogs into a delirium of barking. After which many grave bows and deep curtseyings would prelude the quiet ceremony of entertainment.

But if instead of this peaceful scene the wrong half of the past were to appear! For there were times when the heavy booming and uproar drew ever nearer from without, and then the faces of the señoritas as they peered through the elaborate bars were ashy pale. There were moments, too, when the last doubts had turned to a bitter certainty, when the forms of fleeing men passed the house, and those of others, who stayed, reddened the ground before the door. And last of all!—the apparition of the strange men in hostile garb, the lust of slaughter in their eyes as they rushed on, making another place of the once familiar street. Thirsting for blood, hungry for booty, and for all things beyond—the cheeks of the shuddering señoritas have not paled without reason. After all, perhaps it is better to leave undisturbed the knocker upon the old door.

Such mental apparitions, moreover, could be multiplied indefinitely, for there are a dozen houses of similar design, if of varied ruinous importance, in the town. Indeed, the place breathes strongly of the past. At a street corner here and there is an ancient cannon, buried muzzle upwards into the ground, that serves to fend off from the sidewalk such wheeled traffic as exists. After a while the narrow street falls away, and the wide sweep of the plaza extends to the front.

The place was once the site of a rather peculiar feat of frontier delimitation. The occasion was that of one of the numerous cessions by treaty to Portugal of the town that the Spaniards were wont to win by force of arms. On receiving the order from the Court of Spain to evacuate the province in favour of the temporarily reconciled enemy the staunch old Spanish Governor lost patience. The town, he knew full well, he must surrender, but he refused to give up more even at the command of his royal master. So he raised the muzzle of a cannon in the plaza, fired a shot to right and left, and told the Portuguese that the land within the range of the balls was theirs, but no more. And with this they had to be content.

There are now no cannon in the plaza, where, indeed, the wild shrubs and grasses alone thrive. Passing across it, the river is approached again, for Colonia covers a small promontory. Ere reaching the water on the farther side, however, it is necessary to pass by far the most imposing ruin in the place. By the side of the white lighthouse tower a tall fragment of grey fortress wall rears itself aloft. Some four feet thick throughout, its crumbling embrasures are strongly lit up by the blue sky behind.

From this point the ground slopes abruptly downwards towards the shore. Here are more rocks, more mounds of ruined masonry, more washerwomen—and the forms of a girl and of a man seated apart from the rest upon the stones. The girl is flaming in all the pride of red skirt and kerchief and yellow blouse. For all I know the latter garment may not technically be admissible within the strict category of blouses, but, failing a more intimate knowledge, it must pass as something similar! By comparison with the very brilliant butterfly, the man looms a dusky moth, whose only glitter lies in the great, round, silver spurs that protrude from his high heels. Yet the business of the pair is the same as ever! Though wrought out more frequently when Colonia really lived, it obtains still amongst the ruins. It is comforting to reflect that even the most simple of these rural chains of the affections continues with links far less unbroken than those of war!

Some three miles distant from Colonia, and situated likewise upon the banks of the river, is Real de San Carlo. Although such close neighbours, it would be difficult to find two spots that differed more widely from each other. Real de San Carlo is a mushroom of a place that has only known existence for some two or three years. Since it is planned as a pleasure resort pure and simple, the nature of Real de San Carlo is to a certain extent artificial, and the brand-new buildings have yet to be toned down by the softening process of age.

So far the new bathing-place is deficient in the private dwelling-houses and châlets that characterise the majority of such spots. On the arrival of the steamer at the imposing pier, the eye is arrested at once by the sight of two very large buildings, and by that of one of a more moderate size. Beyond these there is little in the way of architectural development, with the insignificant exception of the cottages that house the labourers upon the place.

THE BULL RING.

To face p. 222.

Of the two great buildings the bullring is the more notable. Indeed, the enormous circular erection of white concrete is visible for a distance of many miles in all directions. One side of the ground beneath, sheltered by the rising spread of tiers that hold the seats, is occupied by an open-air café, while the appointments within are of the usual order to be met with in bullrings. It is here that the periodical bullfights are held, and it is here, moreover, that many of the noted Spanish fighters perform.

In the neighbourhood of the bullring is the pelota-court, which is only just now being completed, in which the famous Basque game is to be played. This is likewise constructed of white concrete, and, although its magnitude cannot rival that of the bullring, it is of an amazing size for a building of the kind, holding galleries above, as it does, that must be capable of seating several thousand spectators. Compared with these two tremendous affairs, the hotel is of modest dimensions and of unpretentious appearance. Nevertheless, were it to stand apart from such overwhelming neighbours, it would doubtless appear imposing enough.

Real de San Carlo is well equipped to cope with the crowds of visitors that the steamers already bring to its shore; it does things, in fact, in a certain elaborate style of its own. A narrow-gauge steam tramway runs between the jetty and the bullring, although the distance does not exceed a quarter of a mile, and behind the miniature engine a number of cars are in waiting, each containing a row of seats facing outwards on either side. At the moment of the visit the bull-fighting itself is undergoing a temporary lull—a fact that, from one's own point of view, is very little to be regretted. So the tramcars, crowded now, roll merrily onwards to a ring devoid of espadas, bulls, horses, and blood, and for the majority of the tourists the chief business of the day is confined to the precincts of the café in the shade of the great building.

Apart from these more artificial attractions, Real de San Carlo will undoubtedly prove popular as a bathing resort. The fine white sands and rippling waters here possess an invaluable auxiliary in the delightful air with which the place is blessed. In this springtime of the year, moreover, the sands themselves are decorated in rather an unusual fashion. From them sprout masses of silver-white, thick, silky leaves, and stems that support blossoms that exactly resemble small sunflowers. The effect that the great stretches of these present is distinctly striking. Thickly spangling the white sand is a silver glow, topped by the yellow of the blossoms above—a colour scheme that gives a strangely fairylike and unreal impression. As though to lend a touch of warmer colour, thousands of butterflies, all of a variety of the painted-lady species, are hovering in clouds about the blossoms.

Just inland, where the undulations of the real country begin, the lanes are ablaze with passionflower and honeysuckle—but the steamer is whistling impatiently in the distance, and the tourists are flocking back to the tramcars. It is time to return, and to mingle with the crowd once more, the great majority of which are returning to Buenos Aires. For it is on the inhabitants of this city, within a couple of hours' steam across the river, that Real de San Carlo depends for its popularity, and consequent welfare.

CHAPTER XIX

THE URUGUAY RIVER

A great waterway—The river compared with the Paraná—Some questions of navigation—The lower stretch of the Uruguay—The stream from Montevideo upwards—Montevideo—The docks—An imposing array of Mihanovich craft—Breadth of the river—Aspects of the banks—Various types of vessels—The materials of their cargoes—The meeting of sister steamers—The etiquette of salutations—Fray Bentos—The Lemco factory and port—A notable spot—The paradise of the eater—The islands of Uruguay—Method of their birth and growth—The responsibility of leaves and branches—Uncertainty of island life—The effects of flood and current—Sub-tropical bergs—The vehicles of wild creatures—A jaguar visitation in Montevideo—Narrowing of the stream—Paysandú—The home of ox-tongues—The second commercial town of the Republic—Some features of the place—Variety of the landscape—The *Mesa de Artigas*—An historical table-land—A monument to the national hero—Salto—A striking town—Pleasant landscape—The Salto falls—The ending of the lower Uruguay—A rocky bed—Some minerals of Salto—Alteration in the colour of the water—The beauty of the upper Uruguay.

As a waterway the Uruguay River is of infinite service to the Republic whose western coastline it serves. It is true that, compared with the Paraná, the stream suffers somewhat both as regards length and navigable facilities. Both rivers have much in common, in that either has its source in the mountain ranges that fringe the coast of Brazil, and either flows first to the west, then southwards until the junction of the pair forms the broad River Plate. But, whereas the Paraná rises in latitude 22° south the first waters of the Uruguay do not come into being until 28° south. The latter, in consequence, has to content itself with a course of a thousand miles, rather less than half the length of its neighbour.

The lower stretch of the Uruguay holds an obstacle to navigation that is unknown in the corresponding waters of the Paraná. At Salto, some two hundred miles above the mouth, falls extend from the one bank to the other, and thus bar the passage of all vessels. Above this place, however, is the starting-point for the lighter draught steamers that continue their northward course for many hundreds of miles.

As though to compensate for the barrier, the first two hundred miles of the Uruguay represent a particularly noble highway of waters, far broader and more imposing, indeed, than the equivalent stretch of the Paraná. Ocean-going vessels here penetrate to Paysandú, and beyond it to the Lemco port of Colón on the Argentine shore, while the really magnificent steamers of the River King, Mihanovich, produce their finest specimens to ply to and fro here. But, as the banks of the stream contain not only some of the most fertile lands in the Republic but much of interest beyond, it is worth while to follow its course, beginning at Montevideo itself, which, as a matter of fact, is somewhat to anticipate the waters of the true Uruguay.

By the quayside of the capital are grouped three or four of the Mihanovich craft, large, two-funnelled vessels with an imposing array of decks surmounted by an unusually spacious promenade that crowns the whole. One of these is bound for Salto—or rather for the Argentine town of Concordia that lies opposite that port—but just now it is not advisable to be tied hard and fast to her broad decks, since she must call at Buenos Aires on her way, and at many other spots outside Uruguay and the scope of this book.

We will therefore perform the strange feat of making a break in the trip ere it is begun. In any case it is necessary to leave the quay over whose broad, paved surface of reclaimed land the cabs are rattling, and where the policeman and porters stand, and where, moreover, a strong group of Salvationists are singing lustily, surrounded by a motley but attentive group such as the precincts of a port attract. But the graceful *Triton* shall churn her way out into the open without us, since we will cling so far as possible to the Uruguayan shore, forging upwards through the yellowing waters, to halt at Sauce with its willow-covered lands and Colonia with its rocky beach, until Carmelo is passed, and at Nueva Palmira the River Uruguay has been fairly entered. Even then, however, it is necessary to accept the fact more or less on trust, and to confide in the accuracy of the map rather than in that of the eyesight. For the faint line that has recently appeared on the horizon to the left might as well stand for a distant streak upon the waters as for the low-lying Argentine shore that it actually represents.

To the right, the Uruguayan bank is well defined. Here the undulations of the land swell boldly out from the edge of the river, while in many places rocks and boulders strew the sloping foreshore as though to accentuate the frontier between stream and land that is so faintly defined upon the opposite coast. Here and there the verdure of the hills is broken by the darker green bands of the eucalyptus plantations, through which from time to time gleam the white walls of an estancia-house. At intervals the chimneys of a saladero prick upwards from the nearer neighbourhood of the bank. About these centres of their doom the speck-like figures of the cattle dot the surrounding pastures, grazing in fortunate ignorance of their end.

The traffic upon the river itself is by no means inconsiderable. Native topsail schooners laden with jerked beef, fruit, and timber come gliding serenely down the stream beneath their spread of sail. One of these craft is especially indicative of the main industry of the land. The vessel is laden as high as the booms will permit with horns of cattle, the bleaching mounds of which must represent the sacrifice of many thousands of animals. There are smart Government tugs, too, that hold the official guardians of the mighty stream, and great dredgers of queer and monstrous shape that steam slowly along to find an anchorage where the bottom is shallow, and there remorselessly to bite out mouthfuls from the unduly lofty bed.

At rarer intervals appear the ocean-going craft and sailing vessels. It would be safe to wager that there is not one of those passing down-stream that is not laden with some portions or other of the bodies bequeathed to humanity by the unconsulted yet generous bovine souls. Nevertheless the exact species of cargo would be more difficult to predict. It might be beef itself, or hides that will make leather upon which to sit while consuming the meat, or horns which will provide handles for the necessary complement of knives, or indeed many other products useful for similar purposes. There never was such a creature as the ox for the provision of a variety of articles that all eloquently urge the benefit of his death!

A tall and majestic structure has come into sight from round a bend in the stream now, and is sweeping rapidly downwards. With grey hull, white upper-works about her rows of decks, and twin black funnels to cap the whole, she is one of the proud fleet of steamers that ply throughout the entire system of the great rivers. If the vessel upon which you may be found bears a corresponding **M** upon its funnel—which in the case of a passenger craft may be taken as a practical certainty—you may be assured that you will not be passed without recognition, even if sheltered by a mere paltry stern-wheeler that is bound for one of the small tributary streams. Combining affability with size, the whale will blow out three deep roars of salute from its great horn, that will be echoed by a like number of shrill notes from the treble whistle of the minnow. Such is the etiquette throughout the entire length of the rivers. The six blows are sounding throughout the day from the tropics of Brazil downwards to where the La Plata and the ocean meet.

Upon the right-hand side Fray Bentos has come into view, marked in the first place by a great collection of tall black chimneys glistening in the sun. Beneath is verdure, and massive white buildings, and streets of dwelling-houses, while to the front is the Lemco port with a small forest of masts rising from its waters. The place, in a double sense, represents the very incarnation of Uruguay's trade. A greedy spot that swallows live cattle by tens of thousands to render them up again in the pathetically diminished form of extract! Even now the odour of soup floats heavily in the air from across a mile of water—a proof that Fray Bentos is busily occupied in turning out its brown rivers of fluid.

The factory, the most notable in the country, is indeed strongly symbolical of the land where starvation in ordinary circumstances of peace has never yet been known. Havana may be the paradise of the smoker, Epernay that of the champagne lover; but the eater's heaven is undoubtedly situated in Uruguay, a paradise in which the spirits of departed and honest butchers might well revel in perfect joy.

Just above Fray Bentos the islands dot the river more plentifully than in almost any other part of the great stream. As is the case on the Paraná, it is difficult enough at times to distinguish between these and the true bank on the Argentine shore; both are equally lowly and each covered with the same density of willows and native scrub. Amongst these larger islands, however, whose surface may comprise several square miles, are numerous smaller pieces of land, and some quite diminutive specimens that can lay claim to no more than a few yards of area. These are baby islands—young territories that have only just succeeded in raising their heads above water. For an island here is conceived, grows, and dies in a fashion that is vegetable rather than purely earthy. The fact is not really curious, seeing that vegetation is directly concerned in their birth.

The conception of one of these is evident even now. A tangle of the thick leaves of the camelota—the water plant with its mauve hyacinth-like flower—has in its downward floating course fouled the earth of a shallow in mid-stream. The arrested clump of green has already inveigled other objects to keep it company in its trap. A few sticks and branches and tufts of grass are already fast in the embrace of the powerful stems and green leaves, while at the end that faces the stream the water-driven sand has risen at the obstacle, and has shyly protruded a small round hump or two above the ripples. The life of the thing is as uncertain as that of a seedling or of a human child. Under favourable conditions it will grow and solidify year by year until from the few leaves and sticks will have extended some square miles of tree-covered soil. On the other hand, it may be swept remorselessly away in its earliest days ere the tentative formation has had time to secure sufficiently firm hold of the earth.

ON THE URUGUAY RIVER.

A URUGUAYAN STREAM.

To face p. 230.

In any case the life of these islands is comparatively short, and fresh floods and currents are forming some and destroying others all the while. During these periods of flood many of them would seem possessed of the characteristics of icebergs. Detached by the irresistible force of the currents, great fragments of the vegetation and camelota plant that cling to their sides go swirling down the stream. Though they can boast no polar bears, they are occasionally freighted with other beasts whose neighbourhood is equally undesirable. On such occasions snakes and many four-footed specimens of northern creatures form the unwilling tenants of these frail rafts of vegetation. It is said that many years ago one of unusually large size struck the shore of Montevideo itself, disgorging four jaguars, who entered the town as much to their own terror as to that of the inhabitants.

With Fray Bentos once left in the rear, the river becomes distinctly narrowed, and, where no islands intervene, the features of either bank begin to be clearly distinguished at the same time. The Argentine shore has broken away from its dead level now, and is rising in gentle undulations; the Uruguayan coast, too, as though in a determined endeavour to retain its physical superiority, has taken to heap itself in far loftier and more imposing hills than before.

The next town of importance at which the steamer halts is that of Paysandú, the great centre of ox-tongues. Indeed, were one to adopt the popular figurative methods of certain magazines, amazing results might well be extracted from the commerce of the place. Thus, supposing a year's accumulation of Paysandú ox-tongues were able jointly to give forth the notes that they were wont to render in life, the effect of the combined roar would probably be to deafen the entire populace of the Republic, and to blow every atom of water from the river! The number of men they would feed, and the distance they would cover if extended in a line I do not know; but it may be taken for granted that the export of these preserved instruments of bovine speech is very considerable.

Paysandú ranks as the second commercial city in the Republic. It is true that, so far as size is concerned, it is altogether dwarfed by Montevideo, since the inhabitants of the smaller town number only twenty thousand or so. Yet, the centre of a rich pastoral and agricultural province, the place is of no little commercial importance, and, although its architecture remains largely of the pleasant but old-fashioned Spanish style, not a few new buildings and boulevards have already sprung into existence. Like the majority of towns of its kind, it is well equipped with electric lighting, telephones, and other such modern appliances, although its tramcar traction is still effected by the humbler methods of the horse.

To the north of Paysandú the stream narrows, the islands become few and far between, and the course of the river is distinct and well-defined. The landscape, too, is more varied now than that of the lower reaches. Among the Uruguayan rounded hills a few well-marked tablelands spread their broad, level surfaces in the way that is characteristic of so many parts of the Republic. Both the inland valleys and river banks are covered with an added density of vegetation, while beaches of shining white sand jut out at intervals from the shore. As for the Argentine bank, it has quite suddenly assumed a marked individuality of its own. It is covered with a reddish yellow rolling soil, tinged only lightly with green, from which close groves of palm-trees sprout upwards for mile after mile. It is as though a portion of Africa on the one shore were facing a rather wooded and broken portion of the South Downs on the other!

The water itself has been growing more limpid all the while, now that the dead-flat, soft, alluvial soil of the Argentine bank has given way to a harder and more stony surface. It has become shallow in parts, too, and the nose of the steamer often gives a tentative turn to the right or left as she cautiously feels her way. The craft has penetrated almost to the limits of the lower stretch of the great river now, and the rising bed is a premonitory symptom of the end.

On the right has now risen the loftiest bluff that has yet marked the Uruguayan shore. It forms one of the walls of a striking and bold table-land. The place is now known as the *Mesa de Artigas*—the table of Artigas. It was upon the summit of this hill that the Uruguayan national hero had his chief encampment, and it has been described as a desolate and lonely spot, haunted by murdered spirits and by the memory of horrors, that no living being cared to approach. The description cannot be said to hold good at the present moment. The green slopes are dotted with grazing cattle and sheep, while at one point the distant figures of two mounted Gauchos are careering to and fro, and the cattle in the neighbourhood are wheeling together and lumbering forward as a result of their manoeuvres.

On the summit of the tableland is a peculiarly tall stone pedestal that rises from a great pyramidal base to soar high upwards against the sky-line. The shaft is surmounted by a bust that represents Artigas himself. The entire structure is on the colossal side, and the effect of the bust poised on high against the blue of the air is curious rather than effective. Viewing it from far below, it is difficult to avoid the impression that the head and shoulders, placed half-way between earth and heaven, are pleading with mute eloquence for a body and legs with which to grasp more firmly the summit of the sustaining shaft. In any case the monument is bold, and affords a strikingly conspicuous landmark for an area of many leagues.

To the north of the Mesa de Artigas the landscape of the river continues bold and hilly. A score or so of miles up-stream from the monument lies the town of Salto, the last place of real importance upon this stretch of the Uruguayan frontier. With its buildings rising to cover the hills of its site, the panorama of Salto is more imposing in its way than that of any other town on the banks of the stream. Indeed, piled on the summit of cliffs and bluffs, the white masses of masonry, crowned by a few steeples and towers, are visible from far inland upon the Argentine territory as well as from the remoter neighbourhoods of its own soil. The river just here is exceptionally populous, since facing Salto from across the waters is Concordia, a large and thriving Argentine town.

The population of Salto is slightly in excess of twenty thousand, and, like every other town along the length of the stream, it serves as a storehouse for the pastoral and agricultural industries of the district. In many respects, however, the situation of the town gives it a commercial scope greater than that of the more southern towns. Although the climate lacks sufficient heat for the production of the banana and similar sub-tropical growths, the variety of fruit is very great. The orange flourishes in exceptional abundance here, and its cultivation forms a valuable addition to the wealth of the district.

CATTLE ON THE ROAD.

A CORNER OF THE FRAY BENTOS FACTORY.

To face p. 234.

Pleasantly situated, with shaded plazas and avenues, and with the orchards, vineyards, orange-groves, and well-timbered country of its outskirts, Salto lies at the end—or, to be more accurate, the beginning—of the lower Uruguay. Just above the town a white foaming line stretches from bank to bank during the periods when the river is low. But these lower falls are navigable during a considerable portion of the year, and not until Salto Grande, at a point considerably higher up, is the permanent barrier to navigation reached. Between Salto itself and Concordia the river is plentifully strewn with rocks, and, although the channels are deep, it is necessary on this head for vessels to use considerable caution, more especially as the tide races fiercely just here. Indeed, the fluctuations of the stream at this point are very great, and account for the tremendously lofty wooden passenger pier that serves the town.

It is in the neighbourhood of Salto that is found the curious water stone that is referred to elsewhere in this book. It is in this province too that exist the topaz and amethyst mines. The visitor, however, need not trouble his head to start out upon any expedition with the object of picking up any of these curiosities. The topaz and amethyst fields are well-defined private property, while the water-stone is as shy and elusive as a four-leaved clover at home. If in quest of these objects, it is wiser to restrict the field of adventure to the Salto shops.

It has been noticeable all the time whilst ascending the river that the water has steadily become less tinged with yellow. Above the falls, however, the distinction is far more marked. The stream here is peculiarly limpid, and the effect at a northern spot such as Santa Rosa, almost on the Brazilian frontier, is entrancing. Here the river is at times of a brilliant blue tint—a broad azure ribbon winding between swelling banks covered now with dense folds of vegetation. Viewed from the rising ground in the neighbourhood, the conviction is inevitable that, although the northern waters may have lost a little in commercial importance, the Upper Uruguay can lay claim to a degree of beauty with which the lower reaches, for all their charm, cannot compete.

CHAPTER XX

THE URUGUAYAN CAMPO

Formation of the land—A survey of the country—Features of the soil—Types of wild flowers—A land of hill, valley, and stream—The glamour of the distance—"The purple land"—Breezes of the Campo—An exhilarating country—The dearth of homesteads—The Uruguayan Gaucho—His physique—The product of the blowy uplands—Matters of temperament—His comparative joviality—The Gaucho as worker, player, and fighter—The manipulation of feuds—A comparison between Argentina and Uruguay—Warrior ancestors of the Gaucho—His sense of dignity and honour—Conservative habits and customs—Costume and horse gear—Strenuous *bailes*—Some homeric feats of dancing—Stirring revelry—The Uruguayan land-owner—Foreign elements in the land—Negro inhabitants of the Banda Oriental—The numerical status of the Africans in the north and in the south—Absence of a racial question—The slavery of former days—The employment of black troops in war—Lenient treatment of negro slaves—Harsh measures applied to aboriginal Indians—A lesson in human economy—Testimony of a contemporary writer—Immigrant colonies.

The Uruguayan Campo is not to be described without a certain amount of hesitation. It would be simple enough for one who had caught only a distant passing glimpse of the land of the pastures to put down the country without further ado as rolling grass upland watered by many streams. That such is the foundation of the Campo is undeniable. Nevertheless to begin and end with such a phrase would be equivalent to a description of the peacock as a bird who wears coloured feathers.

The subtle charms of the Uruguayan Campo are not to be discerned through the medium of the bioscope-like glimpses that so many travellers obtain of it. Very rightly, it refuses to reveal itself fully until a certain amount of familiarity has justified a nearer acquaintance. From an æsthetic point of view it certainly holds far more than might be expected from a country of such comparatively limited attributes.

If you desire to watch the moods of this rural Banda Oriental, ride out to mount one of the higher shoulders of the downland, and wait there, either in the saddle or out of it. You will obtain little sympathy in the task. Eccentric to the mind of the estancieros, frankly mad in the eagle eyes of the Gaucho—a calm survey of the Campo is worth all such merely human depreciation!

The aspect of the country in the immediate neighbourhood of where the observer has taken his stand will be green in the main, although the unbroken verdure by no means obtains throughout. Here and there the ground is strongly marked by the occasional heaps of stones that come jostling to the surface, and that recline in the fashion of small bleak islands in the midst of the green waves. But, should the time be spring, these latter are themselves flecked frequently almost to the extinction of their own colouring. The great purple bands and patches of the *flor morala* lie thickly upon the land. These, however, stand apart, since where they glow the serried ranks of blossom permit no others to raise their heads.

A PASTORAL SCENE.

To face p. 238.

But these, though the boldest of their kind, are by no means the sole occupants of the landscape. Indeed, one of the chief characteristics of the Banda Oriental Campo is the wealth of beautiful and comparatively lowly plants that grow amidst the grasses. They are of the type of English blossoms, peering out shyly from between the green blades, blowing purely and sweetly in their innocence of the heavy sickliness of the tropics. It is where the ground is chiefly dotted with these fresh flowers that the smile of the Campo is most brilliant.

So much for the immediate surroundings up to the point where the more intricate markings become merged in the broader tints of the landscape. Down in the hollows are bands of dark, close green formed by the trees that shade the streams. With scarcely a break in the narrow walls of verdure they run from valley to valley, accurately defining the banks of the small rivers whose waters they conceal. Within these leafy lanes lurk the only spots upon the Campo, save for the rare woodland, that do not stare frankly upwards, exposing all their earthly soul to the blue sky.

Away in the far distance there is a magic glamour. There the lands are no longer green to the eye. The soft waves, as they rise and dip in an accumulation of folds towards the final horizon line, are bathed in warm purple. The Banda Oriental has been called "the purple land" by one who knew it well, and never was a name better applied. Without the foreground—that is itself strongly purpled by the banks of the *flor morula*—all is purple and mystic. The land has its ordinary mirages as well; but here is one that at all times confronts the traveller—that wonderful land of the horizon that, unattainable, dies farther away as it is approached.

Yet, notwithstanding its soft romance, the place is essentially alive. It is a blowy haunt of clean fresh airs that sweep the slopes and open valleys to billow the grass tops and to refresh mankind. It is amidst such surroundings that the Oriental of the country dwells. His type is not very numerous, it is true, and—although the dearth of houses suits the landscape itself most admirably—the scarcity of habitation is a little lamentable in so wealthy and pleasant a land. It is practically certain, as a matter of fact, that the pastures will bear more roots in the near future than they have ever known in the past; but in the meanwhile it is necessary to take them as they are, and their inhabitants as well.

Of these inhabitants the true *paisano*, the Gaucho, decidedly claims the chief share of attention. The Gaucho of the Banda Oriental is not to be confused with his brethren of the neighbouring countries. In appearance he presents perhaps the finest specimen amongst the various kindred families of his race. He is taller in stature, and, if possible, even more athletic in his lithe frame than his neighbour. His complexion, moreover, though frequently dusky and invariably tanned, is peculiarly wholesome and fresh. It was inevitable that the blowy downlands should have produced a fitting and appropriate breed of amazingly healthy, hardy, and fearless men to whom the art of horsemanship has become second nature, while the occasional enforced spells of pedestrianism have degenerated into a mere unwelcome accident of life.

The temperament of the Uruguayan Gaucho shows corresponding distinction from that of the rest. It goes without saying that he is strongly imbued with the grim dignity of the race. Silent austerity here, however, is modified by lighter traits. In the same way as the higher social member of his country, he is more easily moved to laughter than his neighbours, and indulges from time to time in frank outbursts of joviality.

For practical purposes it is necessary to regard this child of the Campo from three standpoints—from that of the worker, the player, and the fighter. It is rare enough that one of them is not called upon to fill all these three rôles on a good many occasions during his lifetime. As stock-rider, he has proved his courage, fidelity, and honesty of purpose to the full; his moments of recreation are taken up by equestrian sports, guitar-playing, and chance affairs of the heart, whilst in warfare he has had only too many opportunities of displaying his reckless brilliancy—frequently, it must be admitted, at the cost of discipline and order.

In his private quarrels the Argentine Gaucho will bottle up his wrath until his overflowing passion culminates without warning in the rapid knife thrust or revolver shot. The conclusion of a serious dispute between his Uruguayan brethren will almost certainly be the same; but the tragic climax will be approached in quite another fashion. The atmospheric effervescence of the Banda Oriental will enter into the case. There will be shouting, vociferation, and not a little abuse. Not until a fair exchange of all this has been bandied to and fro will come the flash of steel or flame—and the red stain upon the grasses of the Campo.

That these dwellers upon the downlands should prove themselves born fighters is no matter for surprise. For the dusky side of their ancestry they claim the Charrúa Indians, the fiercest and most warlike of all the tribes in the neighbouring provinces. With this strain added to the blood of the old Spaniards, and the mixture fostered and nourished by the breezy hills, the result has been a being whose keen sense of dignity and honour were ever in the very active custody of knife or lance.

As is perhaps natural enough in a land whose interests—as compared with the agricultural development of the neighbouring countries—are almost purely pastoral, the habits and customs of the Oriental have remained unusually conservative. His poncho is a veritable poncho, often of a bizarre and daring hue; his spurs are weapons that glitter in huge circles at his heels, while his horse furniture is frequently silvered to the very last degree.

When the Gaucho undertakes a dance—a *baile*—moreover, he enters into the performance with a zest that puts to shame the human products of a later civilisation. In order to witness one of the most homeric of these exhibitions it is necessary to suppose the revellers in the peculiarly reckless and irresponsible mood that from time to time falls to their lot. On such an occasion their wonted strict sobriety is abruptly melted beneath the flow of the native spirit, caña, and perhaps that of wine, and of beer. Then upon the open sward of the Campo they will dance their *tangos*, stepping it manfully for hour after hour.

Indeed, strengthened by the intervals of rest, refreshment, and sleep, it is not unusual for them to continue these tremendous terpsichorean feats for two or three days on end. At the conclusion of which, having danced themselves out and drunk themselves in, these astonishing mortals are perfectly ready for their strenuous work in the saddle!

Having concluded with the Gaucho, it soon becomes evident that the main features of individuality that distinguish the Uruguayan from his neighbours are very nearly finished with as well. The landowner, it is true, still clings in parts to ancient customs and the remnants of national costume rather more closely than elsewhere in the Southern republics. But the distinctions here are less marked, and in the case of the townsmen have disappeared altogether. An important factor in the population is now provided by the large foreign element that has settled itself permanently in the country. By far the most numerous communities of these are those of the Italians and Spaniards; but in addition there is scarcely a European country that is not more or less strongly represented by its emigrants.

The negro race, although its presence is more marked than in the republics to the West, is quite insignificant numerically in the South of Uruguay. Towards the north, however, the numbers of the Africans are much increased, and as the Brazilian frontier is closely approached, the black people tend rather to predominate over the white. It is only in these remote districts that the possibility of a racial question could be involved. As a matter of fact, such an eventuality is quite undreamed of, and nowhere in the world is it less likely to occur. In the absence of any drawn distinction the negro appears to exist in more or less complete peace, and only meddles with the affairs of the country during troublous times when instructed by the true lords of the soil, whose actual superiority would seem all the greater for the fact of its being unexpressed.

Considering the number of slaves that were imported directly into Uruguay as well as those that filtered southwards through Brazil, it is perhaps somewhat a matter for astonishment that these blacks are not numerically stronger than is the case. The explanation lies largely in the numerous wars by which the country has been harassed in the past, and in the policy that prevailed under the old Spanish regime. Black troops were freely employed then, and it must be admitted that they met with far less consideration than the rest. If a desperate situation arose, they were wont to be sent out in search of a glory that was very remote and of a death that was very near, not necessarily because the Spaniards feared for themselves in the attempt, but rather on account of the science of racial economy, and on the principle of sacrificing the pawns before the more aristocratic chessmen. And it is to these wholesale gaps in the black ranks that the existing scarcity of the negro population in the South is largely due.

Not that it must be inferred from this that the general treatment of the African slaves by the Spaniards was severe. Their fate has always been entirely distinct from that of the unfortunate native Indians. The blood of these latter, slain by the first generation of adventurous *conquistadores*, flowed in red rivers almost the length and breadth of South America, while tens of thousands more sank and died beneath the superhuman tasks imposed upon them.

Nevertheless they were not sacrificed from mere wanton love of slaughter. Held as soulless instruments from whom the last possible ounce of labour was to be extracted, these fearful slaughterings were instigated as acts of discipline that should make more pliant and serviceable material of the general body, while the cowed met their slower, toilful death in order that their masters should obtain wealth ere the advent from Europe of further competitors who might desire to share their wealth with them.

After a while the limitations both of the continent and of the labour capacities of its natives became evident, and the first spasms of the remorseless and feverish lust moderated. It was then that the introduction of the negro occurred. With the maturing of the continent came a milder and more settled form of civilisation, of which the dusky imported labourers obtained the full benefit. That they were well cared for in times of peace is testified to not only by the native historians but by perfectly unbiassed English travellers. One of these, who visited Uruguay during the last years of the Spanish dominion, is particularly emphatic on the point.

"There is one trait," he writes, "in the South American Spaniards much in their favour. I mean the mild, humane, and gentle treatment which their slaves receive. This one would scarcely expect from the cruelty they manifest to animals. The condition of the Africans here is without doubt happier than in any other part of the world where they are held in slavery, and I will even venture to say, more so than in their native country. A severe punishment is seldom inflicted; the tasks imposed on them are light, and such as they can easily execute. Indeed, they scarcely seem to be slaves."

If any palliation for enforced human labour were possible it might be looked for in evidence such as this. Nevertheless, since nothing of the kind is admissible, it is well to remember that the slave era in the River Plate countries is now a matter of comparatively remote history. Moreover, as though in compensation for a former servitude, however light, the lot of the African here is now undoubtedly happier than almost anywhere else in the world.

In addition to the ordinary foreign landowners and residents in Uruguay are a few of the regular immigrant colonies the establishment of which has now become so popular throughout the Southern republics. Of these the most important is the Swiss Colony in the neighbourhood of Colonia, to which reference has already been made.

CHAPTER XXI

ESTANCIA LIFE

Similarities between the farming routine of Uruguay and of Argentina—The Banda Oriental a pastoral rather than an agricultural land—Viticulture an asset in estancia affairs—Wheat, maize, and linseed—Scarcity of alfalfa—Excellence of the natural pastures—The possibilities of private agricultural colonisation—Favourable outlook for grazing countries in general—Lemco estancias—The estancia San Juan—A comprehensive enterprise—Cattle, cereals, and viticulture—Stone quarries—A Campo sketch—The cutting out of a bullock—A Gaucho meal.

The Uruguayan estancia life resembles that of Argentina very closely. And of this latter so much has been written in recent years that a too lengthy description of the routine of one of the great cattle farms would almost inevitably savour of repetition and superfluity. The duties of both estanciero and his major-domo are, indeed, almost identical with those of their brethren upon the other side of the great river. There are similar rides of inspection in order to "revise camp," similar great *rodeos*, or gatherings of cattle, and a general method of life that is distinct from the other merely in minor details.

THE BICHADERO ESTANCIA.

HEREFORD CATTLE ON THE BICHADERO ESTANCIA.

To face p. 246.

In the main ethics of the farming itself, it is true, there are some differences. Seeing that Uruguay is a pastoral rather than an agricultural land, the system of setting apart a certain proportion of a private estancia for the purpose of colonisation by crop-raising tenants is almost unknown. On the other hand, as it happens that the soil of a portion of almost every province is suitable for viticulture, a great number of the Uruguayan landowners throughout the republic cultivate vineyards—an industry that in Argentina is confined almost entirely to the two great grape-growing centres of Mendoza and San Juan. In many districts of the Banda Oriental, moreover, fruit-growing forms part and parcel of the industrial programme of an estancia, instead of necessarily forming an entirely separate branch of commerce, as is the case in Argentina.

Although I have referred to Uruguay as an essentially pastoral country, it must not be inferred from this that the cultivation of cereals and the like has no existence in the land. On the contrary, many districts—notably that of Colonia, the most fertile in the Republic—produce really important quantities of wheat and maize, and a certain amount of linseed beyond, although this latter is grown in a minor degree. Very few districts in the country are adapted for the favourable cultivation of alfalfa, a fact that is undoubtedly to be regretted, since the merits of this lucerne for the purposes of fattening cattle are supreme. Yet this disadvantage is to a great extent counterbalanced by the excellent pastures of natural grass with which Uruguay is so plentifully endowed.

It is likely enough, too, that the system of private agricultural colonisation referred to above will in the future be seriously undertaken. At the present moment experiments in this direction are being undertaken, and, should the landowners become impressed with the success of the departure, it is quite possible that the system will spread with the same rapidity as was the case in Argentina.

In the meanwhile the supreme interest of Uruguay remains pastoral; and the bulls and the rams continue to be lords in the land. In a sense this is undoubtedly just as well, for in all probability never was the outlook for grazing countries more favourable than it is at the present moment, when the exports of North America are rapidly dying away, and the markets of Europe are opening their metaphorical mouths in a clamorous demand for further supplies.

Some of the largest and most imposing of the Uruguayan estancias are situated in the western districts of the Republic. Many of these, such as the Bichadero, Ombú, and others, are owned by the Lemco Company, and constitute most imposing estates, stocked by pedigree cattle.

The San Juan estancia is situated in the neighbourhood of Colonia, and, under the able management of Mr. J. Booth, affords one of the best possible examples of an estate whose lands have been aptly utilised to serve various purposes. The estancia is noted in the first place for the quality of its live stock—and with no little reason, since it harbours over a thousand head of pedigree shorthorn and Hereford cattle.

But the energies of the San Juan estancia are not confined to the raising of cattle and the production of maize. Viticulture is a matter of great importance here, for the place enjoys a great repute for the quality of its wine. Its vineyards, as a matter of fact, repose on a subsoil of iron-stone rocks, which lends a particularly pleasant flavour to the vintages. In addition to the great vineyards that spread themselves over portions of the estate, the cellars of its bodega are well worth a visit. The building is specially constructed for the purpose, and contains air-spaces between the inner and outer walls, thus rendering the interior to all intents and purposes damp-proof.

The cellars contain forty-two large casks, each with a capacity for holding 3,600 litres, and, beyond these, twelve giant specimens, in each of which eight thousand litres of wine may be stored. The extent of the vineyards on the place is thirty hectares, and from this area an average 250,000 litres of wine are produced annually. Thus it will be seen that the vineyard industry of San Juan is of no mean importance.

Among the other branches of general industry in which San Juan is interested is that of stone-quarries, the quality and extent of the deposits here being considerable. A large bee-farm is also attached to the place. In addition to this comprehensive programme there are, of course, the ordinary side-issues of estancia production in the way of both live stock and agriculture. Among the horses bred are not a few racers of pedigree stock that have given a good account of themselves in the neighbourhood and elsewhere.

The estancia-house of San Juan is delightfully situated amidst orange, wattle, and paraiso trees, from whose trunks and branches hang festoons of air-plants and masses of yellow orchids. From the picturesque, shaded building itself the view embraces miles of undulating country on all sides, with a few distant peeps of the waters of the River Plate to the south-west. It would be difficult to conceive a pleasanter or a better managed spot.

Such estancias as these, of course, represent the cream of the land, and Uruguayan "camp" life must not be judged as a whole by such particularly favourable examples. Even the foreigner in the Republic, whose life is wont to be rather more fully surrounded with comfort than that of his native-born brother, must perforce make a beginning, and, as in all else, it is always the first steps that are the roughest. It is said that one of the first requisites of a gardener is a cast-iron back. In the same way the primary needs of the budding estanciero are undoubtedly health and a good horse. In these respects he is likely to be well suited, for the climate will attend to the former and his *patron* to the latter.

I have already said that the scenes upon the Uruguayan estancias are much the same as elsewhere, but the following sketch may serve to show a little of the local colour with which the rural Oriental landscape and life are imbued:

ESTANCIA HOUSE: SAN JUAN.

To face p. 250.

The bullock is grazing in the midst of his fellows, plucking stolidly at the spring grass, whose close blades paint the undulations of the Uruguayan Campo in soft green. No pedigree animal this, his lengthy horns, rather pointed nose, and shaggy mottled coat being redeemed by various features that tend to raise him from the mere ruck of the disappearing country-bred. There is a trace of Hereford in the compact form, straight back, and in the symptoms of red-brown and white that endeavour to assert themselves from out of the confusion of his other markings. Representing one of the earlier stages in the forward march of the local breeds, he is of the type known to experts by the cryptic word "useful"—a meritorious physical condition whose reward is wont to fructify in an earlier death than that accorded to those of his brethren who are less liberal in meat. At the present moment the bullock is supremely content, although profoundly unconscious of the charm of his surroundings. This is perhaps just as well, since his ribs would undoubtedly emerge from their plump covering were he to waste the precious moments of mastication in favour of less material delights. As it is, he tramples carelessly on the patches of scarlet verbena, and crushes the life from the white tobacco blossom and the blue lupin flower with a ponderous impartiality. It is enough for him that the warm sunlight beats down upon his back, and that the plentiful grass rises to his cud in a ceaseless green stream. Moreover, the few score of companions that surround him lend a dimly-felt but comforting sense of comradeship.

From the green of the foreground to the blue and mysterious distant swellings of the horizon the face of the Campo has been devoid of humanity. Near by a humble rancho, it is true, raises its diffident walls from the earth, a lowly erection of turf and reeds, enlivened here and there by a small auxiliary patch of corrugated iron, that catches up the sun-rays to flash them back in brilliant defiance. But there are no signs of life about the place beyond that afforded by a couple of hens of worn and frayed appearance that make rapid and spiteful passes at the dust with their beaks. Only when the sun is falling near to the horizon does the first sign manifest itself of more active stirrings. The figures of two horsemen have emerged from behind a distant clump of eucalyptus that stands out like a green island from the midst of a rolling sea.

As the riders draw nearer it is plain that they are Gauchos—Gauchos in a workaday mood, and consequently in attire far less picturesque than that which lends colour to their feast days. Yet they afford striking enough figures of men in their sombreros, kerchiefs, white shirts, broad trousers, horse-hide boots, and giant spurs. Each part and parcel of his horse, they come loping easily along with that curious air of careless alertness that is characteristic of the Gaucho. With the first warning of human approach the cattle have raised their heads in the wary and rather resentful stare that the presence of such visitors demands. When no doubt longer remains that the grim-faced riders are heading directly for their own company, doubt turns to active alarm. There is a flinging up of heels and tails, a bunching together of scattered units, and a surging to and fro, while the horns wave in a panic of indecision. The bullock with the traces of Hereford markings has run to a common centre with the rest.

A moment later the horses are cleaving the ranks of the cattle, and the cumbrous bodies of the horned creatures go floundering to right and left just as they have floundered a dozen times before, with precisely the same degree, moreover, of dread and confusion. Dodging and twisting ponderously, they rush to and fro for a while, then flee with a thunder of hoofs from the impact, ending up in a breathless halt at length to turn their horns upon one another in a fury of terror. All but the bullock with the scanty Hereford markings. He has raced and charged with the rest, only to find on each occasion a horse's flank or chest barring the way to safety, and a threatening human arm raised on high that sent him without further ado to the right-about. And now the situation is doubtless quite inexplicable, since the rumbling of his companions' hoofs has died away, and he is racing across the Campo quite alone save for the horseman who gallops remorselessly on either flank—fatal attendants who are no more to be shaken off than the hairs of his hide. A lasso circles lightly in the air, uncoiling as it goes like an aerial snake: the noose falls with a gentle rattle on the hurrying animal's horns. A terrific jerk shakes him from tail to nostril. But the bullock has kept his legs, and stands firm now, pulling with all his might against the strain that follows, heaving from side to side in his fight with the rope that never slackens. There is a thudding of horses' hoofs at his quarters now. Enraged at the presence of a second foe, the bullock kicks wildly, and the action is the signal for his doom. Another rope has whistled through the air, and has encircled his fetlock in some demoniacal fashion. In consequence, he gives a strenuous jump into the air—his last, for ere his feet have touched the ground his legs are wrenched away from under him, and the heavy body of the creature, flung full upon its side, strikes the earth with a crash. Ere he can move the beat of galloping horses' hoofs has drawn near, and ceased. Two men have sprung to the ground, and are securing his legs with ropes; then one rises to draw the blade of a huge knife from its sheath at his belt. A minute later there is a pool of darker crimson by the side of the verbena patches. A couple of hours later there is a log fire upon the Campo, and the beef is being cut into long strips from where it is spitted above the blaze, and eaten wholesale as Gaucho appetite demands. In the meanwhile the carancho birds are gathering thickly above, for meat is cheap upon the open pastures, and they will be economically-minded Gauchos indeed who do not leave them the greater share of the carcass.

CHAPTER XXII

URUGUAY AS A PASTORAL COUNTRY

Origin of the live stock of the country—Influence of the climate and pastures upon the first animals introduced—Live stock census of 1909—Importance of the breeding industry—Various ramifications—Principal items of home consumption—Articles of export—Quality of the first herds introduced—Type of original sheep and horses—Goats and pigs—The introduction of a superior class of animal—The *criollos* and the *mestizos*—Breeds imported—Durham, Hereford, Polled Angus, and Devon cattle—Dutch, Norman, Flemish, and Swiss cattle—Growth of the dairy industry—Popular breeds of sheep and horses, and pigs—Principal countries from which the animals are derived—Growing value of the local-bred live stock—The manipulation of an estancia—Well-found estates—Uruguayan agricultural societies—Work effected by these—Government support—The Rural Association of Uruguay—Financial results of agricultural shows—Side products—Tallow—Hams—Tanning—"La Carolina"—A great dairy farm—The factory of Breuss and Frey—The *saladeros*, or meat-curing establishments—Number of animals slaughtered—Method by which the meat is cured—*Tasajo*—Countries to which it is exported—The frozen meat trade—"La Frigorifica Uruguaya"—Important growth of the new industry—Shipments of frozen meat.

The great numbers of the live stock which to-day constitute the chief wealth of Uruguay owe their origin to the animals introduced by the Spanish *conquistadores* at the beginning of the seventeenth century.

These animals, which, of course, were drawn from the breeds that existed in Spain at that period, found themselves surrounded by conditions that were eminently favourable. Thus, beneath the influence of a temperate climate and of the rich and nourishing pastures that cover almost the entire surface of the Republic their numbers rapidly multiplied. It is for these reasons, moreover, that the breeding and traffic in these animals constitutes at the present day the principal industry of the inhabitants.

The live stock census organised by the Government in the year 1909 gave the following results concerning the numbers of the live stock that are now in existence in the Republic:

Sheep	16,608,717
Cattle	6,827,428
Horses	561,408
Pigs	93,923
Mules	22,992
Goats	20,428
Total	24,134,896

These figures might reasonably be increased, since it was necessarily impossible for the census to deal with the complete numbers of the animals that exist throughout the country. Thus, without danger of exaggeration, it may be supposed that some thirty million head of live stock actually graze upon the pastures of the land. These figures suffice to show the enormous importance to which live stock breeding has attained in Uruguay.

The ramifications of this industry are naturally numerous. For home consumption and internal commerce meat, milk, and tallow form the principal items. For the export trade the list is considerably more comprehensive. Live cattle, frozen, chilled, tinned, and dried meat, beef extracts, wool, horns, hides, tallow, fat, guano, and the various other products now make up a commerce of an annual value of thirty millions of gold dollars, or of rather more than six million pounds sterling. Chilled or frozen beef and mutton form the principal items of this export trade, after which hides and extract of meat rank next in importance.

The main breeds of animals introduced by the Spaniards at the time of the conquest, although they served their purpose well enough at the time, were by no means of the type which the exigencies of modern times require. The cattle of former years were wanting in many respects. They were wont to possess, for example, a superabundance of bone, were badly built, and were notably backward in development. The sheep were possessed of the same faults, and, in addition, were wont to yield inferior wool.

The horses, on the other hand, although of light build and lacking somewhat in shape, have proved themselves particularly well suited to the country. Hardy and of great power of endurance, they have adapted themselves completely to the natural conditions of the land. From this stock a breed has sprung that fulfils admirably the equine duties of the Campo. The tendency of these horses has been to improve and to increase in size. Both the pigs and goats that were imported from Spain were of an inferior order, although the latter showed favourable results in the yielding of milk.

By the aid of these breeds alone it is certain that the live stock of Uruguay could never have attained to that degree of excellence in quality such as it can legitimately boast to-day. From these, for example, cattle could never have been produced of the class that the freezing works now demand, nor the valuable wool that is characteristic of the day. The beginning of this later progress dates from the middle of the last century. It was then that the more progressive breeders became aware of the limitations of the *criollo* races, as are termed the breeds imported from Spain that have flourished and taken root in the land. To this end these were crossed with others of a superior type, and thus the much-improved *mestizos*, or cross-breds, were obtained. These now preponderate in many regions of the Republic, in which, by the way, no true criollo animals now remain.

In order to effect this improvement in the cattle various English breeds have been introduced. Of these the two most important are the Durham and the Hereford, both of which are excellently adapted for the production of meat. By the crossing of these with the criollo a mestizo steer is obtained, capable of turning the scale at six hundred kilos and more, that provides excellent meat whether for the purposes of live shipment, freezing, salting, or extract. In addition to these more important breeds others have been introduced, such as the Devon, Polled Angus, and a few further varieties—all these, however, in a lesser degree.

It will be evident from this that the improvements in stock have been effected chiefly with the view of increasing the quantity of meat produced. Nevertheless, there are others that have been imported for dairy purposes alone. The chief of these are the Dutch, Norman, Flemish, and Swiss. It must be remarked that the popularity of these is rapidly growing, on account of the progress and extension of the dairy industry.

So far as sheep are concerned, the breeds that have been found most suitable for the country are the Merino, Lincoln, Shropshire, Hampshire, Romney Marsh, and Southdown. The Merino race amidst its new surroundings provides an especially fine class of wool that is appreciated throughout the world; from the crossing of the Merino with the English breeds animals are obtained that provide the best meat for the purposes of export, and those types of wool that are most in demand for general commercial purposes.

The horses principally employed for saddle purposes and for light draught are the thorough-bred, Yorkshire, Anglo-Norman, Irish, and Russian, while for heavy draught the Percheron, Clydesdale, and Shire strains are the most popular.

The improvement in pig-breeding has been effected by the introduction of several English species, such as the Yorkshire and Berkshire, the French animals of the kind being rarely employed.

It is by means of the crossing with all these above-mentioned breeds that the general live stock of the country has been raised in degree. The result has been distinctly favourable, since the healthy climate and the pastures are eminently suitable for the finest strains as well as for the cross-breds.

The annual importation into Uruguay of sires, bulls, and of the remaining stock is now large. The countries whence they are derived are England and other European lands, Australia, Argentina, and North America. Amongst these many valuable animals are to be met with. Thus recently two champion rams have been imported from Australia, various champion bulls and rams from England, while from France came the noted Durham bull "Tamarin."

CHALÊT AT COLONIA SUIZA.

THE VINTAGE: ESTANCIA SAN JUAN.

To face p. 258.

Uruguay, however, does not now depend entirely upon importations from abroad for its pedigree stock. It already possesses a number of *cabañas*, or breeding establishments, from which emerge cattle and sheep of a grade sufficiently high to meet with success in the agricultural shows of other countries. These are to be distinguished from the estancias, the farms of larger area upon which the general live stock of commerce thrives.

The ordinary estancia consists of a number of paddocks, separated the one from the other by wire fences, of the natural pastures that abound in Uruguay. The advance that has been effected in these great enterprises is on a par with that of the rest. They are as a rule well provided with sheds for the housing of the pedigree stock and with plantations of trees for the shelter of the less valuable type of animal, as well as with cattle-dips, water deposits, and stockyards, and, in fact, with every installation that is requisite for the purpose of the industry.

In every department of the Republic societies have been founded in order to encourage scientific breeding, and to organise the agricultural shows that are now held throughout the country. These agricultural meetings have served a most useful purpose in fostering an interest in breeding and in the various other branches of the general national industries. This fact has been recognised by the Government, which, in consequence, has done its utmost to stimulate the holding of such functions. It has thus during the past few years spent an annual sum of fifty thousand dollars in the subsidising of these events, an outlay that has undoubtedly borne good fruit. In providing these subsidies it is stipulated that at least a third part of the sum provided shall be expended in cash prizes, and that the chief attention in this respect shall be devoted to those particular branches of industry that appear in a less advanced condition than the rest, and that, therefore, are the most in need of encouragement.

Many of these agricultural societies possess extensive grounds of their own in the near neighbourhood of the provincial capital. In these places permanent buildings are frequently to be met with that are employed for the annual shows. These usually owe their construction to private enterprise, assisted by the Government. In Montevideo, too, there is a ground specially set apart for this purpose. Here the Rural Association of Uruguay holds the great annual championship meeting, and the Government has just allotted the sum of a hundred thousand dollars for the purpose of improving the spot, and for the introduction of the very latest innovations. These agricultural shows have proved highly successful in facilitating the actual commercial transactions having reference to live stock of all descriptions. Thus during the past few years the principal meetings alone have been responsible for an annual sale of over half a million dollars' worth of animals.

Although, as has been explained, numerous products of the pastoral industry are exported in their natural state, there are others which require special treatment and preparation in their country of origin ere shipment, and which are daily gaining in importance. The most important institutions that deal with these are the meat-curing factories, the freezing works, and the establishments for preserving meat and for extracting its essence. These chief industries we will deal with at some length later, enumerating first of all some of the side products of lesser importance, such as the manufacture of tallow and of hams, and that of tanning.

Another industry that bids fair to be of supreme importance in the future is that of dairy-farming. At the present time this is worked on a comparatively modest scale, since the great majority of farms are content with the breeding and selling of the cattle. Nevertheless, there are several important establishments that produce milk, butter, and cheese for the purposes of both home consumption and of export.

The chief amongst these establishments is that of La Carolina, belonging to Don Francisco Fontana, which occupies an area of eight thousand hectares in the department of Rocha. No less than five thousand milch cows graze on this property, which is provided with steam-driven machinery of the most modern type. In the department of Colonia, too, exists the colony of Swiss, who devote themselves especially to this particular branch of industry. The principal factory here is that of Breuss and Frey, which deals with thirty thousand litres of milk daily, and can turn out twenty-four thousand kilos of butter in a month. This factory likewise contains the most up-to-date machinery, and is provided with freezing and sterilising apparatus. This concern exports cheese as well as butter.

These few facts will give an idea of the point to which the dairy-farming industry in Uruguay may develop in the near future, since there exist several millions of cows of a type eminently suitable for the purpose.

In the Republic there are actually twenty saladeros in existence, of which thirteen are situated in Montevideo, seven on the banks of the River Uruguay, and one at Paso de los Toros, in the interior of the country.

The number of the animals slaughtered at these saladeros will give an idea of the importance of the industry. During the years 1904 and 1908 the total amounted to no less than 2,763,855 head of cattle, thus making the average for the year over half a million head. During these five years 223,872,000 kilos of *tasajo*, or dried meat, were prepared, which represent a yearly average of forty-five million kilos. The average yield of the steers was ninety kilos of tasajo, that of the cows sixty kilos.

The manner in which this dried meat is prepared in the saladeros is fairly simple. After the cattle have been slaughtered and the veterinary examination has proved the absence of any taint or disease the bones are separated from the meat, which is then shaped into various portions known respectively as *mantas* and *postas*. Once dried, these are placed in brine-pans, and piled up, well covered with salt. According to the state of the weather and the condition to which the meat is required to attain, it is placed in special vessels in the sun for a period varying between four and six days, until it is perfectly dry and ready to be baled.

As will be seen from this, salt and sun heat are the two principal agents that enter into the manufacture of tasajo, two powerful agents that, it is claimed, perform their task in the simplest and most hygienic fashion possible. The slaughtering season in the saladeros generally begins in the month of November, and is continued until January of the following year.

Tasajo, when its manufacture is completed, is classified into four grades, in accordance with the fatter or leaner propensities of the meat. The former kinds are exported principally to the markets of Brazil, while the latter are for the most part destined for consumption in Cuba. Beyond these, however, there are various other fields in which tasajo plays a popular part. It is, for instance, sent in fairly large quantities to the Portuguese colonies, to Puerto Rico, and to Spain and Portugal themselves, as well as to numerous less important places whose inhabitants have learned to appreciate this particular form of dried meat. The product contains certain advantages in that its treatment is simple throughout. Thus, when once in the hands of its actual consumers, the salt has merely to be dissolved from the meat in order to render it in a condition prepared for the oven.

It is several years now since Uruguay has commenced to export frozen meat. Six years ago an important freezing establishment, La Frigorifica Uruguaya, was founded in the department of Montevideo on the bank of the River Plate. The place occupies a large extent of ground, and is capable of slaughtering daily two hundred head of cattle and two thousand sheep. This establishment is fitted up with the most recent inventions that have been brought to bear on the freezing process. The frozen beef is classified into three qualities, according to type and weight, and is packed in quarters in a double covering that completely preserves it from the danger of contact with other substances. The carcasses of the sheep, following the usual custom, are shipped entire, and covered in the same way.

The Frigorifica Uruguaya began operations in 1905. The rapid increase in the extent of its shipments may be judged from the following figures. Thus, in 1905, the year of its inception, the establishment exported two thousand tons of frozen meat; in 1906 the shipments had increased to four thousand tons, whereas in 1907 the total amounted to seven thousand and in 1908 to nine thousand tons. This increase has continued unchecked during the past couple of years, and the shipments for 1910 are estimated to have amounted to no less than twelve thousand tons. The machinery has now been added to, and the result will certainly go to swell these figures considerably more in the near future.

The benefit that this concern confers on the pastoral industry is of course very great. Not only does it increase the facilities for sale of the cattle, but its existence tends in addition towards the improvement of breed in general, since only the animals of a superior class are suitable for the purpose it serves.

CHAPTER XXIII

DEPARTMENTS, CLIMATE, AND NATURAL HISTORY

> The nineteen divisions of Uruguay—Their populations, areas, towns, and industries—Canelones—Florida—San José—Durazno—Flores—Colonia—Soriano—Rio Negro—Paysandú—Salto—Artigas—Tacuarembó—Rivera—Cerro Largo—Treinta y Tres—Rocha—Maldonado—Montevideo—Climate—Favourable conditions throughout the Republic—The Atlantic coast line—The summer season—Pleasantly tempered heat—A land of cool breezes—Its attractions as a pleasure resort—Climates of the interior and of the north—Draught—Locusts—Comparative immunity of a pastoral country—Uruguayan fauna—Some common creatures of the Campo—Bird life—The ostrich—Its value as a commercial asset—The trade in ostrich feathers—Measures for the protection of the birds.

A list of the nineteen departments of Uruguay with their more salient features will go far towards explaining in detail the various areas, populations, and resources of the Republic.

Canelones, situated in the midst of the departments of Montevideo, San José, Florida, Minas, and Maldonado, with a coast-line upon the River Plate, possesses an area of 4,751 square kilometres. It is one of the most populous departments, containing over ninety thousand inhabitants. Three railway-lines connect the district with Montevideo. Its chief towns are Guadeloupe, Santa Lucia, Pando, and Las Piedras, each of which contains some eight thousand inhabitants. Canelones is mainly devoted to pasture, agriculture, viticulture, and general fruit-growing.

Florida is situated directly to the north of Canelones. Its area is 12,107 square kilometres and its population fifty thousand. Two lines of railway connect it with Montevideo. The chief town is Florida, the capital of the department, a city of ten thousand inhabitants. Until recent years Florida has been almost altogether given up to the pastoral industry; but of late agriculture has made great strides.

San José is situated to the west of Canelones, and likewise possesses a coast-line on the River Plate. Its area is 6,932 square kilometres; population about fifty thousand. The department is connected with Montevideo by two railway lines. The principal town is San José de Mayo, with a population of just over twelve thousand inhabitants. Rather more than half the department is made up of rich pasture-lands, although the agricultural districts are increasing. In addition to fruit-growing and viticulture, the timber industry of San José is important, consisting of wood both for building purposes and for fuel.

Durazno, to the north of Florida, is the most central department in the Republic, and contains a population of fifty thousand inhabitants. It is connected by a railway line with Montevideo, and its chief city is San Pedro del Durazno, whose inhabitants number eleven thousand. The department is essentially a pastoral one, and is especially well watered, being served by the Rivers Negro and Yi, and by countless tributaries and smaller streams.

Flores, situated to the west of Durazno, contains twenty thousand inhabitants. Almost half this number are residents of the capital, Trinidad. Flores is not yet served by a railway, and it is probably for this reason that so many of its districts, admirably adapted for agriculture, still remain essentially pastoral. In Flores is a very curious grotto, sustained by natural arches and columns, that has been the source of much geological controversy.

Colonia is the richest and most important department of all in the Republic. Lying to the west of San José, it has the advantage not only of railways but of a lengthy coast-line on the River Plate. Agriculture here has attained to a high pitch of development, and dairy-farming constitutes one of the most important industries of the department. Fruit culture and viticulture are in an equally advanced condition, while the quarrying of building stone is now being energetically carried on. In Colonia is situated the Swiss Colony, the inhabitants of which apply themselves to agriculture and dairy-farming.

Soriano lies to the north of Colonia, and its western boundary is likewise washed by the waters of the river—no longer the River Plate, but the Uruguay. The area of the department is 9,223 kilometres, and its population rather exceeds forty thousand. Soriano is connected by railway with Montevideo. Its chief town is Mercedes, the population of which amounts to ten thousand inhabitants. The principal industry is pasture, although agriculture and general fruit-growing is carried on to a certain extent. Timber, charcoal-burning, and stone-quarrying are responsible for a certain amount of labour. A fair quantity of minerals such as iron, silver, copper, and lead is met with here.

Rio Negro is situated on the Uruguay River to the north of Colonia. Its area is 8,470 kilometres and its population twenty thousand. The department is now in the act of being linked up with the main centres by railway. Its capital is Fray Bentos, a town celebrated as one of the chief centres of the manufacture of meat extract, with a population of seven thousand inhabitants. Rio Negro is essentially a pastoral province, and is the chief centre in the Republic for the breeding of live stock, which attains here to an exceptionally high grade of quality. Rio Negro is one of the most favourably situated departments as regards water communication. In addition to its 120 kilometres of coast-line on the Uruguay it possesses 200 kilometres of river frontage on the River Negro.

Paysandú bounds Rio Negro to the north, with a lengthy frontage on the Uruguay River. Its population is forty thousand, of which twenty-one thousand inhabit the capital, Paysandú, the second town of importance in Uruguay. The area of the department is about 14,000 square kilometres. Paysandú is connected by railway both with the capital and the northern centres. Its industries are chiefly pastoral and agricultural, and a number of meat-curing establishments exist.

Salto is the neighbouring province to the north upon the River Uruguay. It contains an area of 12,500 square kilometres and a population of rather over fifty thousand. Its chief town is Salto, that in actual size is said to exceed that of Paysandú, numbering as it does rather over twenty-two thousand inhabitants. The department is served by railway. The principal industry is that of pasture. The department, moreover, is one of the chief wine-producing centres of the Republic. Salto is rich in minerals, and quartz and precious stones are met with in fair quantities here.

Artigas is the northernmost province on the Uruguay as well as in the Republic. Its area is 11,300 square kilometres, its population thirty thousand. Its capital is San Eugenio, situated on the Brazilian frontier, a town of nine thousand inhabitants. The railway runs as far as this point, and thus serves the length of the province. Artigas contains many districts notable for minerals, and is well endowed with precious stones such as the amethyst and topaz. Owing to the northern situation of the department grazing and agriculture are carried on to a lesser extent than in the majority of others. The variety of timber is important here, hard woods being found as well as the softer varieties.

Tacuarembó is situated in the northern centre of the Republic. That is to say, its frontiers extend from the centre to within a comparatively short distance of the Brazilian frontier. The department is the largest in Uruguay, its territories extending over more than twenty-one thousand square kilometres. Its population, however, does not exceed fifty thousand, and it is thus the most sparsely inhabited department of the country. It is served by a railway. The principal town is San Fructuoso, which possesses eight thousand inhabitants. Tacuarembó is for the most part devoted to agriculture. Tobacco flourishes in the province, and recent experimental rice plantations have met with a fair amount of success. Gold and manganese are met with in various districts.

Rivera is bounded on the south by Tacuarembó and on the north by Brazil. It is a fairly extensive department containing comparatively few inhabitants, but the precise figures of neither the one nor the other seem available. The chief town of the department is Rivera, a city situated on the Brazilian frontier that has a population of ten thousand. The industries of Rivera are similar to those of Tacuarembó. The gold mines here are of considerable importance, and are in active working. The department is served by railway, Rivera being the northernmost Uruguayan point of the line from Montevideo.

Cerro Largo is situated on the south-east of Rivera, and is bounded on the north-east by Brazil. The area of the department is nearly fifteen thousand square kilometres; population about forty-five thousand. Its capital is Melo, a town of fourteen thousand inhabitants. It is the terminus of a recently constructed railway-line, the entry of which into the country has had the effect of benefiting local commerce to a considerable extent. The principal industry is pastoral, but, in addition, a certain amount of agriculture is carried on.

Treinta y Tres, which lies to the south of Cerro Largo, possesses an area of 9,550 square kilometres and a population of thirty thousand. It has not the advantage of being served by any railway, although this will shortly occur. The principal town is Treinta y Tres, whose inhabitants are about eight thousand in number. Up to the present time the pastoral industry predominates here, that of agriculture being scarcely known. It is anticipated, however, that the coming development of the province will alter this condition of affairs. The department is well wooded, and the timber industry here is an important one. Treinta y Tres is bounded on the east wholly by the great Lake of Merin, upon the further shore of which lies Brazil.

Rocha, to the south of Treinta y Tres, is also bounded for the great part of its eastern frontier by Lake Merin, although a small portion of Brazil and a long stretch of Atlantic Ocean complete its boundaries in this direction. The department contains an area of eleven thousand kilometres and a population of forty thousand. It is not traversed by a railroad. Its chief industry is grazing; but in some districts viticulture is in an advanced state. The seal fishery affords an important revenue, and the mineral products of the country are considerable. Copper, gypsum, alabaster, marble, and jasper obtain in considerable quantities. The chief town is Rocha, a centre of unimportant size.

Maldonado is situated on the Atlantic Ocean, to the west of Rocha. Its extent and population are not officially given. In a short while the department will be adequately served by the railway, which has already entered its frontiers. Like the great majority of the departments it is principally devoted to pasture. A certain amount of agriculture and wine-growing obtains, and in the southern districts much timber has been planted. The seal fishery in the neighbourhood of Lobos Island, off its coast, is important. The capital of the department is Maldonado, a small coastal town.

Minas, to the north of Maldonado, has a population of about sixty thousand. In addition to its pasture and agriculture, the department is exceptionally well endowed with minerals. The capital is Minas, a city of fourteen thousand inhabitants, that forms the terminus of the railway-line from Montevideo.

The department of Montevideo constitutes the small extent of territory in the neighbourhood of the capital itself, a considerable portion of which is taken up by the outer suburbs of the main town. The country in the neighbourhood here is very fertile and highly cultivated.

There is probably no climate in South America that offers greater attractions than that of Uruguay. Throughout the Republic the conditions are favourable; but it stands to reason that those which obtain upon the coast-line facing the Atlantic are the most ideal of all. The climate in these neighbourhoods is essentially temperate, and may be likened to that of the Riviera of France, without, however, suffering from the occasional winter frosts and intense summer heat that characterise this latter seaboard. Nevertheless the winter temperature of the Uruguayan littoral when a southern wind is blowing can be quite as keen as is compatible with comfort.

As is the case in the majority of temperate countries, there is no accurately defined rainy or dry reason, although the rains are wont to be far more abundant in the winter months. The heat of summer in the south-eastern provinces is very seldom oppressive; indeed, one of the most striking characteristics of the warm season is the continuance of the refreshing and bracing airs that temper the heat, and that render midsummer itself as enjoyable as the delightful spring months. The climate of Buenos Aires is distinctly pleasant, but, so far as the summer season is concerned, the difference between that of the capitals of Argentina and Uruguay is curiously marked, when it is taken into consideration that not more than 120 miles of water separate the two. The exceptionally pleasant conditions that prevail on this portion of the Oriental coast are acknowledged by none more readily than by the Argentines, who flock there in great numbers for the purposes of bathing and general climatic refreshment in January and February.

The wind-swept uplands of the interior are favoured in a similar degree when compared with the districts of the other countries in corresponding latitudes. In the northern provinces upon the Brazilian frontier the increase in the normal temperature is, of course, very distinctly perceptible, and for the first time the vegetation gives undoubted evidence of an approach to the tropics.

STREAM ON THE SAN JUAN ESTANCIA.

To face p. 272.

In consequence of this temperate climate that it enjoys the natural plagues of the Banda Oriental are few. Drought, although it occurs from time to time, cannot be looked upon as a genuinely characteristic chastening influence of the land. The visitations of locusts constitute a more serious matter. These, as in the case of the neighbouring countries, occur in cycles, and the periods marked by the presence of the small winged creatures with the insatiable appetites are unpleasant enough for the agriculturalist. Owing to the great pastoral predominance in Uruguay, however, the country in general suffers far less than one more devoted to the production of cereals. With the spread of agriculture that is now in progress the question is likely to become more serious. But by the time that a reasonable proportion of the Republic has been brought under cultivation it is possible that one of the many plans that are continually being brought forward for the extermination of the locust curse may have taken effect. Nevertheless, too much reliance is not to be placed upon this very desirable consummation.

The great majority of Uruguayan fauna are identical with those of the River Plate countries in general. The animals most commonly to be met with in a journey through the Campo are the carpincho, a large, tailless water-hog; the nutria, a creature that closely resembles a gigantic rat, although its hind feet are webbed; the skunk, the opossum, the iguana, and the armadillo.

In the region of bird life the larger varieties most in evidence are the carancho, a cross between a vulture and a hawk; the chimangu, a smaller carrion-hawk, and a kestrel-hawk with brown body and bright grey wings. Far rarer are the large grey eagle, and the cuerbo, or black vulture. Heron of various species are very plentiful.

Of the smaller birds the teru-tero, a variety of crested plover, is by far the most numerous, although certain districts exist in which the duck and teal run them a close second in point of numbers, while partridge and martineta are to be met with in abundance in others.

Amongst the more gorgeous winged specimens of the country are the flamingo, parrot, woodpecker, humming-bird, and the little black pecho colorado with its brilliant scarlet breast. Both the scissor bird and the *viuda* (window) bird are aptly named. The former rejoices in a very long, divided tail; the latter is of a pure white colour with a well-defined black border to its wings. The "bien te veo, bicho feo" is a mocking-bird whose call closely resembles the phrase by which it is known, and the ornero, or oven bird, is so called from the curious structure of its mud nest. The small owl, too, is a notable inhabitant of the Campo, as are the dainty miniature doves. But to enter fully into the animal life of the Banda Oriental would require a book in itself; therefore it is necessary to be content with a list of the varieties most commonly to be met with.

In dealing with the category of birds I have purposely left the ostrich to the last, as that particular biped stands, as it were, in a class of its own. The *Rhea Americana* represents a commercial asset of no little importance, and the grey companies of these rather awkward-looking creatures are carefully watched now as they strut solemnly to and fro over the pastures. The feathers, it is true, cannot as a rule rival in quality those of the African bird, although occasionally some very fine specimens are to be met with. Indeed, it is said that the large, specially selected feathers are sold at prices that range from fifteen dollars to twenty-five dollars the kilo. The great majority of the coarser feathers are of little value, and are employed for dusting brushes and such similar purposes.

That the commerce in these ostrich feathers is of no little importance becomes evident when the shipments of the article are considered. In 1908 the exports of these to France, the United States, Spain, and Germany amounted to fifteen thousand kilos, while in 1909 they had increased to twenty-five thousand kilos. The numbers of the ostriches themselves, however, have tended to decrease of late years, and it is estimated that at the present time there are not more than fifty thousand in the country. Realising the danger incurred by this diminution, the Government is now taking measures towards the protection of these very useful birds, and there is no doubt that judicious legislation will cause their number to increase once more.

CHAPTER XXIV

INDUSTRIES AND NATURAL WEALTH

England's financial stake in Uruguay—British capital invested in the Republic—Its monetary importance compared with that of other South American nations—General commercial development of the country—A satisfactory outlook—Progress of grazing and agriculture—Marked increase in commerce—Uruguay's exports—Cured meats and frozen carcasses—Diminution of the former trade; increase of the latter—Reasons for the transformation of industry—An outcome of Brazilian protection—The breeding of fine cattle for the European markets—Present situation of the world's meat market—The British Isles as importers of meat—The position in the United States—A change from the rôle of exporter to that of importer—The increase in River Plate shipments—Closeness of touch between South American and English markets—Probable admission of foreign meat into European countries—Intervention of the United States Beef Trust—Purchase of Frigorificos—Possible effects of a monopoly upon the producers—South American views on the subject—Favourable general position of the River Plate—The balance of power in beef—Extract of meat—The Lemco and Oxo Company—Ramifications of the enterprise—The town of Fray Bentos—Agriculture—Wheat—Maize—Barley.

The financial interest that England possesses in Uruguay is not generally realised. As a matter of fact, the amount of British capital invested in the Banda Oriental amounts to over forty-four millions of pounds sterling, and there are thus only two nations, Argentina and Brazil, that possess a greater share of the total of those funds invested in the South American continent. To the ears of the majority, it must be admitted, the names of Chile, Peru, Venezuela, and Colombia sound more familiar than that of the country with which we are at present dealing. Yet in the matter of these investments Chile alone can approach the status of the small Republic on the River Plate, and, indeed, falls behind it only to the extent of a few hundred thousand pounds. Peru, however, is interested to scarcely more than one-half of the extent, while Venezuela, the next in order, cannot lay claim to one-sixth of the amount.

A comparison such as this will show the real financial importance that Uruguay represents to England, and, such being admitted, the condition of its commerce must be a matter of proportionate interest. To deal first of all with the general commercial development of the country, the outlook is undoubtedly satisfactory. In order to obtain the broadest possible survey of the situation it is necessary to lump together the national imports and exports. Taking a recent number of five-yearly periods, the results obtained are:

	$
1862-68	109,886,156
1869-73	158,468,043
1874-78	148,443,857
1879-83	195,757,038
1884-88	234,618,354
1889-93	261,877,934
1894-98	274,137,052
1899-1903	286,580,824
1904-08	338,009,777

The dollar quoted in this table—and wherever this unit is employed throughout the book—is, it should be explained, the Uruguayan gold dollar, the rough value of which may be estimated at four shillings and twopence.

This steady development of commerce is not a little striking in view of the fact that up to the present only a very small percentage of the resources of the country have been brought to bear. It is true that the chief national wealth is likely, in the future as in the past, to remain centred in the rich natural grazing lands. But the progress of agriculture is now such that this branch of industry cannot well fail in the course of a few years to rank as a moderate second in importance to the business of grazing. Moreover, the development of this latter itself is only now being proceeded with in a manner worthy of the great resources that exist. The marked increase in the general commerce that is evident between the years 1899 and 1908 is due to a very large extent to the introduction of modern methods into the estancia life of the country.

It is necessary now to turn to a more detailed consideration of Uruguay's exports. The chief of these, as has already been explained, is represented by live stock, and by meat in various forms. Of recent years these particular branches of industry have been undergoing a certain amount of transformation. For generations, indeed for centuries, Uruguay has represented the chief source of Brazil's supply of animal food. Not only were the herds of cattle and flocks of sheep driven northwards with ceaseless regularity across the frontier, but the millions of bales of dried beef flowed along the same channels too.

Recent events have caused a certain diminution in this commerce. With the course of time Brazil has become more and more desirous of seeing her own southern and comparatively temperate provinces more liberally stocked with cattle. With the idea of fostering the local grazing industry, the northern republic has increased the duties upon both imported cattle and meat. The immediate result naturally proved unfavourable both to Uruguayan graziers and saladero owners. In the end, however, the outcome has proved beneficial rather than detrimental to the landowner. As may be imagined, for the manufacture of tasajo a high grade of cattle is not necessarily required. The secret of the actual quality of the meat is to a great extent lost in the dried and hardened bales of the preserve. Moreover, in order to suit the taste of local consumption in Brazil a far slenderer class of animal was necessary than the fattened type that the colder climates demand.

Thus, when it became necessary to make up for the deficit in these neighbourly exports by the opening up of fresh markets and by catering for the overseas demand, one of the first means to be taken in hand towards attaining this end was a yet more close attention to the question of a quality of meat suitable for European consumption. There were many who foresaw numerous difficulties in attaining to this standard, principally owing to the comparative absence of alfalfa in the land. It is true that this fattening lucerne thrives only in limited areas of Uruguay. But to what extent the excellent pastures of the land have made up for this disadvantage is plain enough from the amount of frozen carcasses now shipped to Europe. The situation as regards the export of pastoral products has, in consequence, become improved. Less dried meat and fewer live cattle are sent to Brazil, but the deficiency is more than counterbalanced by shipments of a superior order to the new markets now established in Europe.

The present situation of the meat markets throughout the world has reached so vitally important a stage that a few comments on the position cannot well come amiss in view of its inevitable direct influences upon Uruguay, and the similar stock-raising countries. Naturally enough, the primary centres of interest are to be found in the United States, and in its Beef Trust. Ere coming to this point, however, it would be as well to review the general situation.

Until the present moment the British Isles have been the chief importers of frozen and chilled meat from both North and South America. The demand has, naturally enough, shown an annual increase corresponding with the growth of the population. A similar state of affairs has, of course, existed in North America, but here the increase of the inhabitants has been so rapid and so overwhelming that the breeding of cattle has been entirely unable to progress in the same ratio. The result of this is that the United States can now produce only a comparatively insignificant surplus over and above the quantity of animal food that is required for consumption by its own inhabitants. Of late, therefore, the shipments of North American beef to the British Isles have decreased with a rather startling celerity, and there can be no question that in the near future the trade will have ceased altogether. Exactly when this will occur—whether in two years or half a dozen—it is impossible for even the experts to tell, since so many elements of the unexpected enter into the question. But that it will come about is certain, and it is, of course, equally inevitable that the conclusion of the period of exportation will mark the beginning of another era when it will be necessary for the United States to import her animal food supply from countries outside her own frontiers.

THE CATTLE DIP.

DRYING JERKED MEAT.

To face p. 280.

In the meanwhile Argentina has stepped into the gap that North America had of necessity left vacant, and the establishment of its frigorifico will now enable Uruguay to take a hand in this business of shipping. The River Plate countries are undoubtedly in a position to cope with the situation for an indefinite period of years, although its effects are already evident to a certain extent upon the local markets of Argentina. In the latter country I have been present at the stockyards in November when the herds of cattle that had arrived from the Campo were being sold. The faces of those estancieros who were present were beaming, for prices were ruling quite exceptionally high. The reason lay in the demand for the London Christmas beef that had sent its stimulus all this distance—an emphatic proof of the closeness of touch that now obtains between the River Plate and the British Isles.

Were the position to begin and end at this point it would be simple enough. Some developments, however, have occurred of late that render the outlook for the future far more complicated. There seems very little doubt that the time will come when England will no longer enjoy the practical monopoly of imported beef. The desire for the admission of this commodity in several of the great European countries is becoming more and more accentuated, and it is highly probable that the agitation that is now being carried on in favour of this new departure will eventually result in the breaking down of the barriers that at present oppose the trade. It is, of course, impossible to estimate the full extent of the consequences of a move of the kind, but that it must cause a rise in the price of beef in the English markets is inevitable.

In the face of these possibilities the prospects of the River Plate countries are, of course, more favourable than ever before. With the markets of Europe open to their cattle and meat, the added stimulus to the industries of these countries cannot fail to be enormous. But here again an element has come into being that, although it will have no effect upon the industry, taken as a whole, must necessarily threaten many of the interests involved. The Beef Trust of the United States has been keenly alive to the great pastoral developments in South America. Accurately foreseeing that the importance of the present day is merely a prelude to what is to come, the great corporation has now descended wholesale upon the shores of the River Plate, has already bought up a number of frigorificos, and it will be through no want of endeavour of its own if it does not sooner or later acquire the remainder.

I have no desire to tilt against the Beef Trust, which is very probably an excellent institution, but one that, since it openly lays no claim to a purely philanthropical policy, cannot be expected to safeguard the welfare of concerns that do not tend towards its own advancement. Should this corporation, therefore, attain its present object of securing the frigorificos, and the consequent monopoly of the purchase of cattle for export, the actual producers of the live stock will find themselves face to face with a situation of which they have previously had no experience. It is quite possible that it will suit the corporation to buy the cattle at prices similar to those which now obtain—or it may not, since it is well known that the estanciero continued to exist in a more or less affluent fashion when his cattle sold at lower rates than is the case at the present day.

In any case the matter seems to be taken fairly lightly in the South American countries most concerned. The prevalent idea is that, should the danger be realised, it is easy to legislate against trusts—a theory that may, or may not, be correct. Putting aside for the moment, however, these possible complications, it will be clear that the position of the River Plate countries as regards the shipment of their beef is quite exceptionally favourable. So much so, indeed, that it is not without the bounds of possibility that the spread of agriculture may at some future period receive a check in favour of the purely pastoral industry. For the wheat and maize-producing lands are considerably in excess of those that raise cattle in sufficient quantities for serious export. Fresh areas suitable for wheat-growing, moreover, are continually being lit upon, whereas the discovery of new grazing lands is obviously more limited. It is true that our own colony of Rhodesia promises to take an important share in the cattle-breeding industry—a promise the fulfilment of which may be anticipated with confidence. With this exception, the countries of the River Plate will undoubtedly hold the balance of power in all matters appertaining to that very, very important article beef.

In addition to that of the carcasses themselves, another very important product of Uruguay is the extract of meat produced by the Liebig (Lemco) Company. Fray Bentos was the original home of this industry, with which the place has been associated since 1865. Of late years the Lemco interests have spread far beyond their original frontiers, for of the total of nearly five million acres at present owned by the concern many hundred thousands of acres exist in Argentina, Paraguay, and even in Rhodesia. As a matter of fact, the working power of the recently constructed factory at Colón in Entre Rios, upon the Argentine bank of the river, exceeds that of Fray Bentos. Nevertheless, the importance of this latter place will be evident enough when it is explained that in 1910 over one hundred and seventy-nine thousand head of cattle were slaughtered there in order to provide the necessary extract of meat.

The Lemco town of Fray Bentos is by way of being a model specimen of its kind. The establishments of the managers here, and the dwellings of the workmen are each admirable of their kind, and very replete with the comforts and luxuries that appertain to the various walks of life. The streets, moreover, are broad and well-engineered, and the schools and various institutions denote a liberal spirit on the part of the directors of the concern.

To turn from the meat industry to that of agriculture, we come, naturally enough, to a far less imposing condition of affairs, but one, nevertheless, that is increasing in importance each year. The chief cereal of Uruguay is wheat. At the present moment nearly three hundred thousand hectares have been devoted to the raising of this crop. Although the discovery of fresh lands suitable to the production of wheat has caused this particular area to increase, the main centres in cultivation up to the present have been rather strictly localised. The provinces that contain the really important wheat districts are those of San José, Colonia, and Canelones. The lines of railway, however, that have recently been constructed to the east and west of the Republic are opening up much land that is undoubtedly admirably suited for the production of this cereal. Wheat, it may be explained, is a crop the nature of which renders it more immune than the majority from the attacks of the voracious locust. By the time the all-devouring insect is wont to make its appearance, the ears of the wheat are as a rule hardened to a sufficient extent to render them unpalatable. Wheat therefore, frequently escapes, wholly or in part, where the maize crop suffers severely from the ravages of the locusts.

The production of maize is only very slightly less than that of wheat. The yield of this commodity in 1909 amounted roughly to one hundred and seventy thousand tons, while that of wheat fell just below two hundred and thirty-four thousand tons. Generally speaking, it may be said that the districts where wheat is grown are suitable for the cultivation of maize, and thus in Uruguay the two are wont to flourish to a large extent side by side. It is worthy of note, however, that whereas the wheat area has remained more or less stationary, although its development is now practically certain, that of maize has increased to a marked extent—from one hundred and forty-five thousand hectares, in fact, in 1900 to over two hundred thousand hectares in 1909.

The production of oats and barley—although that of either still remains comparatively insignificant—has increased rapidly during the past decade. In 1900 the output of oats only just exceeded thirty tons, whereas in 1909 it had amounted to nearly seven thousand tons. Barley has a similar, although a somewhat more gradual, tale to tell, since in the corresponding period its production rose from four hundred to three thousand tons.

CHAPTER XXV

INDUSTRIES AND NATURAL WEALTH (*continued*)

Minerals—Past obstacles to the proper working of mines—Gold—Auriferous prospects—Situation of the goldfields of Uruguay—Past and present workings of the mines—Influence of politics on labour—The Corrales mines—Manganese—Districts in which iron ore is met with—Mineral centres—Minas—Maldonado—Silver—Copper—Marble—Gypsum—Slate—Sulphur—Asbestos—Precious stones—Diamonds and rubies—Jasper—Agate—The amethyst and topaz—The water-stone—A peculiarity of Uruguay—Viticulture—Date of the introduction of the vine—Vicissitudes at the start—Subsequent rapid progress—Vineyard area of the present day—The introduction of suitable plants—Countries of origin—Production of grapes and wine—Departments most suitable to the industry—The seal fisheries—Originally carried on by the Indians—Habits of the seals—Development of the industry—Government grants—Conditions and concessions—Number of skins obtained since 1873—Islands inhabited by the seals—Method of killing and curing—Waste of seal life—Suggestions for the improvement of the industry—Scientific measures necessary—A diplomatic incident in connection with the seal fisheries.

It is quite possible that Uruguayan minerals may yet cause something of a sensation throughout the world. In the past her deposits of the kind have lain comparatively undisturbed, owing to similar reasons that have hampered the industry in Peru and Bolivia—want of transport facilities. With the rapid spread of the railways, however, these disadvantages will shortly become minimised, when no doubt considerably more will be heard of the mineral wealth of the country.

Let it be clear that I am not making the following remarks in the character of a mining expert. The latter profession, according to vulgar report, is at times not averse to fiction; but the gap that separates an author from a goldfield is uncomfortably wide. This apparently frivolous foreword is not altogether uncalled for, since to speak with undue optimism of the presence of the yellow dross is dangerous to the layman writer, and profitable only to the expert. Nevertheless, the auriferous prospects of Uruguay, so far as such can ever be assured, give no small promise of success.

The chief goldfields of Uruguay lie in the northern province of Rivera, and are situated in the neighbourhoods of Corrales, Cuñapiru, and Zapucaya. A district here of from thirty-five to forty miles in length and of about seven miles in breadth is thickly interwoven with auriferous reef. The knowledge of the wealth in this particular spot is no new thing, as ancient superficial workings on the part of the Indians prove. From that time the mines had apparently fallen into disuse until comparatively recent years, when they were in a sense rediscovered by a French company. The concern, it is true, met with a consistent lack of prosperity. The actual working is said to have been carried on in a fashion that was both half-hearted and old-fashioned. The period, moreover, was a peculiarly disturbed one from a political point of view, and the province of Rivera has always been famed as the birthplace and chosen haunt of revolutionary movements. An English company, however, has now assumed control of the mines, a modern plant is at work, and gold is actually being yielded.

Such are the bare historical facts of the chief mines at Corrales. According to the experts, reefs have been met with that will yield five ounces to the ton, and, should the reefs prove deep, the prospects are practically limitless. But this remains to be seen. In the meanwhile the earth has promised! But its promises, like its crust in parts, are sometimes of pielike material. In this case, should the anticipations be realised, there will be no little stir in the province of Rivera—and elsewhere.

In the neighbourhood of these mines are enormous deposits of manganese that are just now beginning to attract special attention. The quantities of iron, too, that are to be met with here are rather exceptional. Rivera, however, constitutes by no means the sole mineral district of Uruguay. The provinces of Minas, Artigas, Maldonado, Salto, Paysandú, Montevideo, and San José are all more or less well endowed with the various species.

Of these remaining centres Minas is probably the richest. Traces of gold are to be met with here, although in a minor degree, and silver, copper, marble, gypsum, slate, sulphur, and asbestos would probably all repay organised handling. Minas also produces lead, but this, too, has suffered from considerable neglect. Indeed, I believe that one of the very few ransackings of the mines that have occurred was for the purpose of manufacturing bullets for the armies during the revolutionary and civil wars at the beginning of the nineteenth century.

The province of Maldonado contains copper, iron, marble, gypsum, sulphur, and slate, and here, too, the mineral field has remained almost unexploited up to the present. Montevideo holds manganese and iron, Salto copper, Florida iron, Paysandú copper, and San José asbestos. These, at all events, constitute the principal centres of the minerals specified, although there are others of comparative insignificance in many other districts.

Uruguay, too, is by no means without its precious stones. Odd rubies and diamonds have been met with from time to time, and the jasper and agate are fairly common. The stones, however, that obtain in really considerable numbers, and that are consequently of the chief commercial interest, are the amethyst and the topaz. Of both these some magnificent specimens are to be met with in the Province of Artigas. These very handsome stones are now attaining a distinct popularity amongst the visitors to Montevideo. To those who have not the opportunity of visiting the remote province of Artigas itself, it may be mentioned that Agosto Wild, in the Calle Veinte Cinco de Mayo in Montevideo, is a most trustworthy and reliable dealer.

A peculiarity of Uruguay is the water-stone that is met with in the neighbourhood of Salto. This consists of a rounded portion of stone, more or less knobbly and opaque or smooth and transparent as the case may be. In the latter the water that is enclosed within it is almost as plainly seen as though it were held within rather dull glass, and with every movement of the crystal-like material the motion and bubblings of the water are very clearly evident. There have been some mental gymnastics ere now concerning the advent of the apple within the dumpling: but the presence of this water within the stone suffices to puzzle the more scientific minds. So far as I am aware, no adequate explanation of the phenomenon has yet been vouchsafed.

Viticulture is one of the more recent industries of Uruguay. It has now, however, obtained a firm hold, and the future of the commerce is distinctly promising. It was as late as 1860 that the first tentative plantings of the vine occurred, and it was not until 1875 that a couple of really important vineyards were established, one at Colon and the other at Salto, in the north-west of the republic. Even then the undertaking did not meet with immediate success, and it was some while ere the type of plant was discovered that would lead to the most favourable results in the local soil.

This, however, once discovered, the progress of viticulture has proceeded almost without a check. The rapidity of its increase may be gathered from the following figures. In 1880 the number of vineyards in Uruguay was 16; in 1890, 181; whereas in 1895 the total had swollen to 748. Since that time the industry has continued to spread. Thus in 1897 the vineyards had increased in number to 824, while in 1905 the viticultural census showed the very respectable total of 1,453.

It is only natural that this great increase in vineyards should have been accompanied by the introduction of a greater variety of suitable plants. The types of vines that now flourish in Uruguay hail from France, Italy, Spain, Portugal, and Germany, the importance of the various kinds being in accordance with the seniority rendered them in order here. Of the French species introduced the most popular are the Sauvignon, Cabernet, Pinot Noir, Castel, Merlot, Verdot, Semillon, Sauvignon blanc, Clairette blanche, and some half-dozen others; of the Italian the Piamonte, Grignolino Negro, Asprino, Docetto, Leonarda, Lambrusca, Cipro Negro, and Verdea. The favourite Spanish varieties are the Cariñana, Morrastel Bouchet, Murviedo, Malvosia Blanca, Pedro Ximinez, while from Portugal have been introduced the black and the white grape, and from Germany the Riesling.

The cultivation of the vineyards is attended by the greatest expense in the south of the country, where the comparatively humid climate lends itself more readily to the propagation of the various diseases to which the vine is subject. Here the American grape, owing to its immunity from phyloxera in a great degree, flourishes admirably. The departments in which viticulture is chiefly carried on are at Montevideo, that possesses a vineyard area of 1,426 hectares; Salto, 719 hectares; Canelones, 699 hectares; Colonia, 490 hectares; Maldonado, 330 hectares; Paysandú, 177 hectares; Florida, 132 hectares; Soriano, 125 hectares; and Artigas, 97 hectares. In the remaining departments the viticultural industry is of small account.

The later increase in the actual production of grapes and wine will be evident from the following table:

	Kilos of Grapes.	Litres of Wine.
1904	16,387,738	10,458,119
1905	20,304,850	11,569,314
1906	16,408,077	9,469,674
1907	19,385,569	11,461,817
1908	28,753,259	18,563,496

The sealing industry of Uruguay is of considerably greater importance than is generally supposed. Mr. C. E. R. Rowland, the British Consul at Montevideo, is the leading English authority on the subject. The following article, then, which he has kindly supplied, may be taken as authoritative:

The aboriginal races of this part of South America were known to have resorted to the coast-line during the summer months for their fishing expeditions, the Indian race of the Charrúas occupying the coastline from above the river town of Colonia to the borders of the Brazilian frontier at al Chue, on the Atlantic.

Traces of their encampment grounds are still to be found along this coast, principally from Maldonado to the Brazilian frontier, where many of their primitive weapons and utensils are still to be met with, and also the remains of what must have been their watch-fires, mounds of burnt bones, containing amongst the rest bones and teeth of seals which crumble under touch.

This coast in these former times evidently abounded in seal life, as the natural conditions offered every attraction to these now timid animals. A storm-beaten coast, with plentiful havens, in the mouth of a large estuary abounding with fish, enticed the seals to the shore and made them an easy prey to the Indians, but time has driven them to the present rookeries which now afford them protection.

The first record of the sealing industry on the coast of Uruguay having been put to practical purposes is that in the year 1834 they were rented by the Government for the period of ten years to Señor Francisco Aguilar for the sum of $80,000. The condition was imposed that he should erect a suitable edifice to be used as a public school in the town of Maldonado. This latter condition was altered insomuch that the building, when completed, was used as a chapel, and has remained so ever since.

A SEAL ROOKERY.

BASKING SEALS.

To face p. 292.

From the termination of this contract up to the year 1858 this industry was worked by various tenants, but in this latter year the Government passed a Law imposing a tax of 20 centavos per skin and 4 centavos per 10 kilos of seal oil, to be paid in equal proportions to the municipalities of Maldonado and Rocha Departments, on whose coasts the islands are situated. A further Law in the year 1896 doubled these taxes, which were destined by the said Law to be applied by the municipal authorities to the public works and the creation of artificial parks.

The following tables will show the number of skins produced from these islands since the year 1873:

Year.	Skins.
1873	8,190
1874	9,449
1875	9,204
1876	11,353
1877	11,066

1878	14,493	
1879	14,093	
1880	16,382	
1881	14,473	
1882	13,595	
1883	12,483	
1884	14,872	
1885	12,245	
1886	17,072	
1887	17,788	
1888	21,150	
1889	15,700	
1890	20,150	
1891	13,871	
1892	15,870	
1893	14,779	
1894	20,763	
1895	17,471	

	Island Coronilla	Island Lobos
1896	11,096	12,543
1897	9,091	10,143
1898	8,908	8,778
1899	9,339	7,796
1900	8,983	9,845
1901	8,023	8,215
1902	9,785	11,468

1903	5,899	7,929
1904	5,114	5,765
1905	2,246	3,387
1906	4,871	7,212
1907	2,880	7,612

The islands inhabited by seals on the coast of Uruguay are:

Castillos Rocks	4 small islands
Polonio	3 "
Paloma	2 "
Lobos	2 "

The Castillos Rocks are very difficult of access on account of the heavy swell breaking on them. The Polonio group consists of three small islands lying directly off the cape of same name, and are called Raza, Encantado, and De Marco.

The sealers' huts and boiling-house are on the mainland in a small bay to the north-east of the lighthouse. The seals when killed on these islands are skinned with the inside lining of fat attached and are brought on shore, when the inside lining of fat is taken off and boiled down. The dead carcasses are left on the island, and in my opinion the presence of so many dead seals destroyed by human agency must have some effect upon those animals frequenting these islands, making them wary and cautious in returning again to a place where the remains of their companions are so visible.

Coronilla Islands consist of two large islands, covered with herbage, and one small "*islote*," or reef, generally awash with the sea.

On the largest of these islands the sealers live during the season for the purpose of salting the skins and boiling down the carcass of the seals for oil. At the end of the season the skins and oil are brought into Montevideo by tug-boats.

On Lobos Islands the killing is carried out in a different manner. A large corral is erected on the middle of the island, and, when seals are plentiful and the wind and weather are specially favourable, a drive is made by about fifty men with clubs, who, getting between the seals and the sea, drive them gently towards the corral. This is done without much difficulty, and perhaps two thousand may be enclosed in one day. Once enclosed they are allowed to wait until all preparations for killing are complete. They are then driven out in batches of twenty or thirty to the skinning-shed and boiler-house, where they are dispatched at leisure.

By this mode of killing I am inclined to think that there must be a great waste of seal life from an absence of a proper knowledge as regards the animal killed. No selection is made from those driven down, and every animal is killed even if the skin is worthless or mangy. The majority of the animals slaughtered are females, consequently the stock of production is gradually lessened. Were a skilled sealer employed for the proper classification of the animals before killing, it would do away to some extent with the extermination of seals whose skins at that season were practically worthless.

On the Paloma Islands very few seals are killed.

The seizure of the Canadian schooner *Agnes G. Donohoe* in the year 1905 on the alleged grounds of sealing in jurisdictional waters—that is, within the three miles limit—caused the intervention of the British Government. The master and men were under arrest for a period of ten months, but the case, diplomatically handled at that time by her Majesty's Representative, Mr. Walter Baring (Minister), and Mr. Robert Peel (Chargé d'Affaires), was finally settled with satisfaction to both Governments by the tactful procedure of his Majesty's present Representative, Mr. Robert J. Kennedy, Minister Plenipotentiary and Envoy Extraordinary.

CHAPTER XXVI

COMMUNICATION AND COMMERCE

British enterprise in South America—The various industries controlled—The railways of the Southern continent—A remarkable record—The opening up of new lands—Some possibilities of the future—Sound basis on which the extension of the lines is founded—Products and transport facilities—Probable influence of communications—Uruguayan railways—A high standard of enterprise—Comfortable travelling—Some comparisons between Uruguay and Argentina as railway countries—Level country *versus* hills—Stone *versus* alluvial soil—Questions of ballast—Importance of the new ramifications—Railway construction in Uruguay—History of the lines—Government obligations—Mileage and capital of the companies—Interest paid on capital—Various railway systems—Areas served—The Central Company—Sketch of lines and extensions—Important developments—The communication with Brazil—Financial position of the Company—Midland Uruguay Railway—Development and extension of the line—Receipts and expenses—The North Western of Uruguay and Uruguay Northern Railway—Montevidean tramways—Local, British, and German enterprise—Steamer service of the River Plate—The Mihanovich line—Ocean passenger traffic—Montevideo the sole port of call—The Royal Mail Steam Packet Company—The Pacific Line—The Nelson Line—Other British companies—Position of British exports—Sound consular advice.

British enterprise throughout South America is admittedly remarkable. If one except the retail and local trades that are carried on by the native-born inhabitants of each republic, or by the Spaniards, Basques, Italians, and Turks, each of which have taken some particular trade under their own protection, there is probably not a single branch of industry in which the British are not interested in a more or less important degree.

From mining and banking to farming and general commerce, the scope is sufficiently broad. In no other kind of enterprise, however, has intelligence and skill been so freely lavished as upon that of the railways. The British have not the sole monopoly of these great undertakings, it is true. There are the local Government lines, numerous French railways, and others of various nationalities that are ably served and administered. Yet almost every one of the most important lines throughout the entire Southern continent owes its existence to British capital, and is managed by British officials. The record is a remarkable one, and the full tale of its magnitude has yet to be written. It is true that in many branches of industry the ratio of British increase has not been in proportion with that of other countries—a falling off that may be inevitable, but that in any case is regrettable. Fortunately, this is not the case with the railways. Indeed, when the progress that is now being made is taken into consideration, it becomes evident that the results that must ensue within the space of a few years cannot well fail to affect the entire world.

Of the feats of this kind that are at the present moment being achieved some of the most important are concerned with Bolivia, Paraguay, and the hinterland of Brazil. The opening up of many of the hitherto inaccessible regions of these countries means more than the enclosing within the fold of civilisation vast areas of rubber, timber, and general agriculture. It promises, in fact, some revelations in the way of minerals and mines that, although the possibility of a disappointment must never be lost sight of, are likely enough to prove of an astonishing nature.

The tales of gold in the untravelled lands where the Indian still holds sway do undoubtedly not emanate merely from the imagination of the few travellers who have penetrated within certain of the districts. The reluctance of the aboriginal to disclose the spots from which they derive the precious metal is an acknowledged phase of his character. But it is not solely upon the unwilling testimony of the Indians that such hopes are based. It is well enough known that when the expulsion of the Jesuits occurred, and when many of the remoter districts in which they had established precarious missions returned to a state of savagery and seclusion, numbers of the mines that were even then known were abandoned when in the full flush of their yield—a yield that the primitive native implements could never make complete.

But it is not in anticipation of such developments as these that the railways have been built. The ordinary products of the countries in question are more than sufficient to demand their existence. The possibility of greater mineral fields than are at present suspected is merely a side issue in the general scheme. The influence of steam transport, however, upon many of the silver-mines cannot fail to be marked, since the utter want of transport facilities now renders imperative an astonishing number of mines of this kind the productive power of which is very great indeed.

The Uruguayan railways form no exception to the prevailing South American rule. The three companies in existence in that Republic are all British, and the standard of each is as high as that of the others in the remaining republics. Although the enterprises naturally enjoy lesser advantages in the way of skilled labour and technical conveniences than those here at home, there can be no doubt that the degree of comfort enjoyed by the traveller on a Uruguayan line compares very favourably with that experienced on an average British railway. The service and observation of punctuality are both to be commended, while the dining and sleeping cars are not only admirable of their type, but extremely well adapted to the needs of the country.

The natural facilities that the Uruguayan country offers for railways differ considerably from those of the Argentine. In the central provinces of the latter many hundreds of miles may be travelled without any gradient whatever becoming apparent. The absence of streams here, moreover, obviates almost entirely the necessity for bridge building. It has already been explained that the characteristics of the Uruguayan Campo are entirely different. Although it possesses few hills of any really imposing height, its stretches of dead level ground are equally rare. Thus, although the gradients may be gentle and sufficiently easy, they are almost continuous. In some places, moreover, the rise and fall of the line is necessarily accentuated, and even abrupt—at all events, compared with the neighbouring areas.

Although, however, Uruguay may not be quite so favourably situated for railway purposes as regards its levels, it possesses one very important advantage over Argentina. In the central and richest provinces of the latter one of the most serious drawbacks lies in the total absence of any local material with which to ballast the track. For hundreds of miles on all sides no stone—not even the merest pebble—is to be met with, since the land consists of nothing beyond the rich, alluvial soil. Thus, if stone be required for the perfection of the tracks, it is necessary to import it from afar, and the haulage of the material inevitably forms a weighty item in the cost and upkeep of the line. In this respect Uruguay is far more favourably provided for. Stone abounds, not only in certain districts but throughout the country—although, of course, there are many centres where the quality of the material is far superior to that of others. Thus the question of ballast and embankments is solved in a very simple fashion here, and in a land of numerous rivers and streams the construction of stone bridges is made possible.

As regards the present position of Uruguayan railways, it is impossible to over-estimate the importance of the new ramifications that are now spreading through the country. Uruguay contains no mysterious hinterland, it is true. But, although every corner of the Republic is known, the resources of many of its regions have of necessity remained quite untapped for want of the railway communication that was essential for the transport of the produce in whatever shape or form it might emerge from the soil.

I am indebted to Mr. V. Hinde, the secretary of the Midland Uruguay Railway, for the following information concerning the railways of the country:

The construction of railways in Uruguay may be said to have commenced in the year 1866, when a concession was granted for a line from the capital (Montevideo) to Durazno, a distance of 130 miles. The construction of this line was followed by the building of a short line from the city of Salto towards the frontier of Brazil. In 1877 an English company, the present Central Uruguay Railway Co., Ltd., was formed to take over the former and complete the line to the town of Rio Negro, which extension was finished in 1886.

In the meantime the Uruguayan Government had devoted considerable attention to the question of railways, and in the year 1884 a law was passed by the Chambers embodying a definite scheme of railway communication with various parts of the Republic, the executive being authorised to contract for lines as outlined, and to guarantee an income equal to £560 per annum per mile of line for a period of forty years. A result of this enactment was the formation of several companies in England, and railway construction was rapidly proceeded with. By the year 1891, 1,000 miles of line were opened for traffic. In respect of which some 670 miles enjoyed the Government guarantee, equal to 7 per cent. on a capitalisation of £5,000 per kilometre.

At this point, however, further development received a check by the Government finding it necessary to rearrange its obligations. This rearrangement took the form of a reduction of the interest on the External Debt, including railway guarantees, from 7 per cent. to 3½ per cent., the service at this reduced figure being secured on 45 per cent. of the Custom House receipts specially hypothecated. Punctual payment of guarantees at this rate has always been made.

In 1889 the Central Uruguay Western Extension Railway Company was formed to construct a line from San José to the towns of Mercedes, Sauce, and Colonia. This line does not enjoy a Government guarantee, and reverts to the Government in the year 1862.

The railway system of the Republic to-day amounts to some 1,432 miles of line opened for traffic and 78 miles in course of construction.

The following shows the capital of the respective companies and length of lines:

	Mileage Open.	Capital. £	
Central Uruguay Railway, including Western Extension and North Eastern of Uruguay Railway Co., Ltd.	482	5,403,018 }	worked by
Central Uruguay Eastern Extension Co., Ltd.	277	2,033,400 }	Central Uruguay
Central Uruguay Northern Extension Co., Ltd.	182	1,627,150 }	Railway Co.
Midland Uruguay Railway Co., Ltd.	229	2,378,462	
North Western of Uruguay Railway Co., Ltd.	111	1,435,517	
Uruguay Northern Railway Co., Ltd.	73	855,562	
Uruguay East Coast Railway	78	309,980	
Total	1,432	14,044,089	

The amount of interest, &c., paid on the above capital may be seen in the table on the following page, which is equal to rather over $4\frac{1}{5}$ per cent. on the whole capital of £13,444,089.

The railway system of Uruguay may be said to be represented by the following companies:

The Central Uruguay Railway and its allied lines.

The Midland Uruguay System, which joins that of the Central and forms a means of communication with the cities of Paysandú and Salto, with a branch to the town of Fray Bentos, now almost completed.

The North Western of Uruguay, continuing the railway from Salto to the frontier of Brazil at Cuareim.

In addition there are the short lines in the nature of branches—that of the Northern Uruguay Railway Company, branching from the North-Western system at Isla de Cabellos connecting with the frontier of Brazil at San Eugenio; and the Uruguay East Coast Railway from a junction with the North-Eastern Uruguay system at Olmos to Maldonado, a distance of seventy-eight miles.

£	Interest paid on Capital.	Per Cent.	£
2,000,000	Central Uruguay Ordinary Stock	5	100,000
400,000	" " Preference Shares	5½	22,000
953,018	" " Debenture Stock	6	57,181
1,000,000	" " Western Railway Extension Debenture	4	40,000
250,000	Central Uruguay 2nd Debenture Stock	6	15,000
400,000	North Eastern of Uruguay Preference Shares	7	28,000
400,000	North Eastern of Uruguay Ordinary Shares	7	28,000
775,000	Central Uruguay Railway Eastern Extension Ordinary Shares	3¾	29,062
775,000	Central Uruguay Railway Eastern Extension Preference Shares	5	38,750
483,400	Central Uruguay Railway Eastern Extension Debenture Stock	5	24,170
1,000,000	Central Uruguay Railway Northern Extension Ordinary Shares	3¾	37,500
627,150	Central Uruguay Railway Northern Extension Debenture Stock	5	31,357
600,000	Midland Uruguay Railway Ordinary Stock	nil	—

600,000	Midland Uruguay Railway Prior Lien Debenture Stock	5	300,000
1,179,462	Midland Uruguay Railway Debenture Stock	5	58,973
120,120	North Western of Uruguay Ordinary Stock	nil	—
293,172	North Western of Uruguay 2nd Preference Stock	nil	—
583,850	North Western of Uruguay 1st Preference Stock	2	11,677
400,000	North Western of Uruguay 1st Debenture Stock	6	24,000
38,375	North Western of Uruguay 2nd Debenture Stock	6	2,302
100,000	Uruguay Northern Railway Ordinary Shares	nil	—
250,000	Uruguay Northern Railway Preference Stock	1	2,500
449,400	Uruguay Northern Railway Debenture Stock	3½	15,729
56,162	Uruguay Northern Railway Prior Lien Debenture Stock	5	2,808
125,000	Uruguay East Coast Railway Ordinary Shares	nil	—
184,980	Uruguay East Coast Railway Debenture Stock	nil	—
		—	
£14,044,089			£599,009

Central Company.—By far the most important system is that of the Central Company, including leased and worked lines. The lines of this system extend from the capital to the frontier of Brazil at Rivera, with branches to the city of Mercedes in the west, and the towns of Melo, Treinta y Tres, and Minas on the Eastern and North-Eastern Extension. The railway from the capital passes through a well-populated agricultural district for a radius of about thirty miles; this radius is gradually extending, stimulated by the increasing importance of Montevideo and the gradual breaking up of lands in the fertile regions of the western and eastern extensions.

The extension now finished to Melo opens up another district suitable to the cultivation of cereals, from which considerable traffic is being derived.

An extremely important matter in connection with the future development of these lines, and, in fact, all the railway interests of the Republic, is to be found in the completion of the port works at Montevideo. Until the port works were taken in hand the embarkation of cargo at this principal outlet of the Republic had been greatly hampered by natural difficulties, and consequently heavy charges in connection with the lighterage from the railway wharf to the ocean steamers. The deepening of the inner port and the construction of extensive wharfs and piers at which ocean steamers can berth will doubtless lead to an increase in traffic, not only from Uruguay but the neighbouring State of Rio Grande do Sul.

An important connection with the railway system of Rio Grande do Sul is made at the terminus of the Central Uruguay Northern Extension Railway at Rivera, and by the completion of a connecting link between the Sao Paulo Rio Grande Railway System and the lines of the Cie Auxiliare de Chemins de Fer au Bresil, a Company which controls practically the whole railway system of the State of Rio Grande do Sul (now almost completed), direct railway communication will be established between Montevideo and Rio de Janeiro.

The following table shows the result of working of the Central Uruguay Main Line, exclusive of extensions, which, as far as expansion in receipts is concerned, may be regarded as indicative of those lines:

Year.	Receipts.	Expenses.	Profit.	Dividend.
				Per Cent.
1904-5	414,228	190,165	223,572	4½
1905-6	442,083	212,465	229,618	5
1906-7	493,682	244,922	248,760	5
1907-8	508,044	272,104	235,940	4½
1908-9	557,122	287,505	269,617	4½

| 1909-10 | 577,489 | 287,959 | 289,530 | 5 |

The increase in gross receipts is perhaps not quite so marked as in the case of neighbouring lines in the Argentine Republic, and a reason for this is to be found in the fact that, favoured by magnificent grazing camps, cattle raising is still the principal industry of Uruguay. Agricultural development, although more marked of recent years, has been slow, but an increase in this is probably due to efforts which are being made by the Government to promote colonisation and the extension of lines in the Eastern provinces.

Midland Uruguay Railway.—This Company's line passes through an entirely pastoral district, and its traffic is principally derived from the carriage of cattle, wool, and general merchandise. An important extension is now practically completed to Fray Bentos, the headquarters of Liebig's Extract of Meat Company. The River Uruguay at this point is navigable for large ocean steamers, and a pier has been erected to accommodate these, which will put the railway system of the north of the Republic in a more favourable position to handle the various products of cattle-killing establishments, both in Uruguay and on the Brazilian side of the frontier of Rio Grande do Sul, an industry of increasing importance.

Year.	Gross Receipts.	Expenses.	Profit.	Dividend.
1905-6	60,533	50,304	10,229	
1906-7	75,887	60,833	15,054	
1907-8	72,172	67,153	5,019	
1908-9	81,503	71,114	10,389	
1909-10	88,165	67,479	20,686	

At the present time a considerable tonnage is transported by river from Salto for shipment from Buenos Aires. It is possible, therefore, that the extension of the Midland Company to Fray Bentos will play an important part in the development of its line and those of the companies north of Salto, and Fray Bentos should very shortly become the second port of the Republic.

The receipts in Uruguay of the Midland Company have shown some expansion of late years, having increased from £55,000 in the year ending June 30, 1904, to £88,165 in 1909-10 (see opposite page).

The North-Western of Uruguay Railway and Uruguay Northern Railway.—The remarks with regard to the nature of the country and the traffic of the

Midland apply also to these lines. At the terminus of the North-Western Line at the River Cuareim arrangements exist for the interchange of traffic with the Brazil Great Southern Railway, and the respective Governments have sanctioned a project for the construction of an international bridge to connect the lines at this point. It is probable that this bridge will be constructed within the next few years, as the interchange of traffic due to the extension of the Brazil Great Southern Railway to San Borju is likely to be considerably enhanced.

The excellent tramways with which Montevideo is served are administered by three companies, local, British, and German. The local enterprise is considerably the smallest of the three, the extent of its lines not exceeding twelve miles. The concern, moreover, is dependent solely upon horse traction, with its attendant disadvantages.

The British enterprise, the United Electric Tramway Company, is the most important in the capital. It possesses eighty-two miles of line, 195 passenger-cars, and sixty-eight trailers. By the terms of the concession at least two-thirds of the employees must be citizens of the country. The Compania Alemania Transatlantia is a German Company, with a length of seventy-five miles of electric tramlines.

The steamer service of the River Plate and Uruguay is almost entirely in the hands of the Mihanovich Company, as, indeed, is that of the entire system of these great rivers. The Company is an extremely powerful one, possessing a very large fleet that comprises all classes of steam vessels from the small, puffing tug to the largest and most modern liner of the fresh waters. Many of these latter are peculiarly fine specimens of their type, graceful in build, powerfully equipped, and provided with broad and roomy decks. Although the larger of these craft will carry between two and three hundred passengers, the cabin and saloon accommodation is contrived on a most liberal and imposing scale. Indeed, there is no doubt that the Mihanovich boats are a credit to the broad rivers on which they float.

So far as the ocean passenger traffic is concerned, Montevideo is the sole Uruguayan port at which the liners call. The capital affords a port of call for the magnificent vessels of the Royal Mail Steam Packet Company that, notwithstanding their size, are now enabled by means of the recent harbour improvements to enter the inner waters of the port. Of the other British lines concerned, the most important are the Pacific (that is now incorporated with the R.M.S.P.) and the Nelson Line, that possesses a fine new fleet of ten-thousand-ton boats. The other great British shipping companies whose vessels call at Montevideo are the Lamport and Holt, Houlder, Prince, Houston, the New Zealand Shipping Company, and the Shaw, Savill.

Thus it will be seen that in all monumental undertakings of the kind the British are holding their own in a satisfactory fashion. As regards ordinary commerce and the exports of manufactured goods, the progress, unfortunately, is by no means so evident. I have so frequently laid stress upon the narrowness of the home commercial ideas in this respect that still obtains in so many quarters that I am glad to be able to quote the words of another that admirably fit the case. The following is from the Consular Report on Uruguay issued in 1910, and the sentences undoubtedly sum up the situation with a commendable accuracy: "It has been pointed out to me that careful investigation into the commercial methods of our competitors reveals several reasons why British trade has failed to retain the proportion of the imports it held a few years ago. For instance, greater attention to detail is paid by the foreign merchant than by his British rival, who, as a rule, adheres in catalogues and invoices to British standard weights and measures and prices, without giving their equivalent in terms of the country. In tenders for public works German firms study the specifications with minute care, and tender for every item, leaving nothing in doubt, besides drawing up their applications in so clear and simple a manner as to give the minimum labour in examination, and the maximum of facility in comparison to the authorities who deal with them; whereas British tenderers sometimes merely quote a lump sum, ignoring all details, and often, when details are given, the price of many items is left vague, 'As may be agreed upon.' When goods are imported into the country from Germany, France, the United States of America, &c., a detailed statement in Spanish of the contents of each package is generally furnished, with metric weights and measures, which facilitates their rapid examination and dispatch, whereas British firms as a rule content themselves with the brief statement, 'Case containing machinery' or 'hardware,' &c., leaving to the Custom House official the task of working out details and calculations.

"Then, again, as regards languages, the British commercial traveller, armed with British catalogues and price lists [although I note with pleasure that some are now printed in Spanish], knows no language but his own, but the German invariably speaks Spanish and English, and he has carefully studied beforehand the needs of the market which he is visiting and the financial position of merchants. This gives him a great advantage over his British rival, who rarely has previous knowledge of his would-be customers, and is dependent on such chance information as he may pick up to be subsequently confirmed by inquiries at the banks. Time is thus lost, and irritation is caused to respectable buyers, who resent what appears to them impertinent suspicion."

CHAPTER XXVII

POLITICS AND REVOLUTIONS

The Constitution of Uruguay—Government of the Republic—Deputies and senators—Their duties—The Civil Code—Marriage—Rights of foreigners—Law—The Commission of Charity and Public Welfare—Hospitals—Orphan asylums—Infirmaries—The charity hospital lottery—The distribution of political parties—The Colorados and the Blancos—Policy of both—Feud between the parties—Old-standing strife—Explanation of the nomenclature—Origin of the feud—Rivera and Oribe—Inherited views—Attitude of the foreigners—Revolutions—Manner of their outbreak—Government precautions—The need of finance and arms—Some rebellious devices—Rifles as Manchester goods—The importance of horses—Difficulties that attend a revolutionary movement—The sweeping up of horses—Equine concentration camps—A powerful weapon in the hands of the authorities—First signs of an outbreak—Sylvan rendezvous—The question of reinforcements—Some desperate ventures—Their accustomed end—Chieftains of the north—Effect of a revolution upon local industries—Needs of the army—Estancia hands as troopers—Hasty equipment—Manner in which actual hostilities are conducted—"The Purple Land that England lost"—The spirit of modernism and the internal struggle—Tendency to localise the fields of strife—Power of the Colorado party—Whence the respective partisans are drawn—Distinguishing insignia—Some necessary precautions on the part of the foreigner—Adventures derived from colour in clothes—Some ludicrous episodes—The expense of revolution.

The Constitution of Uruguay has now stood the test of eighty years, and thus claims to be the oldest in South America, or, at all events, the one that has suffered no modification for the longest period of time. The basis on which this is composed is liberal in the extreme, and the laws undoubtedly concede to Oriental subjects an amount of freedom that can be surpassed in few other countries.

The Republic possesses two chambers, one of deputies elected by the direct vote of the people, the other of senators. In addition to their legislative functions it is the duty of these chambers to elect the President of the nation, whose term of office lasts for four years. The chambers also nominate the judges of the High Court, who, in turn, select the magistrates of the lower courts.

The civil code is largely based upon the Napoleonic model. It may be as well to note rapidly a few of its more salient features. From the point of view of the resident foreigner it is admirable in at least one respect, since it makes no distinction between the civil rights accorded to Uruguayans and those to foreigners. Civil marriage is obligatory, the offspring of a union contracted solely by the Church being considered illegitimate. In commerce the system of arrest for debt is not admitted, the only cases of the kind in which imprisonment is imposed being those in which an element of fraud has entered. In criminal law the death penalty has been abolished, and the various modes of punishment consist of solitary imprisonment, exile, deprivations, suspension from public employment, ordinary imprisonment, and fines.

On the whole, there is a satisfactory absence of red-tape in Uruguayan administrative and municipal affairs. It is true that in litigation the delays are occasionally lengthy; but the popular idea on this point has been much exaggerated, and the dispatch of legal business is far more satisfactory than is generally supposed. The great majority of officials, moreover, discharge their duties in a reasonable and fair-minded fashion that has been heartily acknowledged by many a resident foreigner.

Uruguay possesses comparatively few paupers. Indeed, it would be strange were this otherwise in a land the resources of which are in excess of the population. Nevertheless a certain proportion of the lame, blind, halt, and indigent is inevitable, and these unfortunate human elements are well cared for. Public assistance towards this end is chiefly in the hands of a Commission of Charity and Public Welfare, formed of twenty-one members, two-thirds of whom must be citizens of the Republic.

The powers of this Commission are considerable, and they control a number of important institutions, such as hospitals, orphan asylums, and establishments of refuge for the infirm, indigent, and insane. These are, almost without exception, exceedingly well-organised, and conducted on the most modern humanitarian lines. The financial support necessary for the upkeep of these charities is derived to a large extent from rates and taxes. In addition to this a special lottery has been instituted that is known as the "Charity Hospital Lottery." Twenty-five per cent. of its proceeds are devoted to the institution in question. The support at present derived from this source is not inconsiderable, as will be evident when it is explained that the amount it rendered in 1809 exceeded eight hundred thousand dollars.

We now arrive at the political affairs of Uruguay—a subject that calls for explanation at some length. So far as the distribution of parties is concerned, the matter is simple enough. Shifting parties, fusions and splits between contending sections, and the general complications that attend changing political programmes are to all intents and purposes absent here. The rival parties of Uruguay are the Colorados (reds) and the Blancos (whites). The policy of both is equally well-defined, and, indeed, is amazingly simple. It is to govern! The national programme would almost certainly remain exactly the same whichever were in power. Thus the aim of the party that is "out" is to obtain power in the first place, and to declare their policy of government afterwards.

The feud between the parties is one of old-standing. It commenced with the final wars of liberation, became strongly marked with the establishment of the Republic over eighty years ago, and has continued without intermission from that day to this. The origin of the party terms dates from the war of liberation. General Oribe was the founder of the Blanco party and General Rivera that of the Colorado. The former was wont to ride a white horse, the latter a bay, and the distinguishing colours of the lance pennons of their followers were respectively white and red.

It is a little curious to consider that the present-day party strife in Uruguay is the direct legacy of the disputes between these two generals that broke out in the first instance ere the Banda Oriental had even been proclaimed a nation! In 1830 Rivera was elected first Constitutional President of the Republic; he was succeeded on March 1, 1835, by his rival, Manuel Oribe, and in 1838 there broke out what is known as the *Grande Guerra*, which lasted, with varying results, until 1852. In 1853 a triumvirate was formed, consisting of Rivera, Lavalleja, and Flores, and in the following year the last named, on the death of his two colleagues, was elected Constitutional President. Since that time there have been no less than twenty-three presidents, constitutional and provisional, of whom only two, Perreira and Berro, from 1856 to 1864, have been Blancos. In that year the Colorado party got into office, and have maintained themselves, in spite of the forcible efforts of the Blancos to expel them.

It will be seen that no political principle divides the two parties; men are simply Blanco or Colorado because their fathers and grandfathers were so before them, but they cling to their respective parties with a strange courage and high sense of honour. In the case of foreign immigrants whose sons, born in the country, become Oriental subjects, but who have no Blanco or Colorado traditions to inherit, what happens is this: the youths go to school, form boyish friendships, and by pure accident become ardent supporters of one or other of the two parties. Two brothers may thus chance to become bitter political opponents, and when a revolution breaks out they are to be found fighting on opposite sides. The situation may savour a little of the Gilbertian, but it is sufficiently serious for the families involved. It must be admitted that many revolutions in Uruguay are curious affairs. To one not in close touch with the national movements an outbreak of the kind may appear to burst forth spontaneously, whereas it has probably been anticipated by the Government as well as by the revolutionaries for months beforehand. In these days even the most casual insurrection is not to be effected without a certain amount of forethought. First of all financial sinews are indispensable, and, these once obtained, it follows that a supply of arms is equally essential.

The introduction of these is the most difficult feat of all to accomplish, since the Government adopts methods of precaution, and keeps a sharp look-out for any possible importations of the kind. Thus as a rule the weapons are either smuggled across the Brazilian frontier or over some of the more lonely stretches of the River Uruguay. Occasionally a device is tried similar to that which met with success in the Transvaal Colony previous to the South African War. When I was in Uruguay at the end of 1910 many indications were at hand that went to prove the imminence of a revolution, and the authorities, not only in Uruguay but in the neighbouring countries, were on the alert for any development that might arise. At this period a large number of innocent-looking packing-cases, purporting to contain Manchester goods, were in transit through Argentina destined for one of the northern Oriental ports on the Uruguay River. Through some cause or other the cases came under suspicion, and they were opened ere they had crossed the Argentine frontier. In place of the Manchester goods reposed thousands of grim Mauser rifles and millions of cartridges! The discovery of these weapons must have dealt a bitter blow to the insurrectionist cause; nevertheless, as anticipated, the revolution broke out a few weeks later.

I have said that both weapons and cash are essential for the purpose of a revolution—which is obvious enough in almost every country as well as in Uruguay. But there is a third requisite that is quite as indispensable as either of the former. The Uruguayan is a born cavalryman, and a horse is necessary to him, not only for the partaking in the actions but for the covering of the lengthy distances that have to be traversed. A score of leagues and more frequently lie between a man and his appointed rendezvous. A pedestrian in the midst of the hills and valleys would be a lost and negligible unit.

OX WAGON ON THE CAMPO.

CROSS COUNTRY TRAVELLING.

To face p. 316.

It might be imagined that the matter was simple enough, and that all a revolutionist had to do when the time for the outbreak arrived was to mount his horse, and to ride away over the hills to join his fellows. In actual fact a rising is not to be started in this fashion. It is inevitable in the first place that numerous preparations must occur ere the time for active operations has ripened, and it is equally inevitable that an organisation of the kind, with whatever attempt at secrecy it may be conducted, cannot proceed without becoming known to the Government.

The eve of an outbreak is, in consequence, marked by tremendous vigilance on the part of the authorities. Troopers and police are dispatched to strategic positions throughout the country, and then for a while the nation waits in anxious expectation while the tension increases. With the first hint of the actual banding together of the revolutionary companies the authorities strike a blow—not at the men themselves, but at their means of transport. The troopers and police ride hastily in all directions, and scour the countryside in search of every horse that is available. When the districts have been swept quite clear of their equine population the horses are driven together to the various headquarters, where they remain, strongly guarded.

This very practical measure naturally provides the authorities with a power with which it is difficult for the revolutionists to cope. It is distinctly fatal to a premature or to a belated move on their part, and even should they chance to strike upon the most favourable moment, the horse-gathering policy militates strongly against any likelihood of eventual success. Should the malcontents determine to proceed with the affair in the face of this discouragement, they, of course, follow the lead of the Government, and endeavour to annex all the mounts that the authorities have been unable to carry off in time.

So far as the militant programme of the revolutionists is concerned, the first sign of an outbreak is invariably the riding away of a number of men from townships and estancias to the woods in the remoter and more lonely districts. These sylvan rendezvous are, of course, known to the party in general beforehand, and here the leaders of the movement lie hidden in order to await the advent of reinforcements. The first move is simple enough; but it is the arrival of the necessary reinforcements that is frequently frustrated by the precautionary measures of the Government.

Should the matter appear quite hopeless, it is even then possible for the insurrectionists to disperse and to return to their homes ere the shedding of blood has occurred. The Uruguayan, however, is not noted without reason for his spirit of reckless daring. It frequently happens that a forlorn band, once gathered, will refuse to disperse, and then the result of the campaign is usually short and sharp. In the ordinary course of events the adventurers will lie hidden until a sufficient force has come in, one by one, or in parties of three and four. Then they will ride out and commence active operations, of which the end in these days is invariably the defeat of the party.

Many of the attributes of these revolutions are not a little quaint and picturesque—reminiscent, in fact, of the times when personality counted more and system less. In the remote country districts, more especially in those of the north, are many prominent men who occupy more or less the position of chieftains, or that of the old Caudillos who have left so great a mark on Uruguayan history. Each of these is a power in himself, according to the extent of his following; for each can count upon his own particular body of armed men just as surely as could the feudal knights upon their mediæval retainers. These personalities are naturally marked, and their movements are closely watched in a period of unrest.

A Uruguayan revolution, even when in full blast, has this to be said in its favour, that it does not in the least interfere with the liberty or with the movements of a resident foreigner. If he be an estanciero, however, and should the tide of campaign flow into his district, it is likely enough that it will affect him materially in much the same fashion that a strike influences the fortunes of dwellers in industrial districts. It is obvious enough that when the Government is in need of recruits the claims of neither the pastures nor the shearing-shed can rival those of the cause. Unfortunately for the estanciero, there is almost certainly not a man in his employ who is not admirably adapted for a trooper, and none are more alive to this fact than the Government recruiting-officers. Thus, when the official party arrives its members will be polite but firm, and a short while afterwards the station hands will be bearing rifles instead of lassos, and a *capataz* or two—the foremen on the estate—will find their heads raised a little higher in the air beneath the support of a military title, although it is possible that this may be effected a little at the expense of their pockets, since the pay is not in proportion to the temporary rank.

In the circumstances of haste that obtain at such moments it may be imagined that, with the exception of the Government regular forces, the equipment on both sides knows little of the accepted insignia of military pomp. Indeed, a rifle and a badge in the majority of cases alone distinguish the militant from the ordinary civilian. But at such periods it must be admitted that, putting aside the foreigners, very few ordinary civilians are left in the disturbed areas, since, when the tide of warfare rolls his way, it is practically impossible for an Oriental to remain neutral. Even were he so inclined, it is doubtful whether he would be given the opportunity.

In order to obtain an insight into the manner in which the actual hostilities are conducted no better means could be adopted than the perusal of a novel, "The Purple Land that England Lost," from the pen of a great authority on the River Plate, Mr. W. H. Hudson. It is true that the descriptions deal with a period when the present prosperity of the Banda Oriental had not yet come into existence; but the vivid local colouring must hold good for all the contemporary softening of the national methods.

The spirit of modernism that is now evident in Uruguay has entered to a certain extent into the waging of these internal struggles that themselves by rights should belong to the past. The Oriental is perfectly willing to acknowledge that the dispute concerns himself alone, and the tendency to localise the fields of strife and to respect private property is becoming more and more marked. A certain amount of inevitable damage, however, ensues. In districts where fuel is scarce fence-posts and even railway-sleepers are apt to be employed for the purpose of the camp fires.

So far as the parties themselves are concerned, the tenacity of the Uruguayan character is clearly evidenced in the continued struggles of the Blancos. In view of the fact that this party has not been in office since 1864, it might be thought that forty-seven years of unsuccessful attempts would have cured it of an ambition that has been so costly both in life and purse. Nevertheless, whether openly or covertly, the contest continues with much the same amount of bitterness that characterised it from the start.

PEDIGREE CATTLE.

OVEN BIRD'S NEST.

To face p. 320.

Broadly speaking, it may be said that the Colorado party is made up of the dwellers in the towns and more populous centres, while the Blancos are represented to a large extent by the dwellers in the Campo and the clerical party. Of course, no hard-and-fast rule can be laid down on the subject: there are Blancos in plenty to be met with in the towns, and numbers of the opposing section to be found in the country; but in the main the distinction applies.

The districts in which the Blancos are most strongly represented of all are those of the northern provinces of Tacuarembó and Rivera, more especially the latter, since it offers in case of need the refuge of the Brazilian frontier. Party feeling at all times runs high, and in these districts that are almost altogether given over to the Blanco cause a certain amount of caution is necessary should a revolution actually be in progress. Much stress, for instance, is laid on the insignia that—in the absence of regular military uniforms—distinguish the adherents of one side from those of the other. In a Blanco district, when trouble is seething, it may be laid down as a hard-and-fast maxim that the traveller should wear no trace of red about his person. The precaution may seem grotesque, yet many ludicrous mistakes have occurred through a failure to observe it.

One of the numerous instances of the kind was provided me by a mining engineer, who had himself undergone the experience. Appointed as manager to a goldmine in the far north of the Republic, he happened to arrive, a stranger to the country, during the period of unrest in 1904. Nearing his destination, he had left the railway-line, and was completing the last few leagues of his journey by coach, when he stopped for refreshment at a small *pulperia*, or rural inn.

The place was fairly well filled with *peones*, and with the various types of the local labourer, and no sooner had he entered the doors than it became obvious to the traveller that his advent had caused a deep sensation amongst these folk. The landlord served him with reluctance and a visible show of embarrassment, while the black looks of the rest grew deeper, until the demeanour of a certain number became actually threatening. The mining engineer turned in amazement to the *pulpero*, who in mute accusation pointed a finger at the tie he wore. It was a vivid red! The traveller had learned sufficient of the country's situation to enable him to understand something of the situation. The group of Blancos were fully under the impression that one of their hated political enemies had defiantly come to beard them in their very midst. Explanations produced only a minor result, since these hardy dwellers in the back-blocks were wont to judge by deeds rather than by words. So, perceiving that no other remedy remained, the wearer of the hated badge hurried out to his coach, unstrapped one of his bags, and entered the pulperia once more, bearing beneath his collar a standard of neutrality and peace in the shape of a black tie! On this the local patrons of the inn expressed their entire satisfaction, and profound peace reigned in the pulperia.

It would be possible to mention a number of similar episodes. There have even been cases when the colouring of surveyor's poles has given an unpleasantly political significance to instruments that were never more misjudged. But even such ludicrous side-issues serve to show the amount of bitterness that exists amongst the humblest members of either cause. Such determined struggles, it is true, are not a little eloquent of the virility and energy of a nation. Nevertheless, it will be a bright day for Uruguay when the country can look upon its revolutions as past history. As I have said elsewhere, these minor wars have not succeeded in arresting the forward march of the Republic. Yet their cessation could not fail to produce an even greater acceleration in the present rate of progress. Since every thoughtful Uruguayan admits this to the full, and openly deplores these periodical outbursts of unrest, it is to be hoped that the days of internal peace will not be much longer delayed.

APPENDIX

FINANCIAL AND COMMERCIAL STATISTICS

The increase in Uruguay's trade with foreign countries since 1862—Trade with foreign countries in 1908—Imports of articles destined for commercial purposes—Imports of articles destined for industrial purposes—Ports to which Uruguayan wool was chiefly exported during 1908—Values of imports from foreign countries—Values of exports to foreign countries—Values of goods handled by the various ports since 1909—Proportion of cultivated soil compared with the area of departments—Live stock census of the Republic in 1900, showing the amounts owned by Uruguayan and foreign proprietors—The distribution of live stock in the various departments—Principal articles exported from Uruguay to the United Kingdom in 1909—Principal articles exported from the United Kingdom to Uruguay in 1909—Uruguay's Budget—Distribution of expenditure among the various departments—Services provided for by special revenues—Principal sources from which the revenues are derived—The development of the State Bank during the years 1897-1909—Balance-sheet—Cereal production in tons—Cereal harvest for the year 1908-9—Cable, telegraph, and telephone systems—Postal service.

TABLE SHOWING THE INCREASE IN URUGUAY'S TRADE WITH FOREIGN COUNTRIES SINCE 1862

Year.	Imports.	Exports.	Total.
1862	$8,151,802	$8,804,442	$16,956,244
1864	8,384,167	6,334,706	14,718,873
1866	14,608,091	10,665,040	25,273,131
1867	17,657,918	12,077,795	29,735,713
1868	16,102,465	12,139,720	28,242,195
1869	16,830,078	13,930,827	30,760,705

1870	15,003,342	12,779,051	27,782,393
1871	14,864,247	13,334,224	28,198,471
1872	18,859,794	15,489,532	34,349,256
1873	21,075,446	16,301,772	37,377,218
1874	17,481,672	15,244,785	32,426,455
1875	12,431,408	12,693,610	25,125,018
1876	12,500,000	13,727,000	26,527,000
1877	15,045,846	15,899,405	30,945,251
1878	15,927,974	17,492,159	33,420,153
1879	15,949,303	16,645,961	32,595,864
1880	19,478,868	19,752,201	39,231,069
1881	17,918,884	20,229,512	38,148,396
1882	18,174,800	22,062,934	40,237,734
1883	20,322,311	25,221,664	35,543,975
1884	24,550,674	24,759,485	49,309,559
1885	25,275,476	25,253,036	50,528,512
1886	20,194,655	23,811,986	44,006,641
1887	24,615,944	18,671,996	43,287,940
1888	29,477,448	28,008,254	57,485,702
1889	36,823,863	25,954,107	62,777,970
1890	32,364,627	29,085,519	61,450,146
1891	18,978,420	26,998,270	45,976,690
1892	18,404,296	25,915,819	44,356,115
1893	19,671,640	27,681,373	47,353,013
1894	23,800,370	33,470,511	57,279,881
1895	24,596,193	32,543,643	57,279,881
1896	25,530,185	30,403,084	55,933,269
1897	19,512,216	29,219,573	48,831,789

1898	24,784,361	30,276,916	55,061,277
1899	25,552,800	36,574,164	62,226,964
1900	23,978,206	29,410,862	53,389,068
1901	23,691,932	27,731,126	51,423,058
1902	23,517,347	33,602,512	57,119,859
1903	26,103,966	37,317,909	62,421,975
1904	21,217,000	38,485,000	59,702,000
1905	30,778,000	30,805,000	61,583,000
1906	34,455,000	33,402,000	67,857,000
1907	37,470,715	34,912,072	72,382,787
1908	36,188,723	40,296,367	76,485,090
1909	37,136,764	45,789,703	82,946,467

URUGUAY'S TRADE WITH FOREIGN COUNTRIES IN 1908. A COMPARISON WITH THAT OF SOME OTHER CENTRAL AND SOUTH AMERICAN STATES

Uruguay	$76,485,090	Guatemala	12,567,729
Peru	49,585,000	San Salvador	10,028,237
Bolivia	33,837,000	Panama	9,563,946
Columbia	28,512,636	Haiti	8,180,008
Venezuela	26,540,905	Paraguay	7,661,468
Ecuador	15,296,627	Nicaragua	7,500,000
Santo Domingo	14,613,807	Honduras	4,664,039
Costa Rica	13,386,930		

URUGUAY'S IMPORTS OF ARTICLES DESTINED FOR COMMERCIAL PURPOSES

	Yearly average from 1898 to 1902.	1905.	1906.	1907.
Various foods	$4,938,000	$5,293,397	$6,966,500	$6,530,700
Beverages	2,359,000	1,724,185	1,808,500	2,097,000
Tobacco	218,000	306,142	280,109	697,000
Cotton manufactures	3,265,000	4,900,000	4,400,000	4,555,000
Woollen "	1,203,000	1,523,600	1,814,000	1,879,800
Thread "	155,000	170,086	166,000	226,100
Silk "	276,000	303,286	364,000	521,500
Other "	344,000	1,727,492	1,587,000	955,000
Chemical and pharmaceutical products	507,000	751,993	718,000	1,178,000
Musical instruments	61,000	93,873	106,800	116,600
Paper and cardboard	496,000	615,617	675,100	709,300
Manufactured metal	707,000	1,072,426	1,078,100	593,600
China and earthenware	84,000	163,000	186,800	185,400
Jewels, crystals, &c.	373,000	494,815	546,000	724,000
Various articles	1,271,000	1,635,203	1,948,800	1,384,315
Total	$17,271,000	$20,775,651	$22,645,700	$22,353,615

URUGUAY'S IMPORTS OF ARTICLES DESTINED FOR INDUSTRIAL PURPOSES

	Yearly average from 1898 to 1902.	1905.	1906.	1907.
Livestock	$1,388,000	$1,822,452	$990,000	$754,000
Machine oil	533,000	691,860	781,400	841,400
Coal	1,128,000	1,366,564	1,723,000	1,879,000
Paints and inks	139,000	224,784	223,000	320,000
Timber	1,112,000	1,605,410	1,526,000	1,620,000
Wooden manufactures	134,000	308,175	349,000	418,700
Tanned hides	211,030	310,756	379,000	258,000
Iron and steel	420,000	684,959	883,000	1,688,500
Agricultural machinery and instruments	235,000	299,146	241,300	180,300
Industrial machinery and implements	149,000	247,116	338,000	847,600
Wire fencing	506,000	976,490	721,000	793,700
Manufactured iron	403,000	619,749	737,000	470,000
Portland cement	103,000	237,437	347,000	479,600
Tiles	41,000	59,601	73,000	74,500

Railway and tramway material	490,009	275,889	2,089,000	3,194,000
General factory material	72,000	275,564	407,600	1,295,700
Total	$7,064,000	$10,001,952	$11,808,300	$15,117,100

PORTS TO WHICH URUGUAYAN WOOL WAS CHIEFLY EXPORTED DURING 1908

	Bales.
Marseilles	94,418
Hamburg and Bremen	28,003
Dunkirk	21,901
Ambères	17,926
Havre	12,953
Liverpool	7,003

VALUES OF IMPORTS FROM FOREIGN COUNTRIES

	Yearly average from 1898 to 1902.	1907.		Difference.
Great Britain	$6,447,764	$11,572,152	+	$5,124,388
Germany	2,932,965	6,079,498	+	3,146,533
France	2,290,174	3,924,069	+	1,633,885
United States	2,091,209	3,439,445	+	1,348,236
Italy	2,218,844	2,898,391	+	679,547
Belgium	1,456,469	2,688,520	+	1,232,051

Argentina	3,151,345	2,563,186	-	588,158
Brazil	1,518,800	1,743,731	+	224,931
Spain	1,837,603	1,725,198	-	112,405
Holland	3,625	233,968	+	230,343
Paraguay	145,431	187,989	+	42,558
Australia	—	130,559	+	130,539
Cuba	105,932	121,040	+	15,108
Chile	106,608	108,342	+	1,734
Portugal	15,087	32,668	+	17,281
Austria	3,071	22,178	+	19,107
Total	$24,324,927	$37,470,615	+	$13,145,688

URUGUAYAN EXPORTS TO VARIOUS COUNTRIES

	Yearly average from 1898 to 1902.	1907.	1908.
Germany	$3,401,642	$4,647,866	$5,454,661
England	2,592,613	2,954,529	2,987,759
Argentina	5,194,663	7,295,195	8,143,029
Australia	—	12,750	4,400
Austria	—	116,880	528,568
Belgium	5,084,554	5,551,763	6,138,059
Brazil	6,908,427	2,759,863	3,467,283
Cuba	439,040	1,092,966	848,858
Chile	282,015	289,239	170,924

Scotland	—	38,625	58,846
Spain	531,793	533,674	524,066
United States	1,886,372	1,603,330	2,336,201
France	5,137,192	6,441,631	7,699,927
Italy	663,097	1,155,704	1,310,811
Holland	34,977	11,910	6,071
Paraguay	192,024	9,343	21,618
Peru	106	—	—
Porto Rico	—	—	51,070
Portugal	—	101,784	133,170
Prussia	18,911	—	100,002
Barbadoes	816	330	1,570
Canary Islands	14,234	5,971	2,475
Falkland Islands	3,739	1,483	511
Trinidad	2,051	3,794	1,541
South Africa	2,760	—	12,195
Provisions for vessels	164,400	293,502	291,150
Total	$31,555,422	$34,912,072	$40,296,347

VALUES OF GOODS HANDLED BY THE VARIOUS PORTS DURING 1909

	Imports.	Exports.
Montevideo	$34,251,069	$32,685,267
Paysandú	924,112	2,933,884
Salto	571,371	2,000,038
Fray Bentos	272,535	2,538,870

Colonia	513,684	2,770,862
Mercedes	226,789	1,547,081
Maldonado	21,404	—
Rocha	45,800	—
Cerro Largo	155,000	780,000
Various	175,000	533,700
	—	—
Total	$37,156,764	$45,789,703

PROPORTION OF CULTIVATED SOIL COMPARED WITH THE AREA OF DEPARTMENTS

Departments.	Area in Kilometres.	Cultivated Area Hectares.	Cultivated Area to the whole.
Montevideo	664	1,074	1·61
Artigas	11,378	1,321	0·11
Canelones	4,751	139,721	29·40
Cerro Largo	14,928	11,129	0·74
Colonia	5,681	107,815	18·98
Durazno	14,314	5,100	0·35
Flores	4,518	3,842	0·85
Florida	12,107	33,382	2·75
Maldonado	4,111	11,530	2·80
Minas	12,484	31,079	2·49
Paysandú	13,252	5,707	0·43
Rio Negro	8,470	1,727	0·20
Rivera	9,828	3,986	0·40
Rocha	11,088	7,662	0·69

Salto	12,603	2,202	0·17
San José	6,962	102,866	14·77
Soriano	9,223	21,487	2·33
Tacuarembó	21,015	2,385	0·11
Treinta y Tres	9,539	6,329	0·66
Total	186,929	500,347	2·67

LIVE STOCK CENSUS OF THE REPUBLIC IN 1900, SHOWING THE AMOUNTS OWNED BY URUGUAYAN AND FOREIGN PROPRIETORS

	Cattle.	Horses.	Sheep.	Mules.	Goats.	Pigs.	Total.
Uruguayans	3,135,152	304,381	10,782,057	8,952	15,059	54,877	14,301,378
Argentines	126,796	10,963	347,271	168	219	508	485,925
Brazilians	1,968,188	131,733	2,370,920	7,812	2,522	10,755	4,492,230
Paraguayans	609	112	4,887	—	4	54	5,656
Chilians	11,338	140	3,550	—	—	13	16,041
Mexicans	65	13	—	—	2	—	80
North Americans	6,990	337	5,989	—	2	27	13,345
Spaniards	823,226	58,905	2,769,364	4,080	1,276	15,351	8,672,242
Portuguese	23,122	1,434	36,848	43	6	159	16,612
French	240,494	17,223	1,141,881	564	382	2,339	1,402,883
English	275,183	15,055	514,835	410	119	257	806,859
German	39,544	3,488	121,747	90	54	297	165,220
Swiss	15,033	1,146	23,181	12	12	555	39,939
Italians	158,310	16,226	479,122	836	771	8,631	663,896
Austrians	1,955	203	4,445	21	—	89	6,713
Dutch	25	13	550	—	—	—	586
Danes	15	12	—	4	—	6	37
Belgians	10	3	—	—	—	5	18

Norwegians	25	8	180	—	—	—	213
Russians	6	4	—	—	—	—	10
Arabs	2	9	—	—	—	—	11
Total	6,827,428	561,408	18,618,717	22,992	20,428	93,923	26,134,896

THE DISTRIBUTION OF LIVE STOCK IN THE VARIOUS DEPARTMENTS

Departments.	Cattle.	Horses.	Sheep.	Mules.	Goats.	Pigs.	Total.
Artigas	514,328	43,489	791,969	6,060	1,296	1,501	1,358,643
Salto	614,806	45,819	1,076,878	3,234	1,622	2,957	1,746,316
Paysandú	686,159	44,685	1,071,382	1,881	330	1,734	1,806,171
Rio Negro	525,086	22,346	1,060,344	769	419	934	1,609,898
Tacuarembó	560,406	38,468	922,081	1,683	874	4,406	1,527,918
Rivera	292,704	28,993	207,236	1,063	983	3,234	534,213
Treinta y Tres	382,803	29,160	892,815	384	265	4,158	1,309,585
Cerro Largo	591,007	30,999	662,184	629	67	5,247	1,290,133
Minas	369,172	34,074	1,334,916	290	3,184	6,314	1,847,950
Rocha	336,426	36,735	1,257,495	314	918	8,483	1,640,371
Maldinado	121,176	17,894	695,833	182	1,629	5,472	842,186
Durazno	429,451	31,762	1,978,391	950	140	2,217	2,442,911
Flores	154,776	16,719	1,474,664	154	104	1,346	1,647,763
San José	142,130	12,518	482,436	517	158	1,799	639,558
Florida	338,012	25,037	1,654,940	536	186	2,723	2,021,434
Soriano	407,037	35,968	2,056,795	688	229	1,170	2,501,887
Colonia	225,475	28,868	785,697	1,039	422	4,499	1,043,209
Canelones	112,651	20,808	99,152	917	1,935	29,355	264,818
Total	6,827,428	561,408	18,608,717	22,992	20,428	93,923	26,134,896

PRINCIPAL ARTICLES EXPORTED FROM URUGUAY TO THE UNITED KINGDOM IN 1909

	£
Meat (chilled, frozen, extracts), &c.	732,125
Wool	173,738
Hides and skins (including sealskins, £8,440)	62,703
Bones	10,089
Tallow	76,688
Wheat	20,054
Maize	7,160
Flax seed	26,721

PRINCIPAL ARTICLES EXPORTED FROM THE UNITED KINGDOM TO URUGUAY IN 1909

	£
Coal	699,260
Coke	11,339
Woollens, Manchester and Bradford goods	712,067
Galvanised iron	141,184
Drugs, &c.	70,460
Machinery	337,304
Hardware	26,614
Glass and china	39,105
Jute goods	63,209
Cement	16,000
Stationery	14,000
Paints, &c.	19,140
Metals (excluding iron and steel)	23,675
Hats and millinery	11,335
Woollen articles	29,737

URUGUAY'S BUDGET. DISTRIBUTION OF EXPENDITURE AMONG THE VARIOUS DEPARTMENTS

	Budget of 1908-9.			Budget of 1910-11.		
	Dollars	Cents	£	Dollars	Cents	£
Legislature	541,476	61	115,208	558,864	33	118,907
Presidency of the Republic	77,938	21	16,582	76,471	40	16,270
Ministry of Foreign Affairs	473,280	50	100,698	534,898	37	113,808
Ministry of Interior	2,997,013	36	637,662	3,412,250	88	726,011
Ministry of Finance	1,371,455	84	291,799	1,523,842	57	324,222
Industry, labour, and public construction	1,572,257	46	334,523	2,308,793	75	491,232
Ministry of Public Works	283,887	20	60,401	374,321	91	79,643
Ministry of War and Marine	3,057,377	67	650,506	3,580,739	89	761,859
Administration of justice	445,286	54	94,742	323,353	80	68,800
National obligations	10,255,357	35	2,181,991	10,639,723	80	2,263,771
	—	—	—	—	—	—
Total	21,075,330	74	4,484,113	23,333,260	70	4,964,523

SERVICES PROVIDED FOR BY SPECIAL REVENUES

	$
Municipal Budget}	1,520,000
Montevideo }	
Interior	930,000

National Commission of Charity	1,850,000
University, application of special revenue	140,000
Port works, application of additional duty	1,400,000
National Council of Hygiene	33,000
Miscellaneous	1,200,000
Total	7,073,000

PRINCIPAL SOURCES FROM WHICH THE REVENUES ARE DERIVED

	$	£
Customs Revenue	13,620,000	2,897,872
Property tax—		
Montevideo	1,090,000	231,915
Provinces	1,720,000	365,957
Licensing taxes—		
Montevideo	783,000	166,595
Provinces	571,000	121,489
Profits of the Bank of the Republic	770,000	163,829
Internal taxes on home manufactures—*i.e.*, alcohol,		
matches, beer, artificial wines, tobacco, &c.	1,408,000	299,574
Stamps and stamped paper	830,000	176,596
Post and telegraphs	570,000	121,276
Consumption tax on imported produce	380,000	80,851
Consular fees	233,000	47,449
Lighthouse dues	85,000	18,085

TABLE SHOWING THE DEVELOPMENT OF THE STATE BANK DURING THE YEARS 1897-1909

Year.	Cash.	Notes in Circulation.	Deposits.	Advances.	Capital.	Reserve Fund.	Dividend.
	$		$	$	$	$	
1897	1,659,098	892,430	524,982	2,849,586	5,000,000	—	2·649
1898	3,095,343	2,691,652	834,339	3,418,435	5,020,303	20,303	2·762
1899	4,431,313	4,551,419	1,604,669	4,527,312	5,037,633	37,633	3·273
1900	4,739.788	5,010,388	2,427,891	5,936,920	5,058,243	58,243	4·030
1901	4,633,957	5,223,569	2,704,441	6,353,506	5,083,713	80,713	5·504
1902	6,541,015	6,008,603	3,345,939	7,012,434	5,118,692	118,692	5·410
1903	7,616,593	6,862,538	4,111,762	7,352,943	5,153,302	153,302	5·596
1904	6,120,185	5,256,811	2,472,016	5,460,727	5,223,118	223,118	7·044
1905	9,382,287	8,195,477	4,109,257	6,608,587	5,255,118	255,118	7·107
1906	10,339,651	10,396,740	4,730,672	8,971,758	5,281,626	281,626	6·736
1907	11,362,879	12,323,869	5,032,657	12,483,812	6,326,600	326,600	9·209
1908	13,080,825	13,773,633	5,455,804	15,345,513	6,399,425	399,425	12·754
1909	17,598,920	15,936,961	8,001,301	16,223,624	6,857,901	501,446	11·217

NOTE.—Rate of Exchange: $4.70 = £1.

The following is the balance-sheet of December 31, 1909:

ASSETS.

	$
Cash	20,036,564
Advances	18,921,606
Foreign correspondents	2,927,139
Capital not realised	5,045,947
Sundry stocks and discounts	940,007
National savings bank	400,000

Stocks, &c., for guarantees of judicial and administrative deposits	842,671
Properties	540,596
Branches	4,657,167
Stocks and shares deposited	22,798,736
	—
Total	77,110,433
	£
Equivalent in sterling	16,406,475
	—

LIABILITIES.

	$
Authorised capital	12,000,000
Judicial and administrative deposits	703,641
Notes in circulation	16,692,413
Deposit certificates and silver cheque "conformes"	1,633,000
Reserve Fund	597,599
Deposits	11,000,423
Supreme Government	6,047,270
Dividends (payable to State)	769,221
Branches	4,807,854
Sundries	60,276
Depositors of stocks and shares	22,798,736
Total	77,110,433

	£
Equivalent in sterling	16,406,475

CEREAL PRODUCTION IN TONS

Year.	Wheat.	Linseed.	Oats.	Barley.	Birdseed.	Maize.
	Tons.	Tons.	Tons.	Tons.	Tons.	Tons.
1900	187,553	1,009	33	424	518	77,093
1901	99,719	2,313	68	438	709	141,647
1902	206,936	8,757	115	1,016	1,103	128,539
1903	142,611	20,767	149	658	323	134,335
1905	205,888	14,046	525	588	1,745	121,862
1906	124,344	10,782	543	786	1,908	81,956
1907	186,884	21,930	1,752	1,576	1,638	13,613
1908	202,208	18,372	3,467	1,889	223	———
1909	233,910	13,259	6,710	3,072	119	169,464

CEREAL HARVEST FOR THE YEAR 1908-9

	Amount Sown.	Area Cultivated.	Total Yield.
	Kilos.	Hectares.	Kilos.
Wheat	18,915,529	276,787	233,910,034
Linseed	592,959	18,341	13,259,821
Oats	458,156	6,891	6,710,645

Barley	238,089	3,487	3,072,202
Canary seed	5,319	141	119,130
Maize	2,534,739	203,268	169,464,099

CABLE, TELEGRAPH, AND TELEPHONE SYSTEMS IN URUGUAY

CABLES.

	MILES.
Western Telegraph Company	470
River Plate Telegraph Company	180
Telegraph and Telephone Company of the River Plate	205
National Government cable	10
Total	865

TELEGRAPHS.

	MILES.
National Government Telegraphs	1,740
Oriental Telegraph Company	1,030
River Plate Telegraph Company	328
Telegraph and Telephone Company of the River Plate	300
Total	3,398

TELEGRAPHS (RAILWAY SYSTEM).

	MILES.
Central Uruguay Railway Company	2,138
Midland Railway Company	198
Northern Railway Company	71
North Western Railway Company	112

Eastern Railway Company	32
Local companies	39
Total	2,590

TELEPHONES.

	MILES.
Montevideo Telephone Company (British)	10,845
The Co-operative Telephone Company (Uruguayan)	4,375
National Government lines for police service	2,188
Total	17,408

SUMMARY

	MILES.
Cables (Telegraphs)	865
Public service	3,398
Railway service	2,590
Telephones	17,408
Total	24,261

POSTAL SERVICE

The Revenue from the Postal Services for the year 1909 amounts to £132,307, and the expenditure as authorised by the Government £106,085.

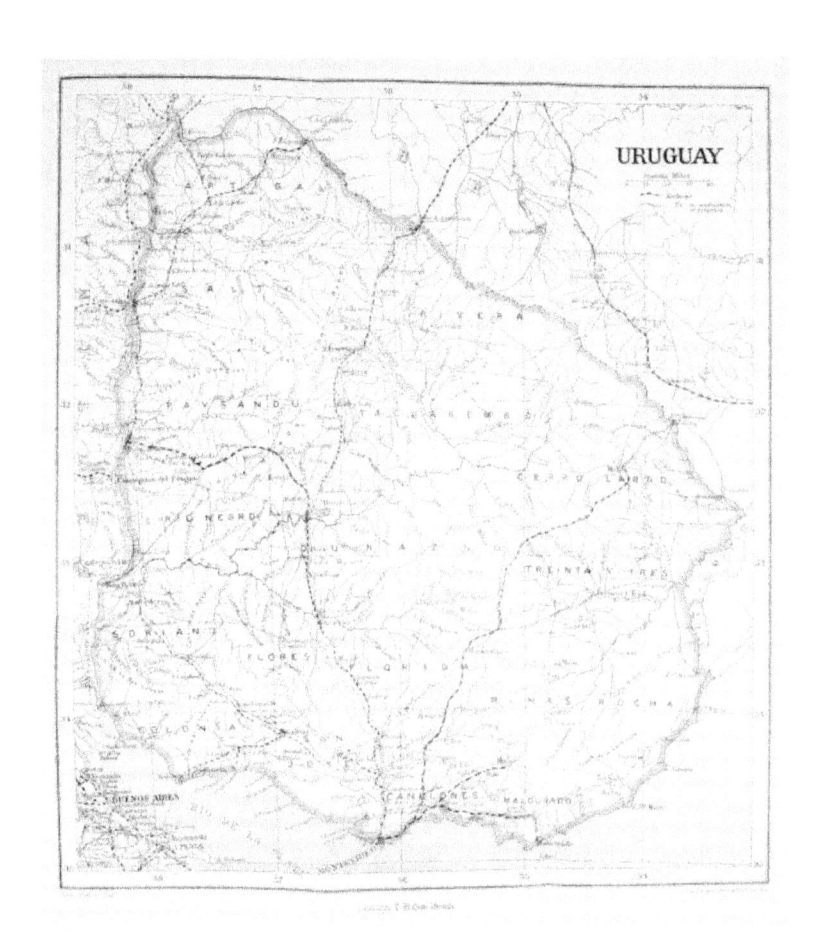

URUGUAY

Milton Keynes UK
Ingram Content Group UK Ltd.
UKHW030623061024
449204UK00004B/385